Moses Foster Sweetser, Moses King

King's Handbook of Boston Harbor

Moses Foster Sweetser, Moses King

King's Handbook of Boston Harbor

ISBN/EAN: 9783744733502

Printed in Europe, USA, Canada, Australia, Japan

Cover: Foto ©Andreas Hilbeck / pixelio.de

More available books at **www.hansebooks.com**

THE THIRD EDITION. 1888. REVISED AND ENLARGED.

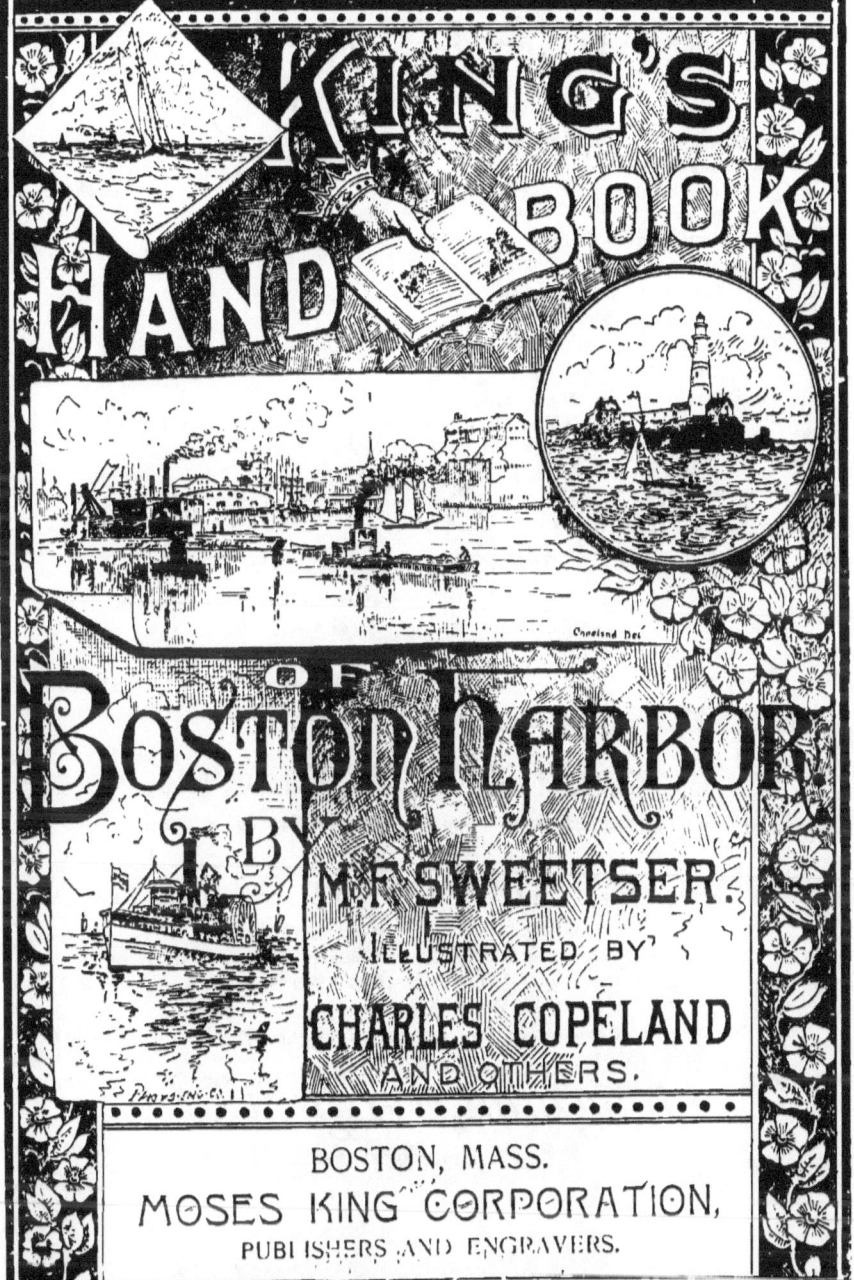

KING'S HAND-BOOK OF BOSTON HARBOR

BY M. F. SWEETSER.

ILLUSTRATED BY CHARLES COPELAND AND OTHERS.

BOSTON, MASS.
MOSES KING CORPORATION,
PUBLISHERS AND ENGRAVERS.

HOUGHTON, MIFFLIN & CO.

DELIGHTFUL BOOKS

BY SARAH ORNE JEWETT.

The King of Folly Island, and Other People. $1.25.

A Marsh Island. A Novel. $1.25.

"A combination of the art of the poet, the painter, and the story-teller. It is at once an idyl, a romance, and a cabinet of exquisite *genre* word-pictures." — *Harper's Magazine.*

A Country Doctor. A Novel. $1.25.

Deephaven. New England Sketches. $1.25.

Old Friends and New. Stories. $1.25.

Country By-Ways. Stories. $1.25.

The Mate of the Daylight and Friends Ashore. Charming Short Stories. $1.25.

Play Days. For Children. $1.50.

A White Heron, and Other Stories. $1.25.

One is almost tempted to say, "Hawthorne *redivivus*," as one lays down this singularly charming little book.... Truly artistic work. — *The Churchman* (New York).

CHARMING OUT-DOOR BOOKS.

BY JOHN BURROUGHS.

Wake Robin. $1.50.	**Pepacton, and Other Sketches.** $1.50.
THE SAME. Riverside Aldine Series. $1.00.	**Fresh Fields.** $1.50.
Winter Sunshine. $1.50.	**Signs and Seasons.** $1.50.
Birds and Poets. $1.50.	**Works.** In 7 vols. 16mo, gilt top, $10.50.
Locusts and Wild Honey. $1.50.	

BOSTON ILLUSTRATED.

An interesting and pictorial description of Boston and vicinity, with a map. 50 cents.

BACON'S DICTIONARY OF BOSTON.

With a map. Cloth, $1.50; boards, $1.00.

This excellent book describes fully, minutely, and compactly the Boston of to-day, and the alphabetical arrangement makes its wealth of information easily accessible.

⁎ *For sale by all Booksellers. Sent by mail, post-paid, on receipt of price by the publishers.*

Houghton, Mifflin & Co.

——BOSTON.——

Index to Illustrations.

Full-page Illustrations.

Atlantic House, 63.
Boston Light, 245.
Boston Yacht-Club House, City Point, 121.
Clifford (The), Plymouth, 293.
East-Boston Docks, 125.
Illustrated Titlepage.
Jerusalem Road, Views on the, 79.
Map of the Harbor, 29.
Nantasket Beach, from Atlantic Hill, 65.
Nantasket Hotel, 61.
Navy Yard, 281.
Noddle's Island, 127.
Nut Island, 213.

Oregon House, 34.
Panoramic Views of the Harbor, 27.
Pemberton, Hotel, 33.
Pleasant Beach, Green Hill, and Black Rock, 73.
Plymouth, Mementos of Ancient, 291.
Quincy, Views in, 101.
Quincy, Famous Houses in, 109.
Savin Hill, Ancient and Modern, 103.
Savin Hill, from Crescent Avenue, 113.
South-Shore Views, 75.
Winthrop's Fleet, Arrival of Gov., Frontispi'e
Winthrop, Views in, 141.

Smaller Illustrations.

Adams Academy, 101.
Adams, Birthplace of President, 101.
Ancient Colonial House, Hingham, 91.
Ancient North Battery, 24.
Andrew House, Hingham, 90.
Arbor in Melville Garden, 81.
At Ease, Snug Harbor, 108.
Atlantic Hill, View from, 269.
Atlantic Hill, Distant View, 275.
Atlantic House, 64.
Atlantic House, from the Hills, 64.

Bather, The, 204.
Bath-Houses near Hull Pier, 31.
Bathing-Car, 77.
Battery, Long-Island Head, 181.
Beach Scene, Nantasket, 80.
Bear-pit, Melville Garden, 87.
Bell Buoy, Harding's Ledge, 280.
Birthplace of the Presidents, 101.
Bits from Life-saving Station, 52.
Blue Hills, 62.
Boat-house at Sunnyside, 141.
Boston, from Winthrop Head, 135.
Boston Light, 245.
Boston Light, from Point Allerton, 56.
Brass Mortar, 80.
Bug Light, 233, 258.

Calf Island, 254.
Cannons, Nut Island, 213.
Capt. James's Landing, Hull, 35.
Carpenter's Shop, Snug Harbor, 97.
Casemate Battery, Fort Independence, 149.
Castle William, 157.
Cliffs on Outer Brewster, 255.
Coaling-Station on Nantasket Railroad, 271.
Constitution, United-States Frigate, 231.
Convicts at Work, 221.
Crescent Beach, 67.

Deane Winthrop House, Winthrop, 131.
Deer-Island Ferry Horn, 224.
Deer-Island, Scene at, 223.

Eagle, 117.
East Boston, Illustrated Titlepage.
Excursion Steamer of 1818, 117.

Ferry at Germantown, 102.
Ferry at Point Shirley, Calling, 224.
Fire-Department Steamer, 265.
Fisherman's Home, Point Shirley, 129.
Flounders, Spearing, Calf Island, 253.
Fort Independence, Main Gate, 145.
Fort Independence, South Front, 149.
Fort Warren, from the Channel, 229.
Fort Winthrop, Governor's Island, 167.
Frigate's Deck, 281.

Germantown, 95.
Going out, Lobsterman, 189.
Going to the Rescue, 53.
Granite Quarries, 101.
Great Head, Winthrop, 133.
Gun from the *Kadosh*, 57.
Gun, Old Signal, 245.
Gun-Park at Navy Yard, 281.

Harbor-Mouth Rocks, 283.
Hauling in Lobster-Pots, 189.
Hingham Old Meeting-House, 89.
House of Industry, Deer Island, 219.
Hulk of the *Passport*, Little Hog Island, 55.
Burying-Ground and Point Allerton, Hull, 44.
Hull Skipper, A, 50.
Hull Yacht-Club House, 49.
Hunt House, The Old, Hull, 41.
Hut on Stony Beach, 57.

Indian Canoe, 23.
Inner Harbor, Illustrated Titlepage.
Inspection by Port Physician, 191.

James, William, 36.
Jerusalem Road, View from, 267.

Leyden Street, Plymouth, 289.
Life-Boat, Stony Beach, 53.
Light-House, 245, Illustrated Title.
Little Hill, 54.
Little Hog Island, 55.
Lively Sea, 222.
Lobster-House, Old, Winthrop, 141.
Lobsterman, 189 279.
Lobsterman's Cabin, Point Shirley, 139.
Lobsterman's Headquarters, Nut Island, 213.
Long-Island Head, 181.
Long-Island House, 183.
Long-Island Light-House, 181.
Lovell House, The Old, Hull, 39.
Lovell's Island, from Gallop's Island, 195.

Magazine, Nut Island, 213.
Melville Garden, from Ragged Island, 83.
Middle Brewster, 256.
Minot's Light, 71.
Moat of French Fort, Hull, 43.

Nantasket Beach, from Atlantic Hill, 65.
Nantasket, Hotel, 63.
Nantasket, Scene near, 274.
Nantasket, Wreck on, 69.
Navy Yard, 281.
New Pacific Hotel, 74.
Nix's Mate, 193.
Nix's Mate in 1700, 192.
Norsemen's Galley, 58.
North Street, Plymouth, 290.
Nut Island, 213.

Ocean Spray, 132.
Old Cemetery, Hingham, 92.
Old Hulks, 281.
Old Sailor at Rest, 99.

Outer Brewster, 247.
Outer Brewster, Rocks on, 177.

Pavilion on Ragged Island, 88.
Peace and War, Nut Island, 211.
Peddock's Island, 209.
Peddock's Island, Pilot's House, 207.
Peddock's Island, View from, 273.
Pews in Hingham Church, 89.
Photographer's Car, 77.
Plymouth Rock, 295.
Point Allerton, Little Hill, 54.
Point Allerton, View from, 56.
Point Shirley House, Taft's, 140.
Point Shirley, Old Mansion, 137.
Point Shirley, View from, 277.
Police-Boat, 264.
Port Physician boarding a Ship, 191.
Port Physician going out, 196.
Portuguese Village, Long Island, 185.
Profile, Squantum, 104.
Pulpit, Hingham Church, 89.

Quarries, Granite, Quincy, 101.
Quincy Bay, from Long Island, 185.

Ragged Island, Melville Garden, 82, 85.
Rainsford Island, 203.
Republicæ Fundamenta, 296.
Rockland Café, Nantasket Beach, 61.
Rope-Reel, Humane Society, 186.
Russ Villa, 251.

Sailors' Snug Harbor, Germantown, 95.
Sally Jones's House, Hull, 37.
Scene on Ragged Island, 85.
Schwartz, Sergeant, 170.
Sentinel, 242.
Signal Station, Hull, 43.
Skipper William James, Hull, 36.
Smith, Capt. John, 122.
South Face of Fort Independence, 149.
Squantum, The Profile, 104.
Standish, Capt. Miles, 106.
Statue of Gov. Andrew, Hingham, 90.
Stony Beach, Hull, 57.
Storm at Minot's Ledge, 71.
Sunnyside, 141.
Sunshade, 30.

Taft, Portrait of, 140.
Telegraph Hill, Hull, 43.
Tewksbury House, Point Shirley, 261.
Thompson's Island, from South Boston, 173.

Unitarian Church, Hingham, 89
U. S. Revenue Cutter, 235.

Whistling Buoy, off the Graves, 249.
Winthrop Beach and Fort Winthrop, 141.
Winthrop, Gov. John, 263.
Winthrop Great Head, View from, 135.
Winthrop's Fleet, Gov., Frontispiece.
Worrick House, 60.
Wreck of the *Grace Lothrop*, 175.
Wreck on the Beach, 69.

Index to Text.

Acadians, 155, 256.
Accord Pond, 86.
Adams, C. F., 100, 103, 170, 109, 228.
Adams, John, 99, 103, 157, 183.
Adams, John Quincy, 100.
Adams, Mrs., 267.
Agassiz, 131.
Alabama, 230, 233.
Albemarle, 271.
Allerton, Point, 51, 54.
Alligator, 156.
Allston, Washington, 277.
Almshouse, 204.
" America," 40; *America*, 189.
Amherst, Sir Jeffrey, 266.
Ancient and Honorable Artillery Co., 145, 229, 237.
Andrew, Gov., 84, 159, 229.
Andrews, Joseph, 87.
Andros, Sir E., 150, 152, 181, 207, 219.
Anti-Slavery Melodies, 87.
Apple Island, 26, 132, 137, 139, 177.
Apthorp, 182.
Arbella, 268.
Arlington House, 78 A.
Atlantic Hill, 67, 86.
Atlantic House, 66.
Atlantic Village, 108.
Atlantic Works, 128.
Attack on Fort Warren, 236.
Auks, 206.
Austin, Gen., 249, 250.
Back River, 90.
Back Way, 181.
Bainbridge, 184.
Baltimoreans, 231.
Baptists, 123.
Bare Cove, 88.
Barrè, Col., 246.
Barron, Admiral, 233.
Bartlett, Gen. W. F., 130.
Bates, Joshua, 92.
Bathing, 76.
Batteries, French, 228.
Beachy Point, 190.
Beacon Island, 244.
Beacon, Nantasket, 48.
Bears, 38, 176.
Beecher, H. W., 38, 145, 261.
Bellamy, Capt., 193.
Bell-Buoy, 253.
Bellingham, Gov., 146, 150.
Bellomont, Lord, 282.
Bells, Convent, 149, 195.
Bennett, quoted, 265.
Bernadotte, 270.

Berthier, Marshal, 270.
Best, Lieut.-Col., 144, 236.
Bethell, 194.
Bill, Samuel, 175.
Billington Sea, 294.
Binney, Amos, 40.
Bird Island, 25, 169, 194, 195.
Black Jack, 178.
Black Rock, 68.
Blessing of the Bay, 192, 282.
Blockade-running, 268, 283.
Blue Hills, 102, 104, 118.
Boarding-house Runners, 247.
Boston and Bangor Steamship Co., 297.
Boston Gas Company, 114.
Boston Jockey Club, 108.
Boston Marine Society, 196.
Boston Massacre, 155.
Bougainville, 49.
Bourbonnais Regiment, 270.
Bradley Fertilizer Company, 89.
Braintree, 228.
Breed's Island, 128.
Brewer, John R., 85.
Brewsters, 243.
Britannia, 274.
British Regiments, 155.
Broad Sound, 26, 179, 188, 220.
Brown, George L., 277.
Brown, James, 187.
Bubbles, 212.
Buccaneers, 194.
Buckner, Gen., 232.
Bug Light, 244.
Bumpkin Island, 28, 214.
Bunker Hill, 259.
Buoys, 188.
Burning Ships, 178.
Burroughs, Stephen, 157.
Burying Hill, 92, 292.
Byles, Mather, 153.
Cabot, Major S., 234, 236.
Calf Island, 253.
Canoes, 262.
Canton Packet, 274.
Capobianco, 259.
Captain's Hill, 294.
Carpenter, Rev. Ezra, 38.
Casemate dungeons, 232.
Castle Island, 39, 119, 143, 246.
Castle William, 137, 143, 152.
Cattle, 284.
Centre Hill, 67.
César, 43, 228.
Champlain, 260.
Chapel, Musquantum, 107.

Charity, 55.
Charles I., 218.
Chesapeake and *Shannon*, 50, 285.
Chevalier, quoted, 208.
Cheviot Hills, 102, 118.
Chickataubut, 99, 105, 109, 219.
Child, Lydia Maria, 151.
Children at Deer Island, 222.
Choate, Samuel, 254.
Christian Indians, 219.
Church, Col. Benj., 49.
City Point, 25, 120.
Clams, 78, 83, 209, 262.
Clap, Roger, 150.
Clark's Island, 290.
Clement, 146.
Cleverly, 205.
Clifford House, 295, 296.
Clinton, Sir Henry, 228.
Coddington, William, 98.
Coffin, Sir Isaac, 156.
Cohasset, 260.
Cole, Foxcroft, 208.
Cole's Hill, 292.
Columbia, 282.
Commercial Point, 112.
Commerce, 279, 282.
Conant, Roger, 46, 165.
Concentrated United States, 238.
Confederates, 231.
Constitution, 139, 184, 272, 280.
Continentals, 246.
Copley, 155, 277.
Cottage Park, 132.
Cottages, 76.
Cotton, 284.
Cotton, Rev. John, 146.
Cow Pond, 217.
Crane, Thomas, 228.
Crescent Beach, 68.
Cromwell, Capt., 195.
Cromwell's slaves, 263.
Crow Point, 81.
Crystal Bay, 136.
Cumberland, 280.
Cunard Line, 284.
Cushing House, Hingham, 84.
Cushing House, Hull, 38.
Dana, R. H., 279.
Davenport, Capt., 147, 148, 150.
David, Sagamore, 219.
Davis, Jeff., 230.
Dean, Hon. Benjamin, 244.
Dean, Thomas, 249.
Dearborn, Gen., 168.
Deer, 217.
Deer Island, 217, 140.
Defence, 268.
Demi-lune, 232.
Demons, 167.
Derby Academy, 84.
De Ruyter, 150.
D'Estaing, Count, 43, 49, 208, 228.

Deux-Ponts, Comte de, 270.
Devens, Gen., 185.
Dimick, Col. Justin, 230, 234, 235.
Docks, 24, 128.
Dominic Brown, 139, 177, 187, 202, 220, 239.
Dorchester, 47, 111.
Dorchester Heights, 119.
Downer Landing, 81.
Downer, Samuel, 81.
Draft-Riots, 234.
Drake, quoted, 151.
Dudley, Gov., 144.
Duels, 126, 158, 176.
Dummer, 262.
Du Portail, 42, 49.
Eagle, 88, 276.
East Boston, 24, 123.
Eastern Head, 179.
East-India Trade, 282.
Eastward Neck, 89, 210.
East Weymouth, 90.
Egg Rocks, 250.
Eliot, Apostle, 105, 219.
Elizabeth, 194.
Emeline, 88.
Emerson, G. B., 130.
Emerson, R. W., 286.
Endicott, 97, 148.
Enterprise, 252.
Escape from Fort Warren, 234.
Everett, quoted, 102, 104, 111, 196.
Excursions, Ancient, 72, 275.
Exports, 284.
False Lights, 55.
Fame's Revenge, 194.
Fanny Pike, 252.
Farm School, 173.
Fiftieth Mass., etc., 191, 275.
Flying Place, 248.
Fly, William, 194.
Fort at Hull, 42, 43.
Fort Hill, 86, 144.
Fort Independence, 35, 143.
Fort Point Channel, 24.
Fort Strong, 126.
Fort Warren, 32, 43, 159.
Fort William and Mary, 151.
Fort Winthrop, 165.
Fourth Battalion, 161.
Fourth Massachusetts Regiment, 185.
Fox Haven, 260.
Fox Point, 114, 116.
Francis, 56.
Franklin, 138.
Franklin, Benjamin, 246.
Freight Rates, Ancient, 282.
French Military Cemetery, 44.
French Fleet, 43, 189, 202, 208, 228, 268, 270.
French Forts, 41, 208, 228.
French Hospitals, 126.
French, Massacre of, 205.
French Nobles, 270.
French Prisoners, 156, 266.

Freneau, quoted, 124.
Friendship Hall, 84.
Frolic, 258.
Fur-Traders, 172.
Gage's Soliloquy, 124.
Galatea, 248.
Galleys, 183.
Gallop, Capt. John, 190.
Gallop's Island, 190.
Gardiner, Sir C., 106, 172.
Garibaldi, 130.
Garrison of Fort Warren, 238.
Gay, W. A., 87.
George, Capt. John, 227.
George's Island, 227.
Germantown, 93.
Ghosts, 234.
Gibbons, Capt., 133, 146.
Gibson, Major A. A., 236.
Gilmour, Harry, 233.
Glad Tidings Plain, 86.
Glass-making, 94.
Godiva, Lady, 218.
Golden-Rod, 210.
Gookin, quoted, 220.
Gorges, Capt. Robert, 91.
Gould, Robert, 35, 40.
Governor Cony, 253.
Governor's Island, 165.
Granite-Quarries, 103.
Grape Island, 89, 208.
Graves, The, 252.
Graves, Thomas, 252.
Great Brewster, 244, 246.
Great Head, 134, 135.
Great Hill, 95.
Greaton, Major, 220.
Great Republic, 126.
Green Hill, 68, 135.
Green Island, 254.
Gridley, Gen. R., 154, 156, 167.
Griffin, 190.
Groton, 131.
Grover's Cliff, 131, 134.
Guerrière, 272.
Gun Rock, 67.
Gurnet, 290.
Gut Plain, 136.
Halfmoon Island, 214.
Hall, Basil, quoted, 247.
Hatsall, W. F., 244, 248, 277, 287.
Hamilton's Battery, 236.
Hancock, 266.
Hancock, Gen. W. S., 163, 236.
Hancock, Gov., 100, 137.
Hancock, Mrs., 137, 268.
Hangman's Island, 214.
Harding's Ledge, 244, 253.
Hardy, Lady, 25.
Harrison Square, 114.
Hartford, 280.
Harvard, 273.
Haswell, William, 39.
Hawkins, Thomas, 114, 193.

Hawthorne, 41, 77, 98, 174, 279.
Hayes, Gen., 144.
Hayman's Island, 214.
Helen, 56.
Hendrickson, Gen., 190.
Highlanders, 184, 268.
Hill, William H., 297.
Hingham, 70, 81, 83, 85, 86.
Hingham Bay, 35.
Hingham Centre, 86.
History, Bits of, 259.
Hobartville, 70.
Holmes, quoted, 38, 217, 278.
Hope, 283.
Hope, Henry, 100.
Hospitals, 191, 201.
Hough's Neck, 212, 295.
Hough's Tombs, 211.
House Beach, 250.
Hovey's "Causerie," 239.
Howe, Earl, 107, 228.
Howells, W. D., 24, 72, 239, 279.
Huguenots, 264.
Hull, 28, 31, 144, 246.
Hull Cemetery, 45.
Hull Gut, 205.
Hull Yacht Club, 35.
Hullonians, 37.
Hunt, Freeman, 100.
Hunt House, 39, 41.
Hutchinson, Anne, 98, 145.
Hutchinson's History, 106, 114, 178.
Hypocrite Passage, 254.
Ice, 284.
Ice Pond, 217.
Immigrants, 284.
Independence, 184, 280.
Independence, Fort, 143.
Indiamen, 283.
Ingalls, Dr. S., 134.
Ironclads, 128, 280.
Jachin, 248.
James, William, 36.
Jerusalem Road, 68.
John and George, 268.
"John Brown's Body," 230.
Jones's Hill, 114.
Jones, Sallie, 208.
Josselyn, quoted, 262.   [246.
Junketings, Ancient, 137, 150, 201, 202, 220,
Kadosh, 56.
Katahdin, 300.
Kelp, 78.
Kidd, Capt., 195.
King Oak Hill, 91, 92.
King Philip's War, 48, 86, 92, 219.
Kingsley, Charles, 243.
Kingston, 294.
Krossaness, 58.
Lady Arbella, 261.
Lady Washington, 138.
Lafayette, 88.
Lafayette, 42, 85, 114, 156.
Lansil, 277.

Larcom, Lucy, 45, 253, 256.
Lathrop, G. P., 40.
La Tour, 54, 123, 133, 166, 189.
Lee, 266.
Leverett, Gov., 243.
Liberty Plain, 86.
Life-Saving Station, 51.
Light-House, 244.
Light-House Board, 187.
Light-House Channel, 45.
Light, Long-Island, 179.
Lincoln, Abraham, 88.
Lincoln, Benjamin, 42, 60, 84, 88, 124.
Lincoln House, 84.
Little Brewster, 244.
Little Calf Island, 254.
Little Hog Island, 57.
Lively, 138.
Liverpool Packets, 284.
Lobsters, 38, 139.
Longfellow, 91, 107, 154, 278.
Long, Ex-Gov., 85.
Long Island, 179, 190, 201.
Long-Island Head, 43, 179.
Loring, Dr., 279.
Lorings, The, 20, 37, 243.
Lost-Town, 261.
Louisburg, 154.
Louisiana, 233.
Love Lane, 37.
Lovell House, 39.
Lovell's Grove, 88.
Lovell's Island, 187.
Lowell, J. R., 194, 278.
Lowlands, 147.
Ludlow, Roger, 107, 116, 145.
Lyford, John, 46.
Lyman, Theodore, 171.
Madagascar Slaves, 264.
Magicienne, 240.
Magnifique, 171.
Manomet, 292.
Map, Outline, 27.
Marine Telegraphy, 38.
Maritana, 223.
Marshfield, 279.
Marsh, Mr., 160.
Martineau, Miss, 276.
Mary, 193.
Mary and John, 43.
Maryland Legislators, 205.
Masconomo, 171.
Mason and Slidell, 206.
Mason, Capt. John, 104.
Massachusetts, 276.
Massachusetts Historical Society, 150.
Massachusetts Humane Society, 47.
Massachusetts Hummocks, 98 C.
Massachusetts Indians, 91, 96, 101.
Massacre, 185.
Massasoit, 56.
Massie's Monument, 144.
Mather, Cotton, 261, 263.
Maverick, S., 91, 123.

Mayflower, 88.
Maypole Revels, 97.
McKay, Donald, 126.
Mears's, 95.
Meeting-House Hill, 114.
Melville Garden, 82.
Merrill, Moody, 40.
Merrimac, 280.
Merry Mount, 48, 96, 98, 279.
Miantonomoh, 282.
Michelet, 76, 135.
Middle Brewster, 248.
Milford, 267.
Minot House, 112.
Mitchell, Professor, 284.
Montague, Admiral, 279.
Montague, Lady, 277.
Moon Island, 107, 108, 118.
Moose, 218.
Morell, Rev. William, 91.
Morris, Lieut., 145.
Morton, Thomas, 38, 46, 78, 90, 96, 97, 98,
    102, 105-107, 172, 205, 212, 218, 260.
Motley, J. L., 98, 106, 111, 114, 218, 279.
Mount Bowdoin, 114.
Mount Dagon, 97, 98.
Mount Wollaston, 95.
Mount Washington House, 25.
Mugford's Fight, 138.
Musquantum Chapel, 107.
Nancy, 266.
Nantasket Beach, 59, 104.
Nantasket Beach Railroad, 31, 80.
Nantasket Hotel, 63.
Nantasket House, 62.
Nantasket Lake, 67.
Nantasket Roads, 29, 255.
Naples, Bay of, 259.
National Sailors' Home, 100.
Navy Club, 273.
Navy Yard, 23.
Negro Slaves, 284.
Nelson, John, 181, 218.
Nelson, Lord, 271.
Neponset, 111.
Newbern, 275.
New Boston, 24.
Newcomb, Peter, 190.
New-England Guards, 114.
New Pacific Hotel, 67.
News-Letter, 137, 193, 194.
Ninth Regiment, 184.
Nix's Mate, 191.
Noddle's Island, 123, 260, 279.
Noddle, William, 123.
Norsemen, 57.
North Battery, 24.
North Brewster, 253.
North Carolinians, 232.
North Weymouth, 88.
Nursery, 222.
Nut Island, 95, 205, 211.
Oceana, 59.
Ocean of Sunrise, 221.

INDEX TO TEXT.

Ocean Spray, 134.
Ocean Thermopylæ, 237.
Old-Colony H...se, 86.
Old-Colony Railroad, 80, 289.
Oldham, John, 46.
Old-Harbor Point, 118.
Old Mansion House, 202.
Old Spain, 90, 210.
Orchards, Primeval, 165.
Ordnance, 211.
Oregon House, 35, 36.
O'Reilly, John Boyle, 42.
Otis Hill, 85.
Otis, James, 40, 137.
Outer Brewster, 249.
Pacific Hotel, 78 B.
Panoramic Views, 27.
Parker, Col. F. J., 234.
Pauper Colony, 204.
Pecksuot, 91.
Peddock's Island, 28, 205.
Peggy, 266.
Pegram, Gen., 233.
Pemberton, Hotel, 28, 32, 33, 205.
Pemberton, James, 48, 227.
Penobscot, 298.
Penobscot Expedition, 268.
Penobscot River, 300.
Pepperell, Sir William, 154.
Percy, Earl, 119.
Peregrine, Peter, 72, 259.
Perkins School for the Blind, 25.
Perry, Nora, 26, 82.
Peruvian, 56.
Peters, Rev. Hugh, 273.
Petition of Hull, 48.
Phillips, John, 134, 194.
Phipps, Sir William, 48, 263.
Pierce, Col., 183, 194, Titlepage.
Pierce's Hill, 112.
Pilgrim Feasts, 107.
Pilgrim National Monument, 290.
Pilot-Boats, 247.
Pine Neck, 112.
Pine-Tree Shilling, 218.
Pirates, 170, 192.
Plains of Nantasket, 69.
Planter's Hill, 85.
Plymouth, 289.
Pochaska, Charles, 252.
Poictiers, 41.
Point Allerton, 51.
Point Shirley, 136, 137.
Portuguese Village, 180.
Pound, Tom, 192.
Powder-Boats, 25.
Prairie Flower, 188.
Preble, Admiral, 230.
President Adams, 100.
President Roads, 25.
Pretty Sally, 269.
Prince, John, 47.
Prince's Head, 205, 211.
Privateers, American, 266, 272.

Privateers, Rebel, 234.
Pulling Point, 133, 135, 136.
Pulsifer, Col. R. M., 40.
Pumpkin Island, 214.
Putnam, Gen., 124.
Quarantine, 191, 193.
Quarries, 103.
Queen Anne Corner, 86.
Quelch, John, 193.
Quincy, 93. 100.
Quincy, John, 99.
Quincy, Josiah, 98.
Quincy Point, 94.
Raccoon Island, 214.
Ram's Head, 187.
Rainsford Island, 201.
Rapid, 87.
Read, T. B., quoted, 36, 248.
Rebel Prisoners, 231.
Resolute, 237.
Revere Copper Company, 139.
Revere, Paul, 156.
Richardson, Hill & Co., 297.
Ringbolt Rock, 77, 86.
Ripley, Col. N., 60, 61.
Riverside, 86.
Robin, Abbe, 259.
Rochambeau's Army, 49.
Rockland, 298
Rockland House, 62.
Romer, Col., 152, 159.
Rose Standish House, 82.
Route of Steamboats, 23.
Rowson, Susannah, 40.
Russ's Villa, Mr., 248.
Sachems' Hummock, 110.
Sagamore Hill, 68.
Sagamore John, 132.
Sagittaire, 270.
Sail down the Harbor, 23.
Sailor's Snug Harbor, 93.
St. George's Cross, 145, 148.
Saints of the Bay, 259.
Sanford Steamship Company, 297.
Saquish, 290.
Savin Hill, 114.
Schwartz, Sergeant, 170.
Sculpins, 38.
Sea-Captains, Old, 194.
Sea-Fencibles, 122, 168.
Sea-Foam House, 70.
Seafort, 282.
Sea-Horse, 194.
Seals, 38, 85, 223.
Seashore Home for Children, 135.
Sea-Weed, 78.
Sewall, 128, 131, 145, 151-153, 275.
Sewer, 118.
Seymour, Gen., 236.
Shag Rocks, 250.
Shed's Neck, 93.
Sheep Island, 214.
Shipbuilding, 94, 126.
Ship Fever, 221.

Shirley, Gov., 137.
Shirley Gut, 138, 139, 193, 217.
Shirley, The, 135.
Shurtleff, quoted, 249.
Signal-Station, Hull, 42, 43.
Six Friends, 263.
Skull Head, 69.
Slate Island, 208, 210.
Slaveholding, 123, 133, 264.
Small-pox Hospital, 138, 155, 201, 203.
Smith, Capt., 186.
Smith, Capt. John, 39, 46, 102, 112, 260.
Smith, Rev. S. F., 40.
Snake Island, 132.
Soldiers, Hull, 41.
South Boston, 24, 25, 119, 156, 190, 211, 112, 237.
Southey, Robert, 286.
South Head, 180.
South Weymouth, 90.
Spectacle Island, 174.
Squantum, 104, 107, 171.
Squeb, Capt., 47.
Squirrel Hill, 86.
Standish, Miles, 91, 97, 105, 171, 209, 260, 294.
Stark, Gen., 124.
State of Maine, 231.
Steamboat Route, 23.
Steamboats, Old-Time, 88.
Stedman, E. C., 243.
Stephens, A. H., 236.
Stoddard, R. H., 87.
Stone Temple, 100.
Stony Beach, 51.
Stoughton, quoted, 262.
Strait's Pond, 47, 67.
Strawberry Hill, 68.
Sturgis & Parker, 139.
Summer Comfort, 23.
Sunnyside, 132.
Susanna Island, 128.
Sweet Singer of the Harbor, 139, 177, 187, 202, 220, 239.
Taft's Hotel, 140.
Talleyrand-Périgord, 271.
Telegraph Hill, Hull, 41, 48.
Temple, Sir Thomas, 181, 218.
Tennesseeans, 232.
Thayer, Gen. S., 169, 228.
Third Massachusetts Regiment, 185.
Thirty-second Massachusetts Regiment, 232, 234.
Thirty-eighth Massachusetts Regiment, 190.
Thompson's Island, 25, 31, 171.
Thoreau, 45, 51, 52, 60, 239.
Thorn-Apples, 45.
Thorwald's Death, 57.
Ticknor, George, 280.
Tilghman, Gen., 232.
Tisquanto, 104, 105.
Townsend, George Alfred, quoted, 25, 90, 100.
Train's Packets, 284.
Trecothick, Barlow, 182.
Trial, 252.

Trumbull, Col., 156.
Tudor, 50, 124.
Tudor, William, 124.
Tug, The, 86.
Tupper, Major, 246.
Turkey Hill, 86.
Turks, 147, 263.
Twelfth Massachusetts, 229.
Urania, 259.
Vane, Harry, 98, 146, 218.
Veazie, Samuel, 39.
Veteran Officers, 158.
Vokes Family, 132.
Vose, Major, 246.
Wabash, 282.
Wachusett, 280.
Walker, Robert H., 228.
Walker, Sir H, 227, 263.
Ward & Co., N., 176.
Ward's Island, 214.
Warner, Charles Dudley, 241, 243.
Warren, 280.
Warren, Fort, 227.
Warren Line, 284.
Warwick, 55.
Watson's Hill, 292.
Webster, Daniel, 59, 68, 71, 85, 279.
Webster Regiment, 229.
Weir River, 28, 47, 74, 77, 85, 86.
Welcome, 263.
West Church, 220.
Western Way, 181, 201.
Weston's Colony, 91, 280.
Weymouth, 88.
Weymouth River, 93.
Whaling, 94, 112.
Wheelwright, John, 98.
Whidah, 193.
Whistling Buoy, 252.
White Angel, 54.
White, R. H., 60.
White Head, 68.
Whittier, John G., 130, 219, 278.
Wiard, Norman, 205, 212.
Wilson, Rev. John, 102.
Williams, David, 168.
Willis, N. P., 259.
Wines, E. C., 259.
Winnipurkitt, 218.
Winnisimmet, 132.
Winter at Nantasket, 78.
Winthrop, 129.
Winthrop, Deane, 131.
Winthrop, Fort, 165.
Winthrop, Gov., 47, 105, 144, 165, 195, 271.
Winthrop, R. C., 168, 218.
Witchcraft, 263.
Wollaston Heights, 102.
Wollaston's Colony, 95.
Wood, quoted, 136, 262.
World's End, 28, 85.
Worrick's, 60.
Worthylake, George, 246.
Zuñi Indians, 220.

The Sail Down the Harbor.

THE perfection of physical comfort is enjoyed, when, on a warm day of summer, one leaves the hot and crowded streets and many cares of the city, and passes down Boston Harbor on one of its luxurious excursion-steamboats. Here, without the distressing motion of the deep-sea swells, or the blank monotony of a level horizon, the bracing and invigorating air of the ocean is enjoyed to the fullest; while on either side are scores of picturesque and historic localities to attract the attention and give high zest to the journey. And if this delicious iodated atmosphere, smelling of sea-weed and surf-beaten rocks, arouses a formidable hunger, there is every variety of means for gratifying that also, from the improvident pop-corn which is sold on the deck, and the frugal but appetizing chowders of the beach-restaurants, to the rich and varied *ménus* of the great hotels at Hull and Nantasket. It is safe enough to say, that no other Atlantic city excels Boston in summer comfort. Its clean, well-swept, and sprinkled streets are frequently visited by delightful sea-breezes, whose refreshing coolness and salty savor are perceptible for a full league inland. And on a day of unusual heat and sunshine, all roads lead to the harbor; and the horse-cars for Atlantic Avenue are crowded with people eager to inhale the bracing air of the ocean. The fares on the steamboats are so small that even the poorest can go: the accommodations are so luxurious that the veriest Sybarite of the Back Bay need suffer no discomfort.

The steamboat has hardly left its pier when the interest of the voyage begins, — the vast and varied panorama commences to unroll. On the right the narrow water-lane of Fort-Point Channel runs off to the South Bay; on the left is the broad mouth of the combined Charles and Mystic rivers, with the picturesque antiquities of the American navy at the head of its vista. The long line of docks and piers, steamships and elevators, on the north, is the water-front of East Boston, the Birkenhead of the Puritan city. (If you wish to know more about this point, or others in the harbor, turn to the Alphabetical Index, at the beginning of the book.) On the right are the great piers and docks of New Boston (often so-called), covered with railway tracks, freight-houses, and elevators, and usually containing several British freight-steamships. This broad and busy plain, dedicated to commerce, has been constructed within a few years, on the melancholy mud-flats, by building high and substantial sea-walls, and filling in with gravel. The veteran master of the British steamship *Sorrento* recently said: "During all my experience as an officer and commander of steamships in the Atlantic trade, I have never before loaded at such magnificent docks. The great depth of water at low tides, and the spacious sheds and elevator, render the most complete facilities for the loading and discharging of large steamships."

At about a mile from the State House, the steamboat usually passes through a fleet of small vessels, weather-beaten coasters, and dainty yachts, anchored off Fort-Point Channel. Mr. Howells has given us this beautiful picture of the inner harbor of Boston: "A light breeze ruffled the surface of the bay, and the innumerable little sail-boats that dotted it took the sun and wind upon their wings, which they dipped almost into the sparkle of the water, and flew lightly hither and thither like gulls that loved the brine too well to rise wholly from it. Larger ships, farther or nearer, puffed or shrank their sails as they came or went on the errands of commerce, but always moved as if bent upon some dreamy affair of pleasure;

the steamboats that shot vehemently across their tranquil courses seemed only gayer and vivider visions, but not more substantial. Yonder a black sea-going steamer passed out between the far-off islands, and at last left in the sky above those reveries of fortification, a whiff of sombre smoke, dark and unreal as a memory of battle. . . . There is always a shabbiness about the wharves of sea-ports; but I must own that as soon as you get a reasonable distance from them in Boston, they turn wholly beautiful. They no longer present that imposing array of mighty ships which they could show in the days of Consul Plancus, when the commerce of the world sought chiefly our port, yet the docks are still filled with the modester kinds of shipping; and, if there is not that wilderness of spars and rigging which you see at New York, let us believe that there is an aspect of selection and refinement to the scene, so that one should describe it, not as a forest, but, less conventionally, as a gentleman's park of masts. The steamships of many coast-lines gloom, with their black, capacious hulks, among the lighter sailing-craft, and among the white, green-shuttered passenger-boats; and behind them those desperate and grimy sheds assume a picturesqueness, their sagging roofs and crooked gables harmonizing agreeably with the shipping; and then, growing up from all rises the mellow-tinted, brick-built city, roof, and spire, and dome, — a fair and noble sight, indeed, and one not surpassed for a certain quiet and cleanly beauty by any that I know."

As the course crosses the line of two miles from the State House, the high hills of South Boston bound the view on the right, crowned by the great building which was erected in 1834 for a summer-resort, under the name of the Mount-Washington House, and has been occupied for more than forty years by the Perkins School for the Blind. In the nearer waters several gray old hulks are moored, containing reserve stocks of powder and other explosives. Farther on, City Point appears, on the right, with its esplanade and fleet of yachts, beyond which towers the large asylum on Thompson's Island, across Dorchester Bay. On the left, observe the spindle, or beacon, rising from the gravelly shoals which mark the site of the ill-omened Bird Island, long since washed away by the tides.

At three miles, in a direct line from the State House, the steamboat passes between the two innermost guardians of the harbor, — Governor's Island (on the left), with its lofty mounds and citadel and low-lying water-batteries, and Castle Island (on the right), almost covered by a handsome stone fort. The view now widens rapidly; and the course is laid for more than two miles across President Roads, which were anciently known as the King's Roads. Here you are tempted to smile at the famous Maryland author who called our maze of pretty islets "a bay like a sterile archipelago of cold gray islands;" and to sympathize with Lady Duffus Hardy, praising "the glorious sail down Boston Harbor." On the right the long asylum on Thompson's Island appears again, and the high barn crowning the bluff of Spectacle Island is nearer at hand. On the left rise the graceful elms of Apple Island, with the diversified shores and villages of Winthrop close beyond. However sultry, dusty, grimy, may be the streets just left behind, here all is cool and invigorating. If the sea gives forth no breath, the forward motion of the boat is enough to make the atmosphere vibrate. If the air will not blow against you, you are blown against the air; and the result is not dissimilar. You may now fairly say, with the old Puritan of two centuries ago, "A sup of New England's air is better than a whole draught of Old England's ale." The sense of refreshment is delicious. On every side the green islands rest, fair emeralds on a sapphire plain, full

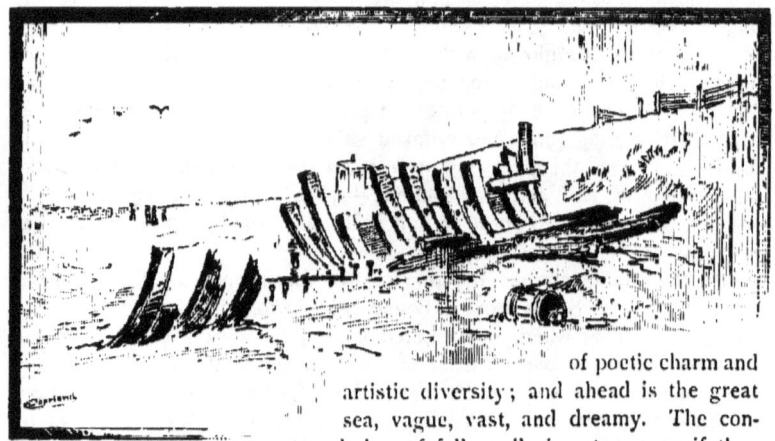

of poetic charm and artistic diversity; and ahead is the great sea, vague, vast, and dreamy. The contemplation of fellow-pilgrims, too, even if they be of "the doughnut democracy," as Nora Perry calls a large part of our harbor-excursionists, adds not a little to the interest of the trip. All types are here, from the wide-eyed rustic, enjoying every minute of the unwonted excursion, to the *blasé* Somerset-Club young man, for whom no harbor this side of the Mersey can possibly have any charms; mothers, with noisy broods of happy children; young couples, whom earth, air, and sea have no power to attract away from each other's eyes; sedate spinsters; rakish commercial travellers; prim clergymen, in conventional black; merry young girls, dressed like incarnate rainbows; care-worn men of business; the old, the young, the grave, the gay, the citizen, the countryman, the hoodlum, the snob, the gentleman, — all enjoying the superlative comfort and coolness which here replace the torridity of the town.

And so we pass between the diversified shores of Long Island, on the

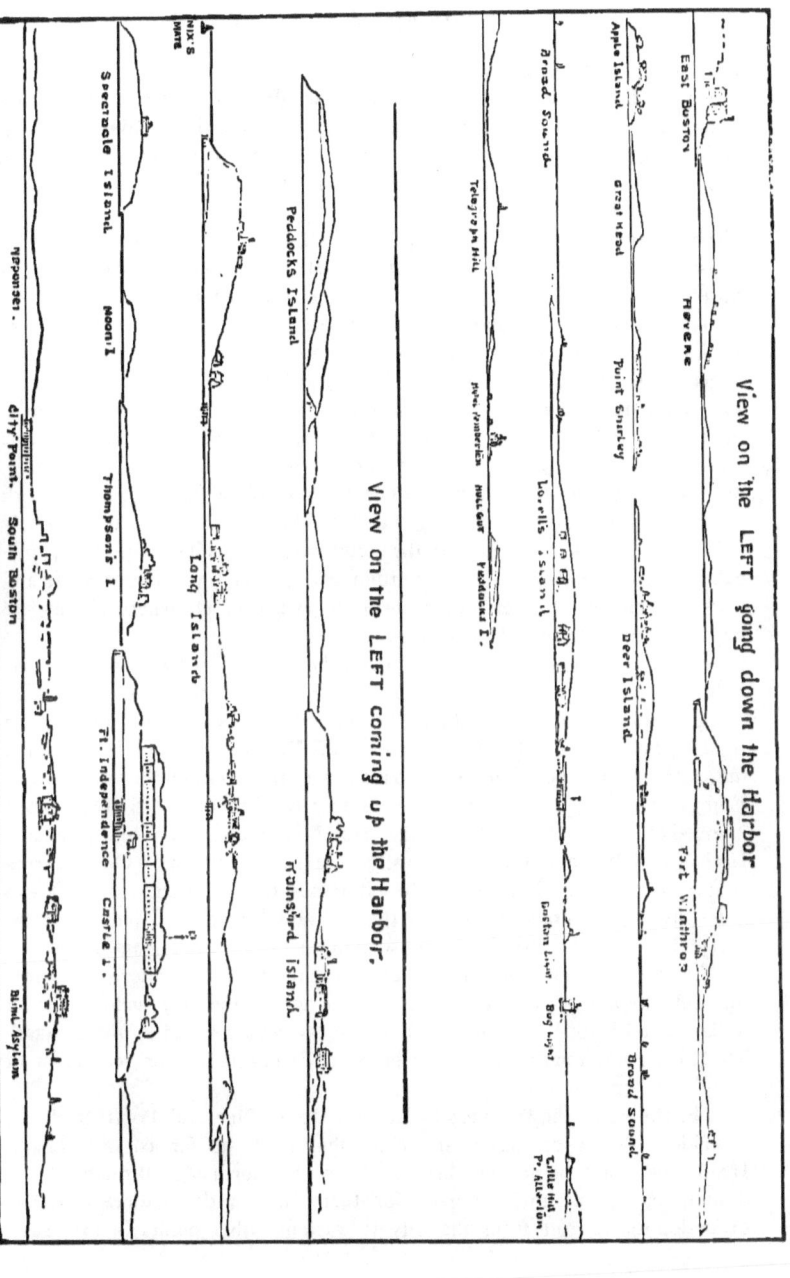

PANORAMIC VIEWS BETWEEN BOSTON AND HULL.

right, the asylum near its centre, and Deer Island on the left, where rise the great brick buildings of the city charitable and correctional institutions. At the sixth mile, in a straight line from the State House, the boat is running south-east, with Broad Sound and the open sea on one side, and on the other the bold bluff of Long-Island Head, crowned by a lighthouse and the green mounds of a battery. She then passes the grim black pyramid of Nix's Mate, and enters the narrow ship-channel, having Lovell's Island, sacred to buoys, on the left, and Gallop's Island, with its hospitals and high bluffs, on the right. If the tide favors, however, the boat leaves the ship-channel just before reaching Nix's Mate, and steers straight for Hull. Beyond the immense and frowning bulwarks of Fort Warren she runs across Nantasket Roads, with the buildings on Rainsford Island conspicuous on the right, and the rocky archipelago about the lighthouse and the open sea on the left. Here the "glimmer-glass" of the inner harbor gives place to a suggestion of the ocean-swell, — only a trifle, not enough to disturb the most delicate, but still a fair suggestion, with brisk little white-caps corrugating the blue ripples. In front are the lonely cliffs of Peddock's Island and the snug village of Hull, with the many-gabled Hotel Pemberton proudly prominent. After traversing a swift and narrow strait, the steamer rounds in at the pier of Hull, where passengers may take the railway to Nantasket.

If you are not inclined to land here, the boat will carry you on across a broad and beautiful bay, with the inner lines of Nantasket Beach on the left, and Peddock's Island and the Quincy and Weymouth shores on the right; past the round green mamelon of Bumpkin Island, and through the narrow pass between White Head and the pasture-hills of World's End; and then up the picturesque winding reaches of Weir River, to the Nantasket-Beach pier, hard by the Hotel Nantasket and the Rockland House, and but a few minutes' walk from the ocean-surf. Other steamboats, after leaving Hull, run south-east across the inner bay for about two miles, leaving Bumpkin Island on the right, and reach the pier at Strawberry Hill, near the Sea-Foam House, and a short distance from the sea.

The boats which touch at the old pier at Hull (the easterly one, near the hill) do not go to the beach, but run across the bay just spoken of to Downer Landing, with its pretty cottages and aristocratic Rose Standish House, and then wind up the crooked harbor to the ancient town of Hingham.

The routes of the steamers to Nahant, Ocean Pier, and Point of Pines, coincide with the course of the Nantasket boats as far as Long-Island Head. Off that point they bear away to the north-east, through Broad Sound, and shape their courses for their various destinations. Other excursion-routes run from the city to various other points in the lower

OUTLINE MAP OF BOSTON HARBOR.

harbor, to Point Shirley, and other well-known localities. The time-tables of the harbor-lines change from month to month, and should be consulted in the Boston newspapers.

The Nantasket-Beach Railroad. — The Nantasket-Beach Railroad is a good enterprise, which is highly appreciated by the people around the harbor, both in Boston and along the beaches. It starts from the steamboat-pier at Hull, and runs around the shore, on the channel side of Cushing's Hill, along the crest of Stony Beach, over the west (or harborward) slope of Point Allerton, and then along the Nantasket plains to the great beach, which is traversed through almost its entire length. There are numerous stations, near the chief points of interest and attraction, at Point Allerton, Strawberry Hill, and beyond. After passing the Rockland House the railway turns inland, among strange rocky hillocks, and meets the Old Colony line in the town of Hingham. On foggy and stormy days, this route is availed of by the people who must go to Boston. The length of the line is nine miles; and the fare is ten cents, over the entire route or any part of it. It is one of the most charming rides imaginable; close beside the cool and salty sea, with the waves breaking so near as to throw spray, at high wind and tide, over the rails, — so near, that, in the winter of 1882, a section of the track was destroyed by a wrecked vessel that was thrown upon it. There is great variety of scenery, too, — the stately procession of vessels in the light-house channel; the Brewster Islands, "green and brown, like cairngorms set in blue enamel;" the lake-like expanses of the inner harbor; and the wide blue ocean, with its surges whitening up the strand beneath the car-windows.

The Ancient Town of Hull.

THE HOTEL PEMBERTON. — HINGHAM BAY. — HULL YACHT-CLUB. — TELEGRAPH HILL. — BITS OF HISTORY.

STRONG and steadfast arm, which, bent on guard, protects Boston Harbor from the easterly gales, is the long peninsula of Hull. The shoulder is Atlantic Hill; the biceps, White Head; the sharp elbow, Point Allerton; the tip of the hand, Windmill Point. From end to end it is not far from seven miles long; but its width will not average a half-mile, and for long stretches a stone can be thrown across it from the harbor to the sea. Hillard complimented the Lido of Venice by likening it to this great natural breakwater of Nantasket. There are summer villages all along the beach; but the only place where those to the manor born dwell, the year round, is a quaint old hamlet on the extreme point, partly hemmed in and sheltered by three high hills. There are about two hundred and ten inhabitants here, with thirty-six on the adjacent islands, and about one hundred and fifty on Nantasket Beach. The

Bath-houses, near Hull Pier.

village is nine miles from Boston by water; and frequent steamers ply back and forth in half an hour, during the summer days. It is twenty-two miles distant by land, with a continuous railway the entire distance.

The Hotel Pemberton looms up alongside Nantasket Roads like some tall castle, over the low beaches of Windmill Point. It is in that quaint and somewhat *outré* form of architecture for which good Queen Anne has been held responsible, with towers, gables, balconies, piazzas, and other picturesque adjuncts. There are upwards of a hundred rooms, with wide and airy halls and parlors, rich furniture and carpets, elevators, wine-vaults, gas-works and lights, vast kitchens, billiard-tables, and a bar of generous proportions. Usually some celebrated band, with a full corps of soloists, gives two concerts daily here, from 3 to 5, and from 7 to 9 P.M.; and every Wednesday and Saturday evenings there are brilliant displays of fireworks. There are broad piazzas around the three lower stories. In front of the house is a band-stand, where the best military music is given; and the scene is very brilliant at evening, when a score of electric lights are flashing through the darkness, and crowds of people promenade in the vicinity. The steamboat-pier and railway-station are in front of the house; and here thousands of visitors debark on every pleasant summer day, in search of the cool breezes and beautiful views for which this locality is famous. The main fronts of the hotel face the south-west, across the broad Quincy Bay to the Blue Hills; and north-east, across Nantasket Roads to the Brewster islands and the open sea. Almost due north, only a mile away, are the massive walls of Fort Warren, whose morning and evening guns and bugle-calls are plainly audible, and whose flag is seen to drop with the setting sun. To the westward extends a broad, open reach of the harbor, with the high and lonely bluffs of Peddock's Island closing in very near at hand, just across the racing waters of Hull Gut. Such are the very satisfactory natural features. An added charm appears in the exuberant life which all summer long throbs about this sea-palace. The little cove close by the hotel is the headquarters of a notable fleet of gallant yachts, of all conceivable models, from the catamaran to the costly schooner-yacht, from the arrowy little pleasure-steamboat to the unwieldy galliot which takes out family parties on safe (but not exciting) nautical excursions. On every side their white sails gleam, as they fly away towards Germantown and Weymouth, or swoop daringly among the light-house islands, or stand outward until they are hull-down on the level horizon of the sea. Among these spoiled pets of the waves and winds the white harbor-steamboats rush in and out, on their half-hourly trips between the half-roasted city and its breezy marine environs. The fishing-vessels are seen skimming out by the Light, or beating down Broad Sound; and the immense British steamships move up the ship-channel with an air of conscious power and importance. All this, and much more, passes within close view of the Pemberton, which is as devoid as Eddystone Light-house of a landward side.

THE HOTEL PEMBERTON, AT WINDMILL POINT, HULL.

THE OREGON HOUSE, HULL

The Oregon House, not far from the Pemberton, was built in 1848, from the materials of the Castle-barracks. When Col. Wright's Massachusetts regiment was coming home from the Mexican war, Major Thayer, then in command of Fort Independence, disposed of the barracks there so that the volunteers (whom he greatly disliked) could not be quartered in them. The material was bought by Rev. Robert Gould, and carried to Hull, where the Oregon House was built. It has received considerable additions during the last five years, and still retains its old *habitués*, who have come hither almost every summer for a quarter of a century. It is a favorite resort for those who seek smelting, in the fall; and no place on the coast can show such good fishing-grounds as the waters in the vicinity of Hull. Of the other boarding-houses in the village, the chief are the St. Cloud, near the Oregon; the Hayes House, fronting on the pond; and the Nantasket, near the bay which extends toward Strawberry Hill. The bold hill on the

Capt. James's Landing, Hull.

south of the peninsula is covered with summer cottages and villas, some of which have much architectural beauty. On the old steamboat-wharf, near the Oregon House (where the boats of the Hingham line stop) is the commodious house of the Hull Yacht-Club, built in 1882, and devoted to the heartiest good-fellowship. This organization, though but five or six years old, has nearly five hundred members, and is the largest yacht-club (with one exception) in the United States. The handsome sheet of water which is nearly enclosed by Nantasket, Hull, Peddock's Island, Hough's Neck and the mainland, although officially recognized as a part of Boston Harbor, is often called Hingham Bay, and covers an area of nearly ten square miles. Of late years this has become a favorite locality for yachtsmen, who can now exercise their white-winged steeds of the sea with but little anxiety. Here many novices are initiated into the noble art, and taught the meaning of the mysterious phrases of nautical science, to the music of "Nancy Lee" and "Yeo ho! lads, ho!" In this regard, the house of the Yacht-Club becomes a college of naval science, with nearly four hundred proficient students, whose boats, with all sail set, are continually skimming over this fair little sea. It is a sight of rare beauty, when, on a bright summer day, the accomplishments of the yachtsmen and the virtues of their boats are tested in the regatta, and the bay is whitened by a long procession of sails, stretching away to some distant goal, and rounding to for the swift homeward voyage. The confirmed landsman, who does not know the difference between a forecastle and a flying-jib, finds a more tranquil joy in sailing out in the local pleasure-boats, with the strong hand of Capt. James, or Capt. Lowe, or Pope, or Tower, on the tiller, and their practised eyes watching the course. One of these veterans, with a boat as clean as the *boudoir* of Lady Clara Vere de Vere, may be hired for two or three dollars, for a long afternoon, to sail whithersoever the wind allows. Free from care of course or current, one may sail on for hours through a deepening peace, dreaming over the legends of the islands, or enjoying such sweet repose as Buchanan Read sang of, in his " Drifting : " —

Skipper William James, Hull.

" My soul to-day
  Is far away
Sailing the [fair New-England] Bay;
  My wingèd boat,
  A bird afloat,
Sails round the purple peaks remote.

" Round purple peaks
  It sails, and seeks
Blue inlets and their crystal creeks,
  Where high rocks throw,
  Through deeps below,
A duplicated golden glow.

" I heed not if
  My rippling skiff
Float swift or slow from cliff to cliff, —
  With dreamful eyes
  My spirit lies
Under the walls of Paradise.

" Under the walls
  Where swells and falls
The Bay's deep breast at intervals,
  At peace I lie,
  Blown softly by,
A cloud upon this liquid sky.

" The day, so mild,
  Is Heaven's own child,
With Earth and Ocean reconciled;
  The airs I feel
  Around me steal
Are murmuring to the murmuring keel.

" Over the rail
  My hand I trail
Within the shadow of the sail,
  A joy intense,
  The cooling sense
Glides down my drowsy indolence."

In the snug little cove, alongside the Pemberton, there are commodious landing-stages, and off-shore scores of yachts have their moorings. Hither they return as the purple haze of evening rises from the eastern sea, folding their wings like weary birds, as they round the point, and glide into the tranquil inner waters. There is a Venetian element in the scene after dusk, when their colored lights shine over the little lagoon, and the sounds of music and mirth float in, mellowed by distance and partly muffled by the manifold and mysterious voices of the sea. It is well to remember, while looking upon this stately Pemberton, that in 1721 the people of Hull voted that there should never be a public house in the town.

The ancient village church stood by the pond, but was destroyed many years ago; and the feeble flock of resident Hullonians worshipped in the little town-hall (also beside the pond) until 1881, when another churchlet was erected. The piquancy of youth, and something of its rawness, is observable in the summer-houses on the hill; but in the ancient homes which closely line the winding street below are fascinating suggestions of venerable traditions of the last century, of French garrisons, of piratical wreckers, of strange adventures on distant seas. What stories could the old Hunt house tell; or Loring's dignified mansion, with its weather-beaten walls half screened by friendly foliage: or the Cushing place, which since 1720 has guarded the inner end of Love Lane; or the legend-haunted old colonial house at the village end of Love Lane, rising from an immense thicket of neglected rose-bushes. Here a Hawthorne or a Whittier might find embarrassing riches of material. The residents are ethnological curiosities. Several of them (or their parents) came from Cattaro, and other harbors of the Adriatic; others from Germany, from Ragusa, from Portugal, from Capri. The person who called himself Mitchell was a Dalmatian, who, after long naval service in the French fleets of Napoleon's time, drifted ashore at Hull, and founded a family, whose present representatives are worthy citizens of the little village.

Sally Jones's House, Hull.

Hull has suffered the fate of most isolated communities in being maligned by many visitors; and startling tales of false lights, merciless wreckers, and pirates, have attached themselves to this salty little hamlet. But the venerable old town is neither an Alsatia nor a Barrataria; and whoever ventures out in the sailboats of the peninsular youth will find good attention, rude courtesy, and shrewd intelligence in their pilots, who dearly love their little town, and, as Dr. Holmes says, are fond of the modest paraphrase, "All are but parts of one stupendous Hull."

Beneath the shadow of the hill stands the Cushing house, built as a parsonage for the Rev. Ezra Carpenter, who ministered at Hull from 1725 to 1756. It is well preserved (his study still being shown), and wears its years with dignity. More than a century ago, when Capt. Souther (formerly of the Royal Navy) lived there, it was frequently the summer resting-place of James Otis, the famous orator and Revolutionary patriot.

From the wharf many small fish are caught, to the great glee of that portion of urban Young America which summers at Hull. Frequently, too, the beguiling hooks bring up atrociously hideous sculpins, which, however, are not without use as lobster-bait. Nay, they have even served a high homiletical purpose also, as when Mr. Beecher bade his startled flock consider, " How many men there are that are like those fish we catch in Boston Harbor, — four-fifths of them are mouth, and the rest is tail."

One or two of the Hullonians devote themselves to hunting seals in the harbor. These strange amphibious animals abound near certain of the islands, and are often seen sunning themselves upon the rocks. They weigh from seventy-five to two hundred pounds each, and produce about two gallons of oil. Several seal-cubs have been captured and tamed, making very amusing pets, and having a bark not unlike that of a dog.

The lobsters of Hull have long been famous. Two hundred and sixty years ago Morton recorded the deeds of their worst persecutors: "The Beare is a tyrant at a lobster, and at low water will down to the Rocks, and groape after them with great diligence." There are thirty or more fishermen at Hull, whose baited lobster-pots are sunk at many points near the islands, and marked by little floating bits of wood. This is the chief port for lobster-fishing in Massachusetts, within whose waters upwards of a million of the delicious crustaceans are captured yearly. The supply is fast decreasing; so that it may not be long with us as when the reverend author of "New-England's Plantation" (*anno* 1630) veritably wrote, "We take abundance of Lobsters, that the least Boy in the Plantation may both catch and eat what he will of them. For my owne part I was soone cloyed with them, they were so great, and fat, and lussious." Visitors at some of the minor summer resorts hereabouts have been heard plaintively expressing the same idea.

In 1700 the town opened the road to "The Point;" and many small wharves, warehouses, and shops were built to accommodate the fishing-trade. There was a goodly fleet of snug little schooners finding here their home port. Thereby were made good the words of Capt. John Smith, written about this coast two and a half centuries ago: "Therefore, honorable and worthy countrymen, let not the meannesse of the word *fishe* distaste you; for it will afford as good gold as the mines of Guiana or Potossie, with lesse hazard and charge, and more certainty and facility."

The Vandal axes which have destroyed the beauty of this region were set in motion in 1644, when the Legislature ordered one hundred and fifty tons of timber to be cut at Nantasket, "to bee ymployed uppon ye ffortifications att Castle Iland." Five years later the planters here petitioned the Legislature "for the encouraging Mr. Mathewes to goe to them and preach amongst them." But the Boston authorities denied them this saving help, and Matthews went without it. It is probable that the old Hunt estate house was built for his par-

The Old Lovell House, Hull.

sonage. It certainly was occupied in 1670 by Zechariah Whitman, a Harvard graduate, who preached here from 1670 to 1726; and Samuel Veazie, pastor from 1753 to 1767, made a painting in the kitchen which is still preserved. Since the Revolution, religious services have been held irregularly in this smallest of Yankee parishes, and no pastor settled here between 1772 and 1881. The church was blown down in the great gale of 1815. In 1657 there were twenty families in Hull, contributing forty pounds to the revenue of Massachusetts, and claiming a notable share in the government of the Bay Province.

After Veazie's demise the old parsonage was the home of one of the most notable local families,—that of William Haswell, a British naval officer, who was wrecked on Lovell's Island in 1767, and settled at Hull, where he lived until the revolt of America. His daughter, who passed her early years here, was the famous Susanna Rowson, some time a sprightly and graceful actress in many cities, and later the foremost teacher in Boston, and a very popular author. Of her novel entitled "Charlotte Temple," twenty-five thousand copies were sold in a few years. She was also the author of the very popular song, "When Rising from Ocean," which was sung to the tune of "Anacreon in Heaven," afterwards applied to "The Star-spangled Banner." Mrs. Rowson thus described Hull one hundred and twenty years ago, in her novel of "Rebecca:" —

"On the left hand of the entrance of Boston Harbor is a beautiful little peninsula, called H——: it consists of two gradually rising hills, beautifully diversified with orchards, cornfields, and pasture-land. In the valley is built a little village, consisting of about fifty houses, the inhabitants of which just make shift to decently support a minister, who on a Sunday ascends the pulpit, in a rustic temple, situated by the side of a piece of water, nearly in the middle of the village, and teaches, to the utmost of his ability, the true principles of Christianity. The neck of land which joins this peninsula to the mainland is very narrow, and, indeed, is sometimes overflowed by the tide. On one side it forms a charmingly picturesque harbor, in which are a number of small, but delightful fertile islands; and on the other it is washed by the ocean, to which it lays open."

About seven years ago the venerable house of Matthews, Veazie, and Haswell was purchased by John Boyle O'Reilly, the Irish-American poet, and editor of "The Pilot" (the chief Roman-Catholic paper of America), who has since made it his summer home. In its yard is the grave of a British soldier, the son of an Old-Country parish curate, who was mortally wounded during the attack on the light-house in 1775, and brought ashore by the victorious Americans. He received tender care from the Haswell family, and was buried in their yard, Susannah herself reading the funeral service.

The Nantasket House, alongside this ancient mansion, was (in part) built in 1675, by Col. Robert Gould; and the quaint old post-office was the birthplace of Col. Amos Binney, for many years naval agent at Boston.

One of the best-known of the summer cottagers, during the last ten years, is Samuel F. Smith, D.D., the venerable scholar, whose poem "My Country, 'tis of thee," has become the national song, and is familiar from Sitka to St. Augustine. Among the blue hills which crowd along the northwestern horizon, he wrote "America," while a student at the Andover school of the prophets, in 1832. Among the other summer residents are (or have been) Col. R. M. Pulsifer, of "The Boston Herald;" the Hon. Moody Merrill, President of the Highland Railway Company; George P.

Lathrop, the novelist and poet, and his wife, the daughter of Nathaniel Hawthorne.

One of the most delightful bits in old Hull was the rude platform around the flagstaff, surrounded with picturesque fragments and names of vessels which had been wrecked on the adjacent strand. Beneath stood a quaint little iron cannon, which might have been brought over on Gov. Winthrop's fleet. This charming group of naval and historic *bric-à-brac* was removed only four or five years ago. Among the ancient trophies of Hull was the great anchor of the British ship-of-the-line *Poictiers*, seventy-four guns, which ran into the Roads during a terrible storm, in 1812, and at early morning cut her cable and fled to sea again. Perhaps she was frightened by that grassy little fort on Telegraph Hill.

The Old Hunt House, Hull.

During the last war, Hull contributed more than her quota, sending twenty-four men to the army and navy, out of a population of two hundred and eighty-five. In 1759, when the militia was enrolled, she reported eight able-bodied men, "and no more;" although even then her people boasted that "Hull had thirty-three houses when Boston had but one." The pulse-beat of the republic was felt nowhere more quickly than in this secluded nook; and in May, 1861, the men raised here a flagstaff one hundred and eight feet high, from which floated an immense new American flag, made by the women of Hull. Two years after the war closed, one of the State militia brigades was encamped here.

The highest of the three hills which diversify the little peninsula is Telegraph Hill, whose summit is occupied by the old French fort, whose walls, bastions, embrasures, and moats are still well preserved. Here also is a well, ninety feet deep, from which the valiant militiamen hoped to get water, should they be invested on all sides. Many a cannon-shot has been fired from this height at the British frigates that sailed up the harbor in Revolutionary times, and many a sailor of his Majesty's service has thereby received his eternal discharge. Inside the fort is a quaint little house, aged and storm-worn, with a two-story wooden tower. Many years ago this station was established for the purpose of signalling to Boston the approach of vessels on the outer sea. A tower stood on Central Wharf, Boston, whence the signals (as repeated from an intervening island) were observed, and repeated to the Old State House. At first the names and characters of incoming ships were indicated by wooden arms, at varying angles, on a tall staff; and later, a set of one hundred and twelve different flags, one for each shipping merchant of Boston, was in use. Vessels entering the Bay bore their owner's colors, and their identity was thus easily made out, and signalled to Boston. Since the invention of the telegraph, this cumbrous system has been abandoned, and marine news passes up by a wire twenty-five miles long, leading around the South Shore. A message is sent every half-hour, and recorded in a great book at the Boston Chamber of Commerce, together with the reports from Highland Light, so that the merchants can tell at any time what is going on in the Bay. The custom-house officers and other harbor-guards are warned in like manner. When large ocean-steamships are coming in at night, they are recognized by their rockets and blue lights. The operator reports the approach of all steamers, West-Indiamen, and square-rigged vessels, but ignores fishing-craft and small coasters. The hull of a vessel can be seen eighteen miles out, and her spars at twenty miles out. In the winter season the little building is rocked and penetrated by the howling storms; and in summer the wires on this lofty point sometimes draw in white shafts of lightning; but the old salts remain here unconcernedly, spinning their unending yarns, and occasionally sweeping the outer Bay with a telescope, as if they were perched on the main-top of a cruiser, on look-out duty.

The surrounding intrenchments are full of interest to antiquarians, being of ancient and somewhat uncertain origin. In 1778 Massachusetts called out three thousand of her militia to finish and garrison the harbor forts; and Washington sent the Chevalier Du Portail, then chief engineer of the United-States army, to superintend the construction of the new works. This officer planned the defences of West Point, and was afterwards Minister of War in France. The fort on Telegraph Hill was armed with several heavy guns, and garrisoned by militia from Hingham and adjacent towns. It was for a long time under the direction of Gen. Benjamin Lincoln, and some say that Lafayette himself made the working-plans from which it was built.

Military engineers find the little fort very interesting, as an example of old French fortress-architecture.

Some part of this work was probably erected in 1778, when the formidable French frigates *César, Provence, Fantasque, Zélé, Sagittaire, Tonnant, Hector, Vaillant,* and others, lay in Nantasket Roads, and the line-of-battle ships *Languedoc* and *Marseillais,* which had been so roughly used by the British vessels *Renown* and *Isis,* off Rhode Island, were being repaired at Boston. Not satisfied with fortifying all the adjacent islands, the Count D'Estaing landed all his marines and large detachments of sailors, at Hull, and erected here a formidable thirty-gun battery. When

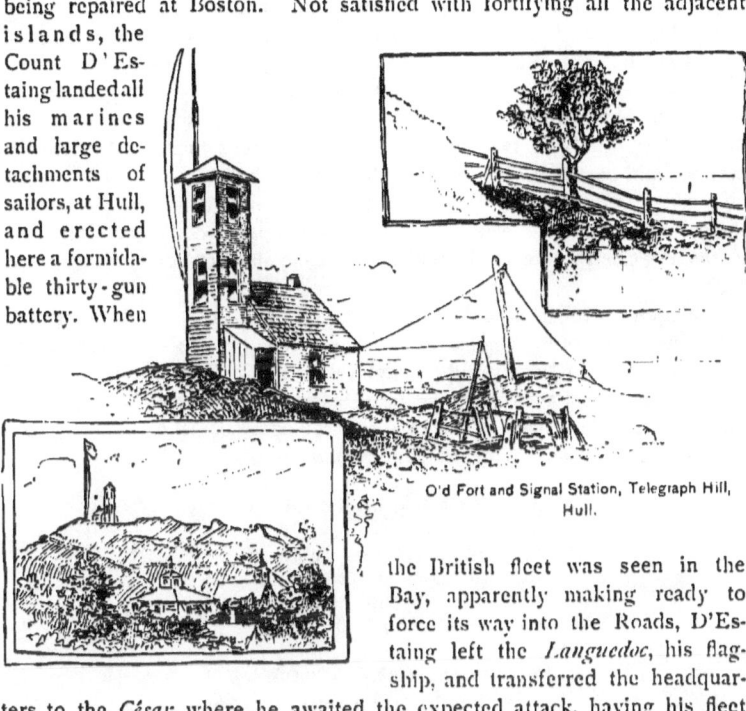

Old Fort and Signal Station, Telegraph Hill, Hull.

the British fleet was seen in the Bay, apparently making ready to force its way into the Roads, D'Estaing left the *Languedoc,* his flagship, and transferred the headquarters to the *César,* where he awaited the expected attack, having his fleet cleared for action, and his batteries shotted, ready for a close and desperate engagement.

On the 17th of July, 1776, the battery on this site, and that on Long-Island Head, fired a salute of thirteen guns, in honor of the promulgation of the Declaration of Independence, which had just reached Boston. In case of war, it would become necessary to fortify and garrison this position strongly; since it looks down almost into the parade-ground of Fort Warren, and a hostile battery here could break "the key of the harbor" in short order. The artillery officers at the fort have recognized the strategic importance of this position, and doubtless have prepared their plans to make of Telegraph Hill a miniature Gibraltar.

The view from this point is magnificent; and on summer days, especially towards sunset, it is enjoyed by many visitors, grouped on the venerable grassy ramparts. It includes all the white summer resorts on the North and South Shores, from Manchester and Magnolia around to Cohasset and Hingham; the long and graceful curve of Nantasket Beach, with its crowded hotels and cottages; the island-studded harbor, bounded by the rolling Blue Hills and the masses of buildings which culminate in the gilded dome of the State House; and, far away in the interior, the azure crest of Wachusett. On a clear day you may see, beyond the black and rocky Brewsters around which the waves whiten ceaselessly, the dim line of Cape Ann and the twin light-houses on Thacher's Island. At night the scene is still beautiful, and includes the warning lights, fixed and revolving, on a wide range of coast; the twinkling house-lamps in scores of villages; the colored lanterns of vessels bound in and out; and the multiform fireworks and electric illuminations with which the summer hotels diversify the night.

Telegraph Hill is owned by an elderly maiden lady of Hingham, who tenaciously refuses to sell or lease it. Were it not so, this glorious height, sacred now to pure beauty and grandeur, would be quickly occupied by dull little *bourgeois* cottages; and the peaceful cattle, browsing the salty grass through which the path leads upward, would be banished to the lonely shores of Peddock's. No more hence could we look out where, —

"At dawn the fleet stretched miles away,
  On ocean plains asleep, —
 Trim vessels waiting for the day
  To move across the deep.
 So still the sails, they seemed to be
 White lilies growing in the sea.

"When evening touched the cape's low rim,
  And dark fell on the waves,
 We only saw processions dim
  Of clouds from shadowy caves:
 These were the ghosts of buried ships,
 Gone down in one brief hour's eclipse."

Near the foot of the hill, on the side towards the open sea, stood the cemetery of the French army which was quartered in and about the deserted village during the Revolutionary War. Here, if the local traditions are not at fault, several hundred of our gallant allies were buried, after the fatal prevalence of an epidemic. Poor boys! the flower of the youth of France, they passed into rest here, lulled to their long slumbers by the moan of the northern sea, and nevermore should see the flowery banks of Seine or Loire, the pleasant hills of Auvergne. Even History herself has forgotten them: but a few wrinkled crones in the neighboring village tell (as it was told to them) how they died; and every springtime kindly Nature adorns their graves with hardy flowers, chief among which is their own royal emblem, the *fleur-de-lys*.

> "By rocky coast, in salty bight,
> Their banners glitter in the light."

The ancient road from Hull to the mainland runs up from the pond over the low *col* north of Telegraph Hill, and down to the shore of Light-house Channel. It is a delightful grass-grown track, so lonely and still that imaginative visitors have called it the Appian Way; flanked on either side by ruined fortifications built by Latin armies (for so we may designate our French allies), and bordered at one point by a diminutive grove of gnarled and wind-wrenched thorn-apple trees (*Datura stramonium*), whose seeds were brought from France. Thoreau noted these very trees, and rejoiced: "At sight of this cosmopolite, — this Capt. Cook among plants, — carried in ballast all over the world, I felt as if I were on the highway of nations. Say, rather, this Viking, king of the bays, for it is not an innocent plant: it suggests, not merely commerce, but its attendant vices, as if its fibres were the stuff of which pirates spin their yarns." Where the road reaches its highest point, a noble sea-view opens out, with the neighboring rocky islets off-shore, and beyond a weltering blue expanse, which stretches eastward, without a break, to the remote Iberian coasts of Pontevedra and Cape Finisterre,

Hull Burying-Ground and Point Allerton.

> "A glimpse of blue immensity,
> A little strip of sea."

On the south-east slope of Telegraph Hill is the old graveyard of the village, recognizable from miles away by its luxuriant trees. The oldest monument bears the date of 1684. Here are the graves of many Cushings and Lorings, and memorial slabs to men who were buried at sea or in distant ports. There were many very ancient monuments here; but the local tradition says that they were carried down to the waterside during the time the French army laid at Hull, and utilized as wash-boards. The soldiers probably used them as the riverside *blanchisseuses* of Paris still do the sides of their barges and quays, by beating the wet clothes against them.

In this locality, where so many of the actors in the long history of Hull have gone to rest, let us contemplate a few episodes in the history of the hamlet.

We have a fair glimpse of the coasts between Cape Ann and Cohasset, before the pestilence nearly annihilated the aborigines, in Capt. John Smith's rather optimistic description of his voyage in 1614: "And then the country of the Massachusits which is the paradise of all those parts: for here are many Iles all planted with corne; groves, mulberries, salvage gardens, and good harbors: the coast is for the most part, high clayie sandie cliffs. The Sea Coast as you passe, shewes you all along large corne fields, and great troupes of well proportioned people: but the French having remained heere neere sixe weekes, left nothing for us to take occasion to examine the inhabitants relations, viz. if there be neere three thousand people upon these Iles; and that the river doth pearce many daies journieis the intralles of that countrey."

It is said that three wandering Englishmen, Thomas and John Gray, and Walter Knights, bought this Hull peninsula from its Indian lords, as early as the year 1622, and settled there. Not long afterward they were joined by John Oldham, John Lyford, and Roger Conant, from Plymouth. The Pilgrims had already built a trading-station here; and these three worthies appointed themselves respectively as chief of traffic with the Indians, Episcopal chaplain, and chief of fisheries. Morton thus narrates the expulsion of John Oldham from Plymouth: "A lane of Musketiers was made, and he compelled in scorne to passe along betweene, & to receave a bob by every musketier, and then a board a shallop, and so convayed to Wessagusus shoare, & staid at Massachussets, to whom John Layford and some few more did resort, where Master Layford freely executed his office and preached every Lords day, and yet maintained his wife and children foure or five, upon his industry there, with the blessing of God, and the plenty of the Land, without the helpe of his auditory, in an honest and laudable manner, till hee was wearied and made to leave the Country."

In time Oldham and Lyford went away; and Conant sailed to the northward, where he founded Gloucester and Salem. When the Winthrop colony arrived, and settled Boston, they spoke of the plantation at the mouth of the harbor as "an uncoth place," which, however, contributed to the costs of the expedition against Merrymount. The little Episcopal flock which followed Lyford from Plymouth had not chosen to go with him to Virginia. Probably the chief settlement was near Straits Pond and Weir River. In 1629 there were four clergymen at Salem, of whom at least two found themselves superfluous; and the Rev. Mr. Smith and his family thereupon "goes to some straggling people at Natasco." The name of *Hull* first appears in 1644, and was derived from the stout old Yorkshire seaport of Kingston-upon-Hull, just then famous for its sieges in the Civil Wars. (Some say, however, that it was named from Joseph Hull of Hingham.)

It was in the pleasant springtime of 1630 that the *Mary and John*, a great ship of four hundred tons, left English Plymouth, and crossed the seas to the western wilderness, bearing many "godly families of Devonshire and Dorsetshire," and their goods. "They came by the good hand of the Lord, through the deeps comfortably," says the record of the voyage. But Capt. Squeb was a careful mariner, and durst not sail his heavily laden ship into an unknown and intricate harbor. So he plumped them and theirs ashore on Nantasket, which the hundred and forty saints stigmatized as "a forlorn place in this wilderness." Here they abode for some days, while reconnoitring parties were sent out (under Southcot, a veteran of the Low-Country Wars), — one which ascended to Watertown, and encamped three days, amicably exchanging English biscuit for Indian bass with the natives; and another which examined the South-Boston peninsula, and secured the removal of the colony thither. The *Mary and John* lay off Nantasket for some time; for Gov. Winthrop called on Capt. Squeb, and was received with a salute of five guns.

After this invasion by the Puritans, the planters at Hull enjoyed peace for two years. In 1632 the Bostonians, "in regard the French were like to prove ill neighbors, being Papists," resolved to build a fort here, "partly to be some block in an enemy's way (though it could not bar his entrance)." So Gov. Winthrop and his four assistants, with three ministers and eighteen citizens, sailed down to Hull, to choose the best strategic point. A stiff north-wester kept them there two winter days and nights, during which time they lived on shell-fish, and slept on the ground, but yet contrived to be "very merry," as the record avers. The natural conclusion of the matter was, that "It was agreed by all that to build a fort there would be of too great charge and of little use; whereupon the planting of that place was deferred."

Some of the founders of New England made their homes here, in those remote days. John Prince, one of the first settlers of Hull, was the son of the rector of East Shefford, in English Berkshire, and received his education at Oxford. He fled to New England when Archbishop Laud's persecutions began, and settled on the sea-girt peninsula. From him descended the Rev. Thomas Prince, the famous author of the New-England Chronology. Another of the ancient worthies was James Pemberton (from whom the hotel is named), a wandering and adventurous fellow, of Winthrop's colony, who finally founded the town of Malden, where he died many years later. Israel Loring was born at Hull in 1682, and became one of the church fathers of New England, occupying the pastorate of Sudbury for sixty-six years. He published over one thousand pages of printed matter, and left behind him MS. records and journals filling thirty volumes of two hundred and twenty-four pages each. From this venerable pastor the Ohio Lorings and other widely scattered branches descended.

In 1673, when Massachusetts was beleaguered by enemies, Hull set up a beacon and watch-house on her highest point, and prepared fire-balls of pitch and oakum with which to send an alarm up the Bay. Telegraph Hill was then covered with cornfields. Two years later, in the thick of King Philip's War, the villagers sent up to the "Honorable Council at Boston" this pathetic appeal: "The Petition off your poore petitioners humbly sheweth, that Whereas the Lord by his prouidence hath cast vs to haue our abode as inhabitants in this towne of *Hull*, in this iuncture of time, where in both this place as well as the Whole Country is exposed to the wasting ffury off the most barbarous heathen, which wee are sensible off, and therfore ffreely willing to spend our care, our strength, yea, wee hope our very lives, in and for the defence off this place, and the Country, yet, beinge persons whose sole employment is ffishinge, and soe att sea, hauinge no lands, nor Cattle to mayntayne ourselves, or familyes, but what wee must haue hitherto done by the blessinge of God on our Labours produced ffrom the sea: beinge therefore now comanded by our Cheife officer, not to goe forth on our imploy, desired then to know, how Wee and ours shall be mayntayned, they hauinge a year's prouision aforehand, Wee none: they hauinge Cattle to giue milke to theire familyes in summer, Wee none; they hauinge Cattle and swine to kill for meats, Wee none; soe that Wee are like to bee put to Extremity, both Wee and ours; ffor they will not support us."

The Nantasket beacon was erected in 1696, and the standing orders to the watchers were to fire it "on the sight of two great ships." In August, 1690, Sir William Phipps and his colonial officers landed here, and had a farewell feast. At evening the fleet of thirty-two sail moved out to sea, and entered upon the mournful and disastrous expedition against Quebec. A few months earlier Phipps had sailed from Nantasket Roads with three war-vessels and seven hundred men, and captured Port Royal with its well-armed fortress. Many other naval expeditions were sent hence against Port Royal during the next half-century, the chief of which was composed of the frigates *Dragon, Chester, Falmouth, Leostaffe*, etc., with twenty transports and five New-England regiments. In 1704 Col. Benjamin Church gathered an army of five hundred and fifty New-Englanders and Indians, and kept them in camp at Hull for several weeks; after which they sailed away to the eastward, convoyed by three frigates, and made a destructive foray on the French settlements of Maine and Acadie.

Perhaps the soldiers and sailors of all these royal fleets did despite to the Hullonian hen-roosts and orchards, for this was one of the first localities to pronounce against the king's government. As early as 1774 the town had protested against British aggression, by an unanimous vote; and, when the Revolution began, the young Dills volunteered in the American army, and received from their admiring townsmen twenty-seven hundred pounds (unfortunately in Old Tenor). At a later date the village was deserted except by a single family, and made a comfortable cantonment for the army of the Count de Rochambeau, which encamped here in quarantine before its embarkation for the Southern battle-fields.

When D'Estaing's fleet lay off in the Roads, in 1778, many of the first gentlemen of France and their Jacobite Scottish comrades met here the magnates of Massachusetts. In October, 1778, Gen. Heath visited Nantasket in company with the Count D'Estaing, and inspected the forts, which had recently been strengthened under Gen. Du Portail's directions, and were under the command of Bougainville, the celebrated circumnavigator of the globe (1766–69). Heath also reviewed the battalion of French marines in garrison, which was commanded by Major M'Donald, a Scottish refugee and lover of the fallen Stuart dynasty. When Lord Howe's fleet reconnoitred the harbor, the town was alarmed by the signal-guns; and Hancock hastened to the fleet, and all the militia of the adjacent towns was ordered to the shores and islands of the harbor. The sturdy minute-men of Norfolk and Middlesex fraternized with the veterans of France, encamping on the grassy slopes of these hills of Hull.

At the end of the war the Hullonians reclaimed the fragments of their homes, and once more became toilers of the sea. Within a single generation, however, the roar of hostile cannon once more shook their windows. It was annoying to the housewives of Hull that the battle between the *Chesapeake* and *Shannon* began at the time it did, for they had just got supper on their tables; but at the first broadside all the men ran from their homes, and clambered up to the hill-tops, to see the mighty naval duel. This fact has been repeated by one of these venerable women, within five years; although, *more feminina*, she stated that the battle was between the *Constitution* and *Essex*, and that the latter was sunk off Point Allerton!

Mrs. Lobdell's public house was opened in 1775; and it has had many successors, until the perfect development of the Pemberton is attained. The point which projects toward Hull Gut was leased by the Tudor family, in 1826, for nine hundred and ninety-nine years, at fifty dollars a year; and extensive salt-works, artificial ponds, dikes, etc., were established there at great expense. But these failed of success, and about forty years ago the Tudors erected the Mansion House from their materials. On a snowy night of 1871 this pioneer summer-hotel was burned; and its successor, the Tudor House, met the same fate in 1875, making way for the Pemberton. And so, within a quarter of a millennium, this obscure Massachusetts peninsula has successively been a desolation, a feeble Episcopal plantation, a Puritan fishing-port, a Continental fortress, a French camp, a wreckers' colony, a semi-Dalmatian maritime hamlet, a Yankee village, and an opulent American summer-resort.

Point Allerton.

STONY BEACH. — POINT ALLERTON. — THE "KADOSH." — NOBLE VIEWS. — THE SEA-KING'S FATE.

EXTENDING from the foot of Telegraph Hill and Vining's pretty cottage, to Point Allerton, is the narrow isthmus of Stony Beach, more than half a mile long, making several graceful curves between the harbor and Nantasket Roads, and giving scant room for the railway and highway between the two strands. Its title is perfectly descriptive; and the weedy rocks on the outer shore exhale the pungent and fascinating odors of the sea, with which they have been for so many centuries saturated. All along these beaches the men of Cohasset make their patrols, after stormy weather, in search of sea-moss. The virtues of kelp were once much extolled hereabouts, and the old hut where Jack Hayden brewed medicines from it is still pointed out. Thoreau says that he found the people of Hull also making potash, by burning the stems of kelp, and boiling the ashes. On the harbor-side is a large wharf, where the United-States engineers landed granite, which was carried thence on a railway, for the construction of the Point-Allerton sea-wall. The wooden house of the Massachusetts Humane Society, on the crest of the beach, contains the large life-boat, the mortar, life-car, and other means to save the crews of vessels which may be wrecked on the adjacent dangerous shores. There are plenty of brave and expert surfmen in the neighboring village, who do not esteem their lives too precious to imperil when vessels are in distress within their reach. The coast of the Bay State is now lined with these life-saving stations, by whose means many lives have been saved from the all-devouring sea.

Little Hog Island, covering about ten acres, and favored by masculine summer-campers, lies just to the south of Hull, — a long, low shape, without even a single tree to mark its low bluffs and winding points. Thoreau said, "As I looked over the water, I saw the isles rapidly wasting away, the sea nibbling voraciously at the continent. . . . On the other hand, these wrecks of isles were being fancifully arranged into new shores, as at Hog Island, inside of Hull, where every thing seemed to be gently lapsing into futurity. This isle had got the very form of a ripple." There is on it little of interest, save the hulls of two old vessels, lying upon their sides on the beach, and fast decaying, inhabited by myriads of spiders, large and small, who have carefully woven their silken webs across every corner, and seem so alert that one hesitates to intrude upon their domain, and turns instead to the other side of the island, where pass the steamboats to Hingham and Downer, and the little fleet of sailboats just out from Hull. Peace to the worn old timbers of the *Passport* and *Virginia!* They have cruised in many seas, and find here their *ultima thule*.

At the east end of Stony Beach is the peninsula of Point Allerton, about half a mile long, and joined to Hull and to Nantasket Beach by isthmuses. To the north it looks on the Light-house Channel; to the east, on the sea.

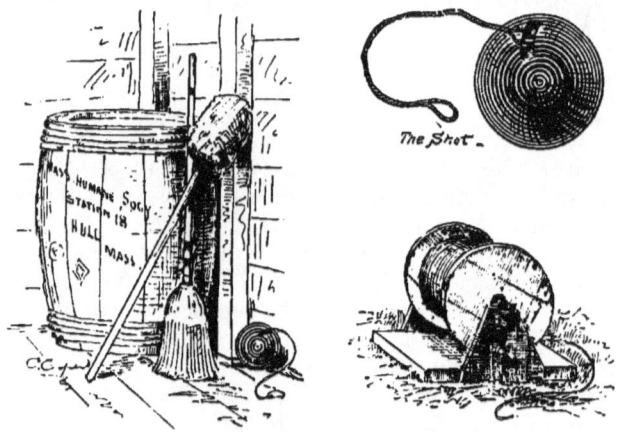

Bits from the Life Saving Station.

It is a high and picturesque promontory, which once extended far out, to the locality now marked by a singular pyramidal beacon, rising from the waves. A part of the second hill, which then swept over to the beacon, still stands, and shows what Thoreau called the "springing arch of a hill suddenly interrupted, as at Point Allerton, — what botanists might call premorse, — showing, by its curve against the sky, how much space it must have occupied, where now was water only." The United States has marked bounds to Neptune's voracious nibbling, by building a long and massive sea-wall around what remains of the Point. Near the verge is a little white farm-house, sheltered on two sides by the hills, and whose narrow fields lie full open to the breath of the sea, so that one would think that the vegetables grown there would need no salting.

The upper part of the great rounding hill is a flowery pasture of several acres, peopled by birds and butterflies, and terminating toward the sea in a sharp and amazing cliff, far below which the waves beat against impassable barriers. Here is a grand view-point. — solitary, far-secluded from the dapper summer-cottages, — where the contemplative man is able

> "Tò musen in his philosophic,
> Sole withouten companie."

It is an enchanted scene, where the narrow-laned harbor opens to the westward, diversified by islands great and small, gray forts, white light-houses, and bluffs gnawed away by the waves; or where the silvery curve of Nantasket Beach sweeps away to the south, fringed by a snowy line of surf; or where, to the eastward,

The Life-Boat, Stony Beach.

the vast open sea stretches into dim blue leagues, holding here and there in its immensity the slow-moving vessels bound on many distant errands, and flecked with shadows of passing clouds. From the edge of the cliff one may comprehend Tennyson's phrase, —

> "The wrinkled sea beneath him crawls."

"Like the promontory of Palinurus, Point Allerton is respectfully regarded as the memorial of an ancient worthy; and the appellation, perpetuating the memory of a man of the greatest commercial enterprise in those early times, is most fitly applied. *Gaudet cognomine terra.*" Thus spake one of the famous orators of New England; and he said well, for Isaac Allerton was one of the leaders in the ancient Plymouth colony. When but twenty-five years old, he went to Leyden, and thence sailed in the *Mayflower* twelve years later for America. He went out with Standish's party, exploring Boston Bay, in 1621; and the name of Point Allerton was probably bestowed at that time. In later years he cruised adventurously along the coasts of Maine and Acadie, in his ship *White Angel*. Once he sailed into Port Royal, and ordered La Tour to show his commission; to which the haughty Frenchman made answer, "My sword is sufficient commission;" and the Plymouth sailor could not impeach the validity of such a document. In subsequent years Allerton fell out with the Pilgrims, and sailed away to New Amsterdam, where he became a magistrate among the Dutchmen. No small part of the trouble at Plymouth arose from his earnest friendship for the merry rascal Morton, whom he brought back from England after the saints had banished him. There is a pretty tradition in the Old Colony, that the fair young May Chilton's foot was the first to press the snow-clad Plymouth Rock; and her friend May Allerton, daughter of our hero, was the latest survivor of the Pilgrim band, having lived until twelve out of the thirteen American colonies had been founded.

Little Hill, Point Allerton.

This locality is designated as *Allerton Poynt* on Wood's map, made in 1634. Some of the ancient charts and deeds speak of it as bounded by the "mayne sea." The history of the Point has been uneventful. It was the site of encampments in 1776, as a remote outer vidette of the insurgent Province. About the year 1880 the locality was discovered by the summer ramblers; and already many pretty cottages have been built on its lower slopes, and many scores of building-lots are for sale, since the passage of the railway along the side of the great hill makes the locality so readily accessible.

While this comely summer luxury adorns the inner side of the peninsular Point, the outer side presents a far different scene to the storm-drenched sailor, whose vessel runs into the harbor on a snowy winter night, steering fearfully between rock and shoal. Many a good ship has left her bones here, to be gnawed away by time and tide. It seems as if the great saints in whose honor the Bay was originally named withdrew their protection when the present heathen title was affixed to it; for many serious disasters took place here in the early colonial days. One of the first relief-ships of the Boston colony, the *Charity* of Dartmouth, a vessel of one hundred and twenty tons, well laden with provisions, was driven ashore on Point Allerton; and in 1636 the barque *Warwick*, ten guns, was wrecked here, where her remains were seen as late as 1804. The *Warwick* sailed to New England before Gov. Winthrop's time, having been sent out by Gorges and Mason to make discoveries; and afterwards came within a

Hulk of the Schooner "Passport," Little Hog Island.

span of being wrecked on the Brewsters, while on a voyage from Portsmouth to Boston. During the two and a half centuries which have ensued, the sea has thrown many a costly sacrifice on this altar, sweeping off their rich cargoes and their gallant crews into the deep outer gulfs. There are grim old-time traditions of false lights having been displayed on the Point, with intent to lure vessels to destruction. But the dangers of this rocky elbow, with its long bars projecting like traps, need no human malignity to give them fatal power. From a part of the wrecks of the last decade, the circle of destruction since 1630 may be imagined.

In 1870 an Italian bark was wrecked on the Point; and all but one of the crew perished miserably in the waves, finding hereaway no soft Mediterranean breezes, but the unrelenting terror of the storm-king of the north. This has also been a fatal shore for East Indiamen, several of which have here found the end of their long voyages. Here the *Massasoit* was lost, with part of her crew, while just entering the home harbor after the weary voyage from Calcutta; and her cargo of indigo and hides was strewn along the beach for miles. It was in 1872 that the barque *Kadosh*, from Manila, came ashore here, in a blinding snowstorm; and her captain and seven sailors were lost. She broke up immediately on the fangs of those terrible rocks; and her cargo of sugar, hemp, and sapan-wood was thrown up along the beaches. It is said that several Cohasset men bought sixteen hundred bales of hemp, floating about in the wreckage. They paid one hundred and forty dollars for it, and realized ten thousand dollars,— a very pretty profit, indeed, for the South-Shore syndicate.

Boston Light and the Brewsters, from Point Allerton.

In the same storm the ship *Peruvian* and the barque *Francis*, both bound in from Singapore, were wrecked on the other side of the Bay. The *Peruvian* had a cargo of East-India goods, valued at one million dollars. A year later the *Helen*, with pine timber from North Carolina, ran on to the Point in a tremendous sea; but its crew was saved by a life-boat from the shore, manned by a volunteer party of the bravest of the brave. It is dangerous to approach this coast in a small boat, even on quiet days, so formidable are the rocks and shoals off-shore: but to make a landing from the reeling and splitting deck of a ship stranded on the bar requires superhuman courage, skill, and good luck.

The splendid sea-wall which defends the bluff against north-eastern waves was built by the United States, at a cost of one hundred and fifty thousand dollars, and seems calculated to defy the elements for centuries, with its long lines of heavy masonry. Here one may promenade comfortably, and without fear of meeting other passers, save perhaps a sea-gull or a butterfly.

On one side is the great bluff, rising overhead with inaccessible steepness; and on the other are the kelp-covered rocks, amongst which the sea swashes back and forth ceaselessly. Here let us consider the legend of this locality, as it was sung in far Norway eight centuries ago.

Many famous antiquaries believe (and make great show of argument to prove) that Point Allerton is the locality called "Krossaness" in the Icelandic sagas, where the Viking Thorwald was slain and buried in the year 1004. He was the son of Eric the Red, who sailed from Norway to Iceland, and thence (in 985) to Greenland, where he founded a colony of warriors and heroes. Thence the leaders, in their little galleys, made frequent excursions along the wild and unknown coasts to the south-

Old Gun, from the Barque "Kadosh"

ward, seeking some new Drontheim Fiord on which to found a Norway of the West. Thus Thorwald cruised down the present New-England coast, finding there a race of men small in stature and yellow in color, very much like the Esquimaux. The victorious advance of the powerful red men from the mysterious mountains and prairies of the West had not yet begun. That date takes us well back into history; for it was before the Norman conquest of England, or the First Crusade, or the Guelphs and Ghibellines had been heard of, or Portugal, Bohemia, Switzerland, or Turkey had become nations. The Roman Empire still survived in the East; and, in the West, King Ethelred was vainly trying to beat off Sweyn's fierce Danes. Centuries were to elapse before Dante wrote, and Giotto painted, and Rienzi spoke, and Richard Cœur de Lion swung his battle-axe.

On Stony Beach, Hull

The Icelandic sagas tell how Thorwald sailed from the point he called *Kialarness* (Cape Cod) toward the mainland, where he came to anchor not far from a hilly promontory overgrown with wood, and was so much pleased with the place that he exclaimed, "Here it is beautiful, and here I should like to fix my abode." He met there nine men of the aborigines, "eight of whom they killed, but the ninth escaped in his canoe." Some time after, there arrived a countless number of canoes, laden with Skrællings, — as the Scandinavians called the aborigines, as well of Greenland as of Vinland, — and a battle ensued. It was the first bloodshed between Europeans and the indigenous Americans. The Norse battle-shields were arranged along their bulwarks; but the undaunted Skrællings fired flights of arrows at Thorwald and his men for some time, and then quickly retired. After the battle Thorwald asked his sailors whether any of them had been wounded. Upon their denying this, he said, "I am! I have an arrow under my arm, and this will be my death-blow. I now advise you to prepare for your departure as soon as possible. But me you must take to that promontory where I thought to have made my abode. I was a prophet. For now I shall dwell there forever. There you shall bury me, and plant there two crosses, one at my head and one at my feet, and call the place *Krossaness* [the promontory of the crosses] for all time coming." Thorwald, upon this, died; and his men did as he had ordered them.

The place where they buried him, and erected the crosses, must have been one of the headlands not far south of Cape Ann. It is known that it was near the harbor of Boston; and the only question at issue is, whether it was Point Allerton or the Gurnet (near Plymouth). De Costa, Dr. Kohl, Guillot, and others, favor Allerton. It was surely a worthy burial-place for a Scandinavian viking, — this noble and lonely height, —

"Islanded in the immeasurable air."

The Norsemen's Galley.

Nantasket Beach.

THE ROCKLAND HOUSE, HOTEL NANTASKET, AND ATLANTIC HOUSE.—
STRAWBERRY HILL.—BEACH NOTES.

ANTASKET BEACH faces the open sea for a length of about four miles, running nearly north-north-west, slightly curved, and diversified by several picturesque hills and narrow plains. On the north, it ends at the hills which form one side of the main ship-channel into Boston Harbor; on the south, it is joined to the mainland of Plymouth County, the venerable and historic Old Colony. Upon this arm of sand, hardly more than a natural breakwater, with the restless sea on one side, and the quiet waters of the harbor on the other, is the summer park and playground of Boston; and the constantly plying steamboats daily land thousands of people at the wharves on the harbor side, within a few hundred feet of the ocean. The downward slope of the beach is so gradual that the waves have a long sweep between the tides; and the wet gray sand is firm and hard, affording secure footing. At low tide a splendid boulevard, many rods wide, lines the surf-side, and is occupied by carriages of every description, driving along this highway of nature's grading, and by groups of urban promenaders, moving leisurely up and down by the side of the breaking waves. At other seasons, here is the paradise of bathers, who scurry down from all manner of adjacent bath-houses, clad in motley garments of every cut and hue, and plunge into the cold, clear, green waves.

On all the long miles from Atlantic Hill to Point Allerton, the beach is unbroken,—a wide and almost level belt of sand, with low tufted banks on one side, and the curling waves on the other. Looking off from this large section of her eastern front, one sees how just was the conception of the ancient Provincial dignitaries, who tried to change the pagan and incuphonious title of Massachusetts to *Oceana*. Close beside is the sea, in all its beauty and mystery.

> "The tide slips up the silver sand,
> Dark night and rosy day:
> It brings sea-treasures to the land,
> Then bears them all away."

The development of Nantasket as a summer resort has been a work of gradual and rational extension, advancing through many decades of time.

Nearly a century ago the people of the inland towns used to drive down to the sands, and indulge in the mild dissoluteness of family picnics; where, perchance, they discussed the contemporary policy of President Washington, the campaigns of Austerlitz and Moscow, the dismemberment of Poland, or the daring advance of New-England colonists into the vast Ohio wilderness. Gen. Lincoln, who commanded the harbor-defences during the Revolution, and often rode across from Hingham to the forts at Hull, wrote that "between Nantasket Neck, so-called, and Point Allerton, is a beach of three miles, very hard, and a pleasant ride in summer." In 1826 Mr. Worrick opened a public house near the south end of the beach, and called it "The

Worrick House, at Nantasket, owned by George L. Damon.

Sportsman." This old-time inn was the resort of Daniel Webster, and other distinguished men, during the presidencies of Adams, Jackson, and Tyler, and doubtless witnessed many an interesting scene in those far-away ancient days. Here the magnates of the Old Colony used to assemble, during the dog-days, to discuss those grave questions of local policy which are now as far forgotten as the debates of the town-council of Sybaris or Assos; and under these sturdy old rafters there was, doubtless, much talk of Hunkers, and Barn-burners, and Locofocos, and other long-defunct political parties. Some twenty years ago (or more) this old tavern passed into the hands of Mr. Arthur Pickering, of Boston. It is now owned and used as a summer-house, by Mr. George L. Damon, of Boston, the celebrated manufacturer of safes and burglar and fire-defying bank-vaults.

THE HOTEL NANTASKET AND ROCKLAND CAFÉ.

The Rockland House was established in 1854 by Col. Nehemiah Ripley, who conducted it for nearly thirty years, while it increased from 40 rooms to nearly 200, and from a plain 60-foot front to an imposing façade of 275 feet. In its early years the average number of visitors to the beach during a pleasant week of summer was 200. In those old days Thoreau wrote: "On Nantasket Beach I counted a dozen chaises from the public-house. From time to time the riders turned their horses toward the sea, — standing in the water for the coolness, — and I saw the value of beaches to cities, for the sea-breeze and the bath." The Rockland was successful from the first, although all its guests had to be brought down by stage from Hingham. As a result of the remodellings and improvements of so many years, the hotel is

The Blue Hills of Milton from the Lower Harbor.

now one of the best and most commodious on the coast, with all the modern necessities of aqueduct-water, gas, steam-heat, richly furnished parlors, billiard-rooms, music-rooms, etc. So gradual is the upward slope of the wide lawn, from the beach to the house, that it does not seem to be on a height; but when the piazzas are reached, the splendid view downward and outward, across the verdant *glacis* to the blue and dazzling sea, shows how marked the ascent has been.

The Rockland Café is situated at a respectful distance from the great hotel, at the head of the main road leading from the steamboat-pier, and close upon the edge of the beach. It exists for the convenience of the great crowds of transients who visit Nantasket; and is an airy and attractive building of large area, with wide piazzas, dining-halls, parlors, dancing-hall, bowling-alleys, shooting-galleries, swings, and other accessories to

ATLANTIC HOUSE, NANTASKET BEACH, OWNED BY L. DAMON & SONS.

divert the mind from too-engrossing contemplation of the grandeur of Nature. Yet even the dancers and bowlers and diners — in the intervals of their amusements — may look off over the cool sea, into —

'The ever-silent spaces of the East,
Far-folded mists, and gleaming halls of morn."

The Atlantic — From the Beach

The Atlantic, from the Hills.

A long arcade, extending parallel with the surf line, roofed, floored, and lined with seats, joins the Rockland Café to the Hotel Nantasket, both being under one management. The former is devoted mainly to fish-dinners and chowders; the latter exhausts all the resources of the market to furnish out its luxurious tables with choice game, meats, and other attributes of a metropolitan *menu*.

The Hotel Nantasket is the Aladdin's Palace of this region, — a new and beautiful house, half pavilion and half hotel, rich in towers, gables, and balconies, and fretting the sky with scores of pinnacles. It is charmingly irregular in shape, and unique in architecture, and in many other ways attractive to the casual visitor. Toward the sea is the band-stand, where the famous Cadet Band of Boston renders sweet music, overpowering even

NANTASKET BEACH, FROM ATLANTIC HILL.

the deep monotone of the neighboring surf. Broad platforms, promenades, and piazzas line the front; and heroic and costly attempts are made to plant here gardens, English parterres, lines of trees, and beds of geraniums. The hotel is conducted on the European plan, and mainly devoted to the use of transient guests, although a certain number of regular boarders are accommodated in the airy rooms up-stairs, above the great dining-halls. Extensive plans for the beautifying of the adjacent lands have been made by Bowditch, the expert landscape-gardener. The scene in the vicinity, on a fair summer evening, is truly bewildering in its brilliancy and fulness of life. Electric lights banish the darkness, the music of the band floats over the beach and plain, the cool and bracing breath of the sea dispels the parching heats of the day; and thousands of happy visitors regale themselves with the choicest viands and beverages, merrily chatting, and waited on by a small army of negro servants. Here is the nineteenth century at sport, the modern table of Lucullus, the temple of gastronomy and social mirth.

As the evening grows old, the rising winds from the Bay overpower the smoke of countless Havanas, the fusillade of corks drops into a desultory skirmish fire, the deep roll of the waves booms through the *pianissimi* of the band, and the invigorated citizens and *citoyennes* seek the neighboring railway-station and steamboat-pier, and within a short hour are in Boston. Thus also retire Patrick and Michael, from the roystering saloons toward Sagamore Hill; and Timon and Zenobia, the lovers of Nature, who have rambled along the beach until their shoes are full of sand.

It is said that there is a beach near the city of New York, with more than one hotel not unlike this; but the true Nantasketer accepts this statement with much kindly doubting. A tart New-York newspaper remarks, nevertheless, that " Bostonians are justly proud of Nantasket Beach, where one can get cultured clams, intellectual chowder, refined lager, and very scientific pork and beans.... It is far superior to our monotonous sand-beach, in its picturesqueness of natural beauty, in the American character of the visitors, and in the reasonableness of hotel-charges and the excellence of the service."

The Atlantic House crowns the bold rocky ridge which makes out into the sea, at the southern end of the beach, and is the most conspicuous object in the views from distant points, with its lofty roofs and striking forms of architecture. It is an immense building, with rich parlors, broad piazzas, and attractive surroundings, and has always been well-filled with guests during long summer seasons. The view hence is very grand, including a long reach of the South Shore, picturesque and island-dotted sections of the harbor, the entire extent of Nantasket Beach, and an illimitable expanse of open sea. It is a prospect so diversified, so replete with elements of nobility, so alluring, that one never wearies of it. If Peepy Marshmallow in her easy-chair on the piazza tires of her embroidery, or of Birdie's gossip about the last ball, she has but to lift her pretty eyes, and the fairest panorama of sea and sky lies spread out before her. From many points in Boston, Roxbury, and Dorchester, this stately Palace of Indolence is seen, with its gables cutting sharply against the eastern sky.

The rocky eminence whereon the hotel stands is known as Atlantic Hill, and is also occupied by several handsome cottages. Around its landward side runs Atlantic Avenue, which was laid out in 1873, and leads from the beach to Nantasket Lake, and thence connects with the road to Hingham. Just south of Atlantic Hill is Centre Hill, rocky and sea-beaten, with

Crescent Beach.

several small hotels and cottages. Farther along stands the handsome New Pacific Hotel, a large modern house, on a bold cliff over the sea. Close at hand on the west is Nantasket Lake (until recently known as Straits Pond), a singular lagoon two miles long, on which boat and tub races and other aquatic sports are often conducted. This rather pretty sheet of water has been suspected of malarial influences; and the contiguous towns spend considerable sums upon it yearly, in the interests of sanitation. In old times it was known as *Lake Galilee*, and Atlantic Hill bore the name of *Mount Zion;* certain reverend pilgrims, returning from the Holy Land, having reported that the hills of this region bore a singular resemblance to those of Palestine. From the craggy peninsula of Gun Rock, whose hotel was destroyed by a fire years ago, Crescent Beach extends toward Green Hill, and is largely occupied by the cottages of Bridgewater and Abington manufacturers, and other inland citizens. Many years ago this was a strip of farm-land and pasturage; but successive storms have reduced it to a pebbly beach, between Nantasket Lake and the sea. Here, also, are three or four small hotels and boarding-houses. Beyond lies Green Hill, a high and graceful promontory, projecting into the blue ocean, towards Black Rock, and occupied by many neat cottages, whose windows and piazzas command exquisite marine views. In one of these secluded houses, haunted by bobolinks and robins, dwells the author who (in her "Boston-Journal" letters) has interpreted more clearly the spirit of Nantasket than any other writer.

Yonder is the famous old Black-Rock House, from which the Jerusalem Road runs for miles down the coast, toward Cohasset, high on the cliffs, lined with costly marine villas, and rich in inspiring views over leagues of open sea. Nothing this side of the Riviera can compare with this avenue of vistas. You may thus enter the Old Colony, and pass by Daniel Webster's farm at Marshfield, and Standish's high tower at Duxbury, and the graves of the Pilgrims at Plymouth, and so out into the primeval and deer-haunted forests toward Cape Cod.

Sagamore Hill rises from the beach between Atlantic Hill and Strawberry Hill, not far from the Weir-River steamboat-pier; and its far-viewing crest is occupied by several cottages and a picnic-garden, not unknown to Sunday-school excursions, and affluent in swings, pavilions, and other appurtenances of summer-day joys. On this height one of the ancient Indian sachems had his wigwam, and held his savage court; and great councils of the harbor clans were held here. Many remains of their camps and gatherings have been found in the vicinity. Along the seaward foot of the hill straggles a motley group of small hotels, cafés (so-called), and cottages, lining the edge of the beach for a considerable distance. Among them is a large hall, sacred to fish-dinners and clam-bakes, where may be seen the original Rhode-Island method of cooking the favorite bivalves, buried amongst hot stones, and covered with sea-weed. To the northward the long promontory of White Head projects into the harbor, with many dreary undulations and abandoned fields. Its chief productions are hay and birds.

Strawberry Hill is a conspicuous elevation, nearly midway between Sagamore Hill and Point Allerton, rising like a great wall across the beach-plains, and extending from the harbor almost to the line of the breakers. It is said that strawberries once abounded in the vicinity, and gave reason for the name. The water-tower seen on its summit is a well-known landmark for pilots off the coast. Here centre the official surveys and triangulations of the harbor, for the elevation is so considerable and so isolated that it gives a prospect of vast extent and beauty. On this site stood a very large barn, in 1775; and it contained eighty tons of hay, which the Americans burned, to grieve the British garrison of Boston. The harbor was splendidly illuminated by these patriotic flames. The south side of the hill appears very steep; but the ascent from the north is easy, and leads up from the vicinity of the Sea-Foam House to the airy crest, whence one may see, afar,

"The tides of grass break into foam of flowers,
And the wind's feet shine along the sea."

The plains extending toward Point Allerton have been called "the Belgium of the neighboring tribes in savage times;" and there are traditions of many sanguinary battles having been fought thereon. Probably the

Wreck on Nantasket.

harbor Indians chose this as a favorable point to attack the Tarratines, who used to make pitiless forays hereabouts, in their fleets of swift sea-going canoes. On and near Skull Head, great numbers of human bones have been found, with arrow-heads, tomahawks, and other weapons of war. When the English first came into these parts, the plains were held as commons of the people of Hull. Two hundred years later (or about 1840), the county of Plymouth bought this almost worthless territory, and resold it, at a handsome advance, to Litchfield, Ripley, Wheatland, and other speculative gentlemen. After costly litigation, the plains have passed into the hands of the Nantasket Land Company, and are laid out in streets and avenues, along which cottage-lots are offered for sale. There are four well-graded avenues parallel with the beach, crossed by many streets running east and west — designated by letters. Promising clusters of Swiss cottages have already been erected, most of which are leased to summer visitors at from two hundred to four hundred dollars for the season. Several thousand shade-trees have been set out along the avenues; and it is hoped that this narrow sea-blown plain will sometime become a great cottage city, inhabited by families who wish to avoid the vast hosts of transient visitors overflowing other localities on the beach. Although it has many natural advantages, the embryo town does not yet compete with Newport or Oak Bluffs in prosperity, or with Chautauqua or Old Orchard in tranquil pietistic fervors. As the Independent Corps of Cadets have not been in the habit of encamping here, the climate remains unspoiled; and it seems only necessary for the Land Company to devise some new and original attraction, say a summer school of poetry, or an Episcopalian camp-meeting ground, to cover these charming lowlands with the desired cottages.

On the harbor-side is a pier, which is visited many times daily by steamboats from Boston; and near by, about fifteen hundred feet from the sea, stands the spacious Sea-Foam House, which was built in 1870, and, after passing through many vicissitudes, now keeps open hall for summer travellers. Close to the sea are several smaller hotels and restaurants, once freely patronized by excursionists from Boston and inland, but recently closed (for the most part) by the Land Company, in order to secure a more thorough quiet and decorum for this region. The summer village near Strawberry Hill is locally known as *Hobartville*, and is quite distinct from the adjacent settlements at the north and south ends of the beach. Steamboats began to run to this point in 1867, during which year the First Brigade of militia held its annual encampment here, and was reviewed by Gen. B. F. Butler. A project has been developed of crowning Strawberry Hill with a hotel of a thousand rooms; but probably it will not be realized until the twentieth century is well along. The plains near the north part of the beach have been aptly described thus: " It is a desert of sage-brush, as like the alkali wastes of Nevada as any thing so limited can be. The sand around is white as salt; and the stunted gray growth covers it close, except where here and there a hand's breadth of oasis in the shape of a clump of green bushes breaks the sameness. The sea is so far off, and you are on such a dead level, that it shows not much more than a blue line." Arid as these plains are, they have given rise to a great amount of controversy among the old Puritan yeomen. In 1641 Hingham and Nantasket (Hull) contested about a part of the beach lands, and Joseph Peck was the leader of the Hingham agitators. Certain citizens made the following deposition, " That which wee doe testifie Concerninge m^r Peck his Speech is this, That wee heard hime Say, That pride and malice were the foundation that sett us a worke about Nantascett, and if that were the foundation it would easily apeare What the buildinge Would be ; alsoe that we did Conspire together about it, and it was like unto those that Conspired together to kill Paul." In 1643 the General Court ordained thus : " The former grant to Nantascot was again voted and confirmed, and Hingham was willed to forbear troubling the Court any more about Nantascot." This law still remains upon the statute-books of Massachusetts, and has been called into service within ten years, when Hingham had again taken issue with Hull, and the selectmen of the latter town threatened an appeal to the law of 1643.

Over this silent heath, in the remote days when the only visitors to Nantasket were sportsmen, Daniel Webster often rambled, with gun on shoulder, in search of birds. At night, thoroughly tired, he would seek sweet sleep at the little inn at Hull. His biographer testifies that "he was a keen sportsman. Until past the age of sixty-five he was a capital shot; and the feathered game in his neighborhood was, of course, purely wild. He used to say, after he had been in England, that shooting in 'preserves' seemed to him very much like going out and murdering the barn-door fowl. His shooting was of the woodcock, the wild duck, and the various marsh-birds that frequent the coast of New England. . . . Nor would he unmoor his dory with his 'bob and line and sinker,' for a haul of cod or hake or haddock, without having Ovid, or Agricola, or Pharsalia, in the pocket of his old gray overcoat, for the 'still and silent hour' upon the deep."

When freed from the cares of diplomacy and statecraft, and happily removed from the throngs of politicians which even then filled the little city by the Potomac, he seemed to desire seclusion in such a place as Jeremiah describes: "A land that no man passed through, and where no man dwelt."

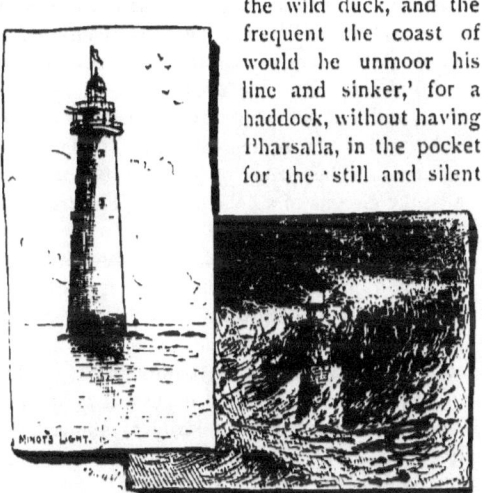

A Storm at Minot's Ledge.

Here, in the immense solitude, amid the pure spiritual air, with the solemn roll of the sea beating without cease near by, some of his noblest thoughts were conceived, and prepared for such utterance as would electrify the nation. It is a tradition in Boston, that he thought out his celebrated apostrophe to the veterans of Bunker Hill while fishing in Massachusetts Bay, and first delivered it to a gigantic codfish which he just then drew from the waves. In the annals of oratory, Nantasket should hold as honorable a place as that Greek beach whence Demosthenes flung his noble sentences into the senseless storm.

On this famous strip of coast, from Point Allerton to the Jerusalem Road, there are many objects of interest, for visitors of different temperaments, and many scenes in varying moods of sea and sky, which arouse emotions of diverse kinds. Sir Arthur Helps well says "that the traveller will often find an exquisite delight in what the guide-books pass by with indifference;" and nowhere is the remark so applicable as in a place like this, which is visited for any purpose rather than the pursuit of knowledge.

As many as three-fourths of the excursionists land at the pier in Weir River, or alight at the adjacent railway-station, and seek their recreation on the southern mile of the beach, between Atlantic Hill and Sagamore Hill; and it is on this stretch that the largest amount of human interest may be found.

The emotions of Peter Peregrine, forty years ago, were so similar to those of myriads of other visitors, that they may well be reported here: "The Nantasket beach is the most beautiful I ever saw. It sweeps round in a majestic curve, which, if it were continued so as to complete the circle, would of itself embrace a small sea. There was a gentle breeze upon the water, and the sluggish waves rolled inward with a languid movement, and broke, with a low murmur of music, in long lines of foam against the opposing sands. The surface of the sea was, in every direction, thickly dotted with sails, the air was of a delicious temperature, and altogether it was a scene to detain one for hours."

Forever gone are the days he chronicled, when the Norfolk-County and Old-Colony farmers and villagers drove down the fragrant country roads to the lonely beach, with their old-fashioned families, and made huge kettles of spicy chowder over drift-wood fires, while the delighted children raced barefoot over the wet sands, and bathed in the gentle waves. All is now changed; and the beach has a half-dozen crowded hamlets, a score of hotels, a daily newspaper, an aquarium, a score of shops, avenues and parks, sewers and aqueducts, and other appliances of our luxurious, complex, and painful modern civilization. Here now appear the flying horses, goat-wagons, and Punch-and-Judy shows of the city parks; and innumerable peddlers of candies and fruits, peanuts and pop-corn, pink lemonade and foaming beer, whips and fans, small red balloons, and other incomprehensible adjuncts of modern festal days and places. Now there are all manner of excursions *en masse*, armies of basket-bearers from Worcester and Berkshire, and even from farthest Albany; lodges and encampments of mystical organizations, yearly dwindling societies of veterans of the Secession War, cohorts of Hibernian merry-makers, the banded populations of Weymouths and Bridgewaters and Braintrees without number. Howells also tells us of a loftily philanthropic society in Boston, demonstrating that "ten thousand poor children could be transported to Nantasket Beach, and bathed, clam-baked, and lemonaded three times during the summer, at a cost so small that it was a saving to spend the money."

PLEASANT BEACH, GREEN HILL AND BLACK ROCK.

At the arrival of the late afternoon boats the long pier is covered with all manner of barges, wagons, and carriages, which presently dash away over the adjacent roads, bearing to their summer homes groups of happy citizens. When Ripley first suggested that the steamboats should come directly to the beach, by ascending the narrow and crooked channels of Weir River, he was saluted with guffaws of laughter. But he persevered, and in 1868 the first steamer crept cautiously up the devious stream, and tied up at the new pier. Now seven boats each way daily are hardly enough for the summer visitors. Their straggling and many-colored columns move from the pier or railway-station to the edge of the beach, and there melt away in

New Pacific Hotel.

squads; some drifting down to the edge of the surf; others seeking the kindly shelter of adjacent restaurants, whose broad roofs and open sides insure shade and free air; and others settling on the sands, with the venerable family umbrella and the crammed family lunch-basket to comfort them. The vast beach seems unchanged by their presence; for it has room for millions, and here are but a few thousands, here and there a few black dots on the glistening gray plain. Yet each, in his own way, is drinking in new life, and feeling the joy of an unwonted experience. He will return homeward at evening, reddened by sun and wind, tired in every muscle, perhaps a trifle confused in digestion; but a sound sleep awaits him, and an awakening to a new day of vigor.

KING'S HANDBOOK OF BOSTON HARBOR. 75

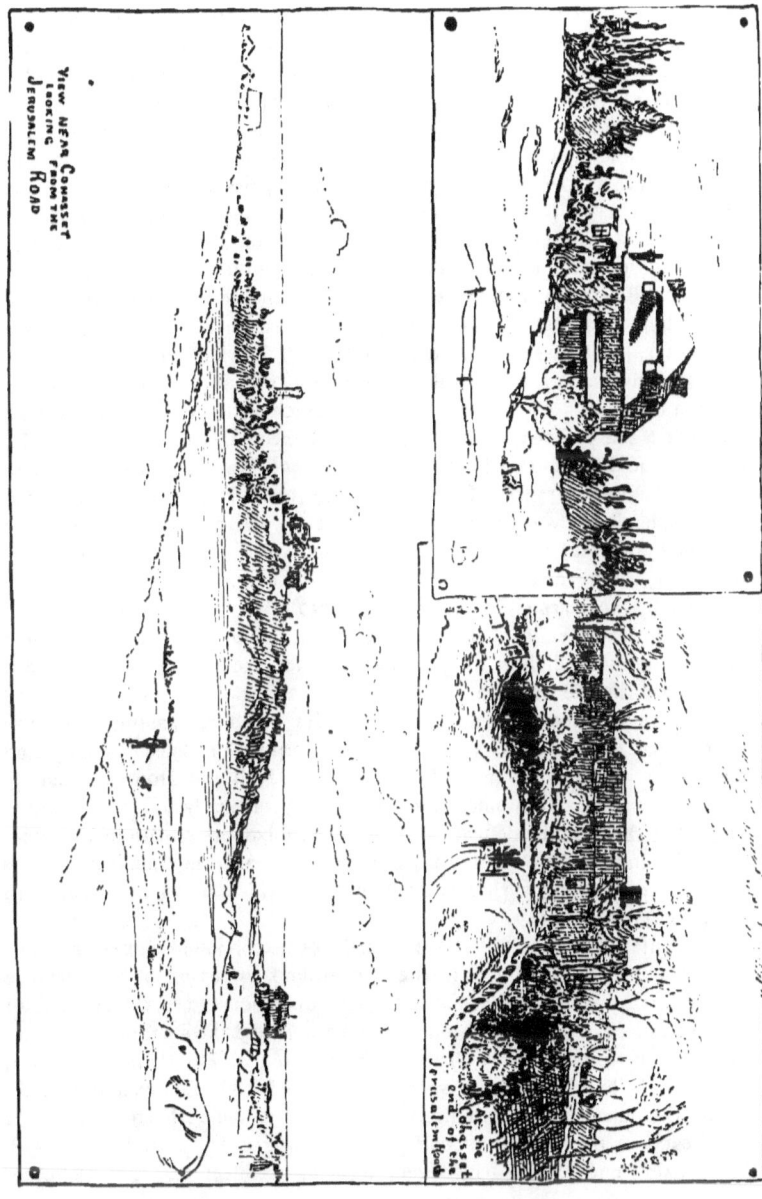

VIEWS ON THE SOUTH SHORE.

We are assured by Homer that Hercules delighted in banquets (he wandered far on the Mediterranean beaches); and so the Bostonian turns with confidence to the feasts in the adjacent shore-houses, from the humble chowders of the multitude to the epicurean repasts of the great hotels. Other groups, the rustic swains in whose breasts all the storms of the equinox cannot quench the flame of love, seek the rocks at the foot of Atlantic Hill, and there divide into sequestered pairs, and enjoy the sweets of bucolic courtship. Others, disguised in the unmitigable hideousness of bathing-suits, rush down over the sands, and enter the waves, where, with many outcries and a nervous hilarity, they endure the buffets of the mighty Atlantic. There are hundreds who avail themselves of the bath-houses, which line the crest of the beach, toward Sagamore Hill. Here, for a trifling fee, one may secure a small wooden cell, in which to doff the habiliments of civilization, and don the scantier apparel appropriate for a promenade in the surf. The waters of the Massachusetts sea are always cold, and give a sharp shock to the bather; but he who takes a fearless header through the first approaching wall of surf, and then battles sturdily with the successive rollers for a few minutes (not exceeding ten), will come out with a splendid glow of health, a keen appetite, and a sense of renovation. Michelet attributes the revivification of the worn-out English race to the discovery of the medicinal virtues of sea-bathing, which was first commended by the learned Dr. Russell, in 1750. "It is necessary," he said, "to drink sea-water, to bathe in sea-water, and to eat sea-weed; clothe your children as lightly as possible, and let them have plenty of air. The ocean breeze and the ocean water; there you have the sure cure." This heroic treatment, recommended first for glandular wasting, has since been found efficacious in a hundred other forms of sickness, debility, and decadence. There are many bath-houses at Hull and Downer Landing, also, where the water is much warmer than that off the beach, and produces very little shock to the delicate system. There bathers remain in the quiet (yet salty and iodated) waters for twice or thrice as many minutes as they could in the chilling surf, "that hell of cold, which, in its re-action, gives such a glow of heat."

The life of the hotels and the drift of excursionists, great as they appear, are rapidly falling into the background, by reason of the increase of the cottagers. The prices at the chief public-houses are rather high for the average citizen to bear throughout a season, and the smaller hotels here are almost uniformly very shabby affairs; so that Paterfamilias finds it expedient to build or lease a snug little place for his family, and transfer hither the housekeeping essentials from his city home. From one end of the beach to the other new cottages are rising every year, brilliant with fresh paint, and exemplifying every form of architecture. The clatter of hammers resounds on every side. "There are big houses and little, houses like the Chinese pagodas in old Canton blue ware, houses like castles with towers and battlements, houses like nests, and houses like barracks; houses with seven gables, and houses with none at all. It is marvellous what pretty interiors some of these nondescript, plain-boarded, deal-floored, rough-hewn cabins make, and what good effects a few common stage properties create." In such sheds, huts, villas, and mansions do the citizens "loaf, and invite their souls," relapsing a little way toward our original and happier barbarism. There is the sea, and that is the main thing. Even Hawthorne once said, "Oh that Providence would give me the merest little shanty, and mark me out a rood or two of garden-ground, near the sea-coast!" and again, "I am going to begin to enjoy the summer now, and to read foolish novels, if I can

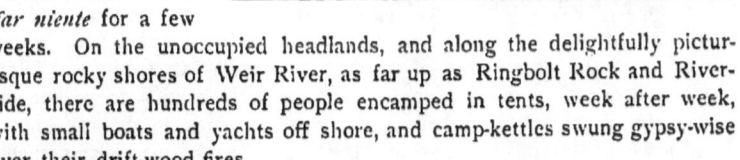

get any, and smoke cigars, and think of nothing at all." With such deep designs thousands of inland people come hither, and in their little cabins live a life of *dolce far niente* for a few weeks. On the unoccupied headlands, and along the delightfully picturesque rocky shores of Weir River, as far up as Ringbolt Rock and Riverside, there are hundreds of people encamped in tents, week after week, with small boats and yachts off shore, and camp-kettles swung gypsy-wise over their drift-wood fires.

All seasons (except the infrequent days of still heat) have a charm for the true Nantasketers. Hear how one of these optimists extracts comfort from elemental gloom: "There is, besides, a cleanliness in our foggy days,— an absence of sticky mud under foot, a fresher green on the grass, a pearling of dew on the small forests of weeds, that is in itself charming. . . . And such a harmony of grayness, such a symphony of blended shades, from the white of pure light to the black of thunder-cloud, even Whistler himself never imagined." The blithe spirit which finds such comfort in a damp gray fog must be aroused to ecstasy by the fair early hours, filled with the freshness of morning; or the breezy afternoon, when easterly winds carry the savor of the sea abroad; or the sunset, unspeakably brilliant in the west, and filling the east with violet shadows; or the white moonlight, adorning ocean and shore with mysterious beauty; or the intermittent starry midnight, when the last reveller has sought his troubled sleep, and the solemn anthem of the breaking surf rolls on through the darkness.

During the heavy easterly gales of the winter, vast quantities of kelp and sea-weed are thrown upon the shore. This material is valuable for fertilizing farm-lands, and a single gale has piled up here upwards of ten thousand dollars' worth of it. In some places the heaps are five feet high and fifty feet long, and hide the sand for great distances. At the same time myriads of sea-clams and quahaugs are torn from their submarine homes, and landed on the beach, where they are gathered into baskets by the South-Shore men. These worthies inherit the taste of their Indian predecessors, of whom it was said, "The Salvages are much taken with the delight of this fishe [clams]; and are not cloyed, notwithstanding the plenty." In winter, also, huge piles of snow and drift-ice line the high-water mark, presenting an aspect of fierce desolation and grandeur. More grim and repulsive even than the high-crested sea, or the ruin-heaped strand, are the deserted summer villages, abandoned to the gales, and relieved by no *entourage* of trees, or pleasant suggestion of smoking chimneys. This is the time of peril on the sea; and many a stately vessel has been driven up on these shores, where her timbers, half buried in the sand, have crumbled away during the slow succeeding years. In the great gales of December, 1839, when the islands and beaches hereabouts were strewn with wrecks, and ninety vessels and two hundred lives were lost in Massachusetts Bay, the stately barque *Lloyd*, bound from Havana to Boston, was driven ashore on Nantasket, the sea making a clean breach over her; and all on board (except one) were lost. A year later the *Hoogly*, laden with coffee, drove up on the beach near Strawberry Hill, and went to pieces. Long is the roll of schooners and coasters whose keels have been broken on these shining sands, while their crews scuttled ashore in the convenient dory, or were taken off by the securer life-boat. One of the most pathetic incidents in the Nantasket annals occurred in 1722, when the Rev. John Robinson of Duxbury thus wrote: "My dear, pious, virtuous, loving wife Hannah, and my dear and lovely daughter Mary, were both of them drowned in the sea near Nantasket Beach." It is only a single sentence, but how full of sadness! It comforts us to know that both the bodies were found (one of them having floated to Cape Cod).

Near the base of Sagamore Hill on the beach is the well-known Arlington House, with a beautiful and extensive view over the sea and shore. It has twenty-five well-furnished chambers for permanent boarders, who seek moderate-priced quarters along the beach. The house is provided on all sides with broad verandas where visitors may enjoy the sea air amid comfortable and commodious surroundings. But the great feature of the Arlington is its spacious dining-room. Here are served the famous clams of this region, baked on rocks and amid sea-weed in the good old-fashioned way, as ancient as the Colony days, and never yet improved upon. The meals are served on the American plan at a uniformly low price. The dinners are served from noon until nine in the evening, at 50 cents a head (children

Arlington House, Nantasket Beach.

under ten years old, half price), and include clams cooked in various ways, and several kinds of fish, with vegetables, green corn, melons, etc. The hotel also has a number of bath-houses, where guests can conveniently prepare for a dip in the breakers that roar and foam along the beach, and afford such luxurious coolness in the blazing days of summer. The proprietors of the Arlington are S. L. Chessman & Co.

The Pacific House is finely situated on the high and rocky promontory to the southward of Atlantic Hill, well apart from the localities frequented by the thousands of summer-day excursionists, and therefore more quiet and restful than the open beach to the north. It commands very interesting views toward Crescent Beach and the famous Gun Rock, and westward over the favorite boating reaches of Straits Pond, and along farther to the southward to the Jerusalem Road and Green Hill. From the sea front there is a noble view of the blue waves, stretching from the foot of the cliffs, almost at your feet, clear out to the level horizon, and flecked here and there with the white sails of passing vessels.

Pacific House, Nantasket Beach.

The hotel has a frontage of 100 feet, and is entirely surrounded by commodious verandas. The rooms are well furnished, and supplied with the well-known Accord Pond water. The facilities for bathing, fishing, yachting, driving, and the favorite in-door amusements are good. The proprietor of the Pacific is William B. Hathaway.

SCENES ON THE JERUSALEM ROAD.

The land route to Nantasket is over the Old-Colony Railway, and the time from Boston to the beach is about 45 minutes. The line runs through a country rich in picturesque scenery and historical associations, and abounding in ancient and populous villages. After leaving the city, it follows

the shore for several miles, with pleasant views of the harbor on the left, with the dark groves of Thompson's Island and the villa-crowned ridge of Squantum. After traversing Savin Hill and Harrison Square, it crosses the Neponset River, leaves the hill-village of Wollaston Heights on the right, and runs through venerable Quincy, the home of the Presidents, with the Adams Academy on the left, close by the track. The train passes thence into the rural region to the southward, and at Braintree leaves the main line, and passes on to the rails of the South-Shore branch, where it follows through the rich villages of Weymouth, and into Hingham. A mile or so beyond is the Old-Colony station (18 miles from Boston), whence the new Nantasket-Beach Railway diverges to the beach, running through a quaintly desolate region of rocky hillocks and level salt-marshes. The South-Shore train continues on to Cohasset, Scituate, Marshfield, and Duxbury, in the very heart of the land of the Pilgrims.

Brass Mortar, Life-Boat Station.

Hingham and Weymouth.

DOWNER LANDING AND MELVILLE GARDEN. — THE OLD SHIP. — WEYMOUTH'S STRANGE HISTORY.

DOWNER LANDING is the pretty summer-resort on the headland at the mouth of Hingham Harbor, with the spacious Rose Standish House at the head of the pier, and a score or two of cottages on and about the hill beyond. Fifty years ago this was one of the least-visited localities in the Bay; and perhaps its former name of Crow Point indicates that it was then chiefly the habitat of the useful but unmusical *corvus Americanus*. When the sailing-packets were unable to ascend Hingham Harbor, their passengers often landed here, and reached the village by a foot-path through the woods. The point was purchased in 1854 by Samuel Downer, who intended to remove his great oil-refinery hence, from South Boston. It proved unsuitable for the purpose, being frequently, during the winter, inaccessible by water; and in 1870-71 it was laid out in avenues, as a summer-resort, and a hotel, wharf, pavilions, and many cottages were built. Within five years Mr. Downer spent two hundred and seventy-five thousand dollars on his pet summer-resort; and since 1875 he has laid out nearly one hundred and fifty thousand dollars more. He was one of the original abolitionists; and in 1877 a re-union of the old anti-slavery leaders was celebrated here, with orations by Adams, Hoar, Bird, and others. Mr. Downer was also a man of Puritan piety, and occasionally brightened the quiet summer Sundays at the Landing, by what he called lay sermons, sometimes rich in reminiscences of Mann, Parker, and others of his old-time friends.

In Melville Garden.

The Rose Standish House is a spacious and comfortable summer hotel, which has always been the resort of such as are called in the adjacent metropolis "nice people." Mr. Downer was often urged to move this house from its place down by the edge of the water to the crest of the sea-viewing mound close by; but he always firmly refused. "It will probably be moved very soon after I am dead," he said, "but it never shall be before." From a distance the house looks like some old-time three-decker, drifted ashore under the hill. Really noble views, however, are commanded by the hill-cottages above, where the foot of the amateur casual rarely intrudes, and the basket of the picnic-party is not seen. Foremost among

Ragged Island, Downer Landing.

these is a small boarding-house, which overlooks a hundred square miles of harbor; and farther back, and around the pretty cove to the westward, are other comfortable and substantial little summer homes. Nora Perry thus daintily touches the nerves of the Crow-Point villagers: "Downer Landing is a retreat for the cottagers chiefly; and, still and high, it looks down upon Nantasket's whirl and bustle with a little of the holier-than-thou-ativeness that comes so natural to the Bostonian. Ask these quiet dwellers enthroned upon their height, if they visit Nantasket frequently for a day's junketing, and see with what a superior air of pity for your ignorance you will be answered. You might as well ask them if they spent Fourth of July on Boston Common."

Melville Garden, the most famous picnic-resort in the harbor, is reached by a covered walk, four hundred and fifty feet long, leading from the Rose Standish House. On this twenty acres of pleasaunce are all manner of means for summer enjoyment, — groves and shrubberies, hill-top observations, ponds with many boats, a rocky island with mazy paths leading to cosy *tête-à-tête* pavilions and arbors, bath-houses, boats and yachts, bowling-alleys, shooting-galleries, croquet-lawns, bear-pits, billiard-halls, swings, flying-horses, and other sources of unbounded joy for young and old. The veterans of the Grand Army, the rank and file of the various mystic societies, the multitudes of family parties, who wend their way here of summer days, find their chief delight in the three spacious and handsome buildings beyond Lake Walton, — the café, with a hall seating six hundred persons; the music-hall, where many feet keep time to the rollicking melodies of the band; and the clam-bake pavilion, where eight hundred persons can take their places at once, and partake of ship-loads of clams cooked in the genuine and unmodified manner of Rhode Island. The first white men who came to Crow Point found huge mounds of clam-shells, indicating that the Indians had long enjoyed the delicious products of the adjacent shores; and the traditions of the locality have been so worthily respected, after three centuries, that if Chickataubut and his red sachems could revisit this favored corner of their ancient domain,

Melville Garden, from Ragged Island.

they would find at least one comprehensible observance. There is probably more fun to the acre in Melville Garden than in any other piece of Massachusetts ground.

The delightful old town of Hingham, for many years a favorite resort of summer ramblers, is about three-quarters of an hour from Boston, by steamboat or railway. It is a quiet, staid, and conservative place, with something of an English air, as if some Kentish or Devonshire hamlet had been transported across the sea by Puritan angels, and dropped among the hills and coves of the South Shore. There is much wealth among the old families, who lead tranquil and somnolent lives in their pretty wooden houses, surrounded by trim old-fashioned gardens and orchards, and within sound of many church-bells. Streets shaded with long lines of century-old elms lead almost imperceptibly into fair rural highways, among the comfortable farms of the countryside; and these, again, give place to narrower roads, hard by the bright waters of the coves, or solemnized by the shadows of the woods. Every thing speaks of peace and plenty, health and salubrity, industry and thrift. The town has about four thousand five hundred inhabitants, distributed in and between half a dozen villages. The chief of these is grouped around the old churches and the railway-station, some ways west of the steamboat-pier; and has a very neat and comfortable hotel, the Cushing House, much resorted to by Bostonians, who find the drives in this vicinity full of varied interest and beauty, while the resident society is of the best. Here stands the quaint old Derby Academy, founded by Madam Derby in the last century, and famous throughout the South-Shore towns. Nearer the harbor is the Lincoln House, a well-known summer-resort, which is much affected by Bostonians.

Some one has hit upon the happy phrase, "a marine Old Hadley," with which to describe Hingham; and it possesses colonial houses and ante-colonial trees enough to merit the title. The very quaint and venerable meeting-house of the First Church, was built in 1681, at a cost of four hundred and thirty pounds, and has been used as a house of worship ever since. The pyramidal roof of this delightful structure, "the oldest church in Yankeedom," is crowned by a quaint little colonial belfry and spire; and the interior of the building is pervaded by the solemnity and dignity which pertain to its years. The chief ornament of the ancient hill burying-ground, behind the church, is the statue of John A. Andrew, the war-governor, "the civilian Miles Standish of Massachusetts" during the Secession War. It is of Carrara marble, and was executed by Gould, at Florence. As a work of art this statue has received high commendation from capable critics. Andrew was for many years a resident of Hingham, and his grave is near the monument. Elsewhere in this high-terraced cemetery are the monuments to the ancient pastors of the village,— Norton, Ware, Gay, Lincoln, and other fathers of the church. An obelisk commemorates the seventy-six soldiers and sailors of Hingham who died in the Secession War; and another tall shaft, surrounded by a circular redoubt, is a memorial to the early settlers. Gen. Benjamin Lincoln's grave stands on this beautiful hill.

There are many rare old colonial houses on the quiet streets and roads of Hingham. The Perez Lincoln place, built of hewn oak before 1640, is still standing, and occupied by direct descendants of Joseph Andrews, its builder. The Thaxter mansion, on South Street, is more than two hundred years old, and contains many curious old painted panels. The great beams overhang the low parlors in antique power. It is but a few years since the Sprague mansion, on Main Street, built in 1654, was demolished. Another of these houses, at the corner of North and Lincoln Streets, was Gen. Benjamin Lincoln's home; and Gov. Andrew's old home stands near the pier.

As the steamboat winds up the serpentine channel of the harbor, it passes four islets so small that not even a bit of history or legend has stranded upon their rocky shores. The long peninsula on the left, on which stand Planter's Hill and Pine Hill, and the strange lenticular mound of World's End, projecting high and far into Weir River, pertains to the manorial estate of John R. Brewer, whose mansion is seen on the south side of Hingham harbor. The hills have recently been planted with a great number of shade-trees, and will thus become, years hence, a beautiful fea-

Scene on Ragged Island.

ture of the lower harbor. There is a fancy among some of the fishermen that the king seal of the harbor has his habitat off World's End. On the west side of the harbor rises the high mound of Otis Hill, with its egg-shaped swell, occupying a long stretch of the shore towards Downer Landing. This hill was the object of Daniel Webster's profound admiration, and he made several attempts to buy it. The new carriage-road to Downer runs around the harbor-ward side, and affords charming water-views. On the commanding hill to the right, at the head of the harbor, is the handsome many-gabled villa of Ex-Gov. John D. Long, built in 1870, and occupied every summer by the former official head of Massachusetts. Here, where his view commands the beauties and strongholds of the metropolitan bay, the Governor enjoys his great library, enriching his mind with the English and Latin classics, and surrounded by charming colonial antiquities.

The pretty upland hamlet of Hingham Centre, about one and a half miles from Hingham, has several stately old mansions, a venerable cemetery, and a fine new public library with reading-room and art-gallery. The broad boulevard of Main Street keeps on to the southward, by the hamlet of Glad Tidings Plain, to Liberty Plain, which received its name in 1774, on the occasion of the raising of a liberty-pole. South Hingham has a famous magnolia-tree in its burying-ground. Still farther southward is Queen Anne Corner, a group of ancient houses, rich in bits of picturesque eighteenth-century work, and on the old highway which leads down through Assinippi and toward Marshfield. Farther south is Accord Pond, a long-drawn blue lakelet, high up along the plateau. From this secluded pond the Hingham water-works supply delicious water to the villages near by, and to most of the hotels and houses at Nantasket Beach.

Fort Hill, on the Weymouth road, commemorates the little fort which was erected on its summit in 1675, one of three appointed for the defence of the people against the hostile Indians. Nevertheless, several houses were burnt, and some bloodshed was caused in the town, by marauding parties of King Philip's red warriors. From other heights, such as Turkey Hill and Squirrel Hill, beautiful views are afforded over the "rumpled and uneven" township, the variegated green and blue harbor, and the wide estuaries on either side.

It is not far from three miles from Hingham to Nantasket Beach, by a broad and pleasant road, over which many carriages and barges pass throughout the summer days and evenings. The Old-Colony House was built in 1832, on the crest of the hill between Hingham and the beach; and the beauty of the view from this point, and the coolness of the air, made it a favorite resort for several decades. Thousands of summer visitors sojourned here before the adjacent resorts were dreamed of. On an October afternoon of 1872 this paradise of the ancients was burned, and several unavailing attempts have since been made to raise capital to reconstruct it.

Descending the long hill beyond the site of the Old-Colony House, the highway traverses a level reach for a long distance, passing the spacious old farmhouse and summer boarding-house of Riverside, secluded on a rocky knoll on the left. Weir River, here narrowed into the dimensions of a brook, curves around the house, and may be followed by boat down to Nantasket, by Ringbolt Rock and a score of summer camps. As the Hingham road approaches the beach, it traverses the little cross-roads hamlet called The Tug, and then sweeps around Atlantic Hill and into close view of the Atlantic Ocean.

This quaint little Hingham, with its salty bays and murmuring woods, has given a dozen eminent men to the learned professions, and several gallant officers to the army and navy. Two of her children are known in art, — W. A. Gay the marine-painter, and Joseph Andrews the engraver. There may be something revolutionary in the air, mingled of pine and brine; for here, when abolitionism was sedition, in 1843, Jairus Lincoln printed a volume of "Anti-Slavery Melodies; for Friends of Freedom," wherein the

The Bear-Pit, Melville Garden.

ringing liberty songs of Whittier and Pierpont and their brethren were set to appropriate music. It was at Hingham, nearly sixty years ago, that Richard Henry Stoddard, one of our foremost poets, was born. He was a boy of boys about the harbor, enjoying the full flush of youthful life in a seaport town, and idling away many a day about the gray old wharves. In later years his tender memories of this region were fruitful in flowing and melodious verses.

The little harbor has not always been as dull as it now appears. At one time there were ninety sail of fishing-vessels hailing from this port; and between 1815 and 1826, a hundred and sixty-five thousand barrels of mackerel were landed from their salty decks. For fifty years — from 1811 to about 1860 — the *Rapid* sailed as a packet between Hingham and Boston, making the trip on one occasion in sixty-seven minutes. In the War of 1812 she was carried up Weymouth River, and covered, masts and hull, with green bushes, so that marauding British cruisers might not find her. In 1881 this venerable vessel was refitted, and made ready for another half-century. The earliest steamboats in the bay wormed their way betimes into Hingham Harbor, — as when the puffy little *Eagle* came hither in 1818. Ten years later the *Lafayette* ran regularly between Boston and Hingham, twice a day, charging thirty-seven and a half cents each way, and taking two hours for the trip. Once this gloomy little vessel was caught in a harbor-squall, off the Castle, and put back to Hingham in great trepidation. The old salts of the village had a mean opinion of her, and many were the obscure marine jokes of which she was the object. In 1831 a new steamboat-company was organized, which, it was predicted, would, in time, carry thirty thousand passengers a year; but this sanguine prophecy fell short of the present result by over a hundred thousand. The first boat of this line was the *Gen. Lincoln*, which had two engines, — one to back, and the other to go ahead, in the narrow and tortuous channels near Hingham. The *Mayflower* was the next boat; and was succeeded in 1858 by the *Nantasket* (now the *Emeline*) which went into the national service during the Secession War, and ploughed the muddy waters of many an historic Southern river.

On Ragged Island.

The town received its first settlers in 1633; and two years later its name of *Bare Cove* was changed to *Hingham*, in memory of the English village from which most of the immigrants came. Among the pioneers were the Lincolns, whose local descendants included Gen. Benjamin Lincoln, famous in the Revolutionary campaigns at the South; Attorney-Gen. Levi Lincoln; Gov. Levi Lincoln, and other notables. Abraham Lincoln was descended from the same family. Here also dwelt the Nortons, the Wares, the Gays, the Hobarts, and other well-famed Puritan clans of strong and steadfast pioneers, whose successors in the land lead placid and tranquil Unitarianized lives, and levy a formidable annual tribute on Boston by leasing their houses to city merchants during the heated term.

West of Hingham lies the venerable town of Weymouth, on the south shore of the harbor, little visited by summer voyagers, but not without attractive coast and lake scenery, and rich in historical reminiscences. Until within a year or two, a large steamboat plied several times daily between Boston and the picnic-grounds (Lovell's Grove) at North Weymouth; but her passenger-lists grew smaller and smaller, year by year, until at last it became evident that the Bostonians no longer craved the mild excitements of Pine Point; and the quiet waters of Quincy Bay have since remained unvexed by the paddle-wheels of the *Stamford*.

Eastward Neck runs far out into the harbor, nearly to Grape Island, and is occupied by the extensive works and wharves of the Bradley Fertilizer Company, and the village in which dwell its ten-score employés. This business was founded in 1861, and now produces annually sixty thousand tons of fertilizers, which are used throughout the United States. There are odors issuing from this establishment which savor not of

The Old Meeting-House, Hingham.

Araby the Blest; and, crossing the harbor on the unwilling wings of a southerly gale, they enwrap the cottages of Hull with a mild malaria. It is well to know that this effluvium is not unhealthy, but acts in some cases as a curative agency. On the east of the Neck is the narrow estuary of Weymouth Back River, running up for three miles to East Weymouth, the seat of the iron-works. There are several well-known camping-grounds among the rocky bluffs and wooded banks of this picturesque stream, which affords some of the most charming nooks near the harbor. Farther westward is the more important Weymouth Fore River, on which, beyond Germantown and Quincy Point, is the flourishing commercial village of Weymouth Landing. Between the rivers is North Weymouth; and several miles inland is the wealthy hamlet of South Weymouth. The manufacture of shoes is the chief industry, and occupies fully eighteen hundred persons, while the rich farms which fill the spaces between these thronging villages have hardly a hundred and fifty men to care for them. A well-known Southern author recently made a pretty sketch of life in this ancient town: "As the head of each family generally has a house and garden, the industrial class is tolerably well off, and with money in the savings bank. At Weymouth, too, clams may be had for the labor of digging them, and fish for the sport of catching them. Nantasket is in full view, and the fishing-ground within a short sail. When Morton, of Merry Mount, set up his Maypole, to the scandal of his neighbors in Plymouth, he little dreamed what a paradise his wilderness would become in two centuries. Intersected by tidal rivers of great depth, and by the Old-Colony Railway, its surface diversified by lofty hills, commanding enchanting views of sea and land, a highly cultivated soil, innumerable orchards, great elms, — the growth of a century, — roads as smooth as an asphalt pavement, and all fanned in summer by the invigorating east winds, the people of Weymouth have no reason to envy the inhabitants of any other town or State."

Statue of Governor Andrew.

Old Governor-Andrew House.

The hamlet of Old Spain, three miles from Quincy, and near the foot of King Oak Hill, was the site of the second settlement in Massachusetts, Plymouth being the first. Here, in May, 1622, landed a party of ten men, "rude fellows, made choice of at all adventures," and sent out by Thomas Weston, an enterprising commercial adventurer of London, who designed to found here a great trading-post. They came down from the Maine coast in an open boat, and explored Boston Harbor carefully, pitching upon the Weymouth region as the best, and purchasing the land of a local Indian sagamore. They then went to Plymouth, and a few weeks later returned with sixty more "rude fellows," sent out by Weston. During the ensuing winter, this half-starved and improvident *canaille* begged and stole from the Indians, until the latter, hating and despising their white neighbors, formed a conspiracy to exterminate them. Miles Standish barely saved the colony by marching up from Plymouth, with a band of Pilgrim soldiers, and killing the hostile chiefs Pecksuot and Wituwamat (as narrated in Canto VII. of Longfellow's "The Courtship of Miles Standish"). After this disastrous season, the settlement was broken up. In 1623 a new colony came over under Capt. Robert Gorges, a veteran of the Venetian wars, and son of Sir Ferdinando Gorges, the head of the Council for New England; and

Ancient Colonial House, Hingham.

under the patronage of King James, the Dukes of Buckingham and Richmond, and many other powerful English nobles and gentlemen. There were in this company traders and farmers and mechanics, many of them bringing their families; with the Rev. William Morrell, an Episcopal divine, as its spiritual head; Francis West, as Admiral of New England; and other grandiose officials. Gorges took possession of Weston's abandoned blockhouse and clearings; and, with the title of Governor-General, endeavored to found here the capital of a feudal palatinate. Here dwelt Blackstone, afterwards the pioneer at Boston; Walford (probably), the first settler at Charlestown; and Maverick, who afterwards ruled at East Boston. But this show of mediæval rank was rather laughed at by the New-Englanders; and within a year Gorges returned to England, and was soon followed by the amiable Morrell. Wessagusset was shown to be an impractical point for a trading-post, on account of its long and devious channel; and most of the settlers soon went away. In 1635 a third settlement was established here, by twenty-one families (one hundred and five persons), who had been induced by the Rev. Joseph Hull, their leader, to emigrate from Dorsetshire. About a month after arriving at Boston, they took ship again, and sailed down the harbor, and through the southern islands, and into Fore River, which they ascended for several miles, and formed a settlement, named Weymouth in memory of the old English village from which they had emigrated. Fragments of the colonies of Weston and Gorges remained in occupation of Wessagusset, tilling their lands, and enlarging each his individual domain. The pleasant heights of Burying Hill and King Oak Hill, overlooking the harbor expanse, were surrounded by their farms; and on the summit of the former soon arose the village church and watch-house, the Acropolis of the new colony.

During King Philip's War, Weymouth suffered from several Indian attacks, and many of its outlying houses were burned. A hundred years later there was a flurry of battle on the Weymouth islands; and peace has since reigned, although the monument to ninety-nine of her citizens, who died as soldiers in the Secession War, attests the patriotism of the town. Among the natives of Weymouth was Joshua Bates, the famous London financier, and benefactor of the Boston Public Library.

In the Old Cemetery, Hingham.

Quincy.

GERMANTOWN. — HOUGH'S NECK. — THE BLUE HILLS, AND SQUANTUM. — MORTON OF MERRY MOUNT.

WESTWARD for a thousand leagues the star of empire has taken its way, since the locality was so strangely christened; but the name of Germantown still clings to the little peninsula which projects into Weymouth River from Quincy, and looks down the estuary to the north-east, and out across the islands. The Sailors' Snug Harbor was founded here in 1856, in a charming location, among grand old trees, under which the blue waters of the Bay are seen. During the past fifteen years, about two hundred and fifty weather-beaten tars have been received here, ninety of whom died in the Harbor. There are accommodations for about twoscore. The sentiment of the place is well expressed in Lunt's poem, read at its dedication: —

> "Here may the veteran mariner repose,
> When on his craft the life-storm fiercely blows;
> Here let him turn a-port, and, furling sail,
> Run for a harbor through the driving gale;
> Here, rounding to, drop anchor near the shore,
> And ride in safety till life's voyage is o'er.
> From cape to cape, search round our noble bay,
> No lovelier sight than here can eye survey;
> From yonder hill, when sunset's blazing sheen
> Sets in a golden frame the pictured scene,
> Let the eye wander freely as it will,
> Landward or seaward, all is beauty still."

From the lawn near the Home rises a tall flag-staff, with a small cannon at its base. Elsewhere on the drowsy little peninsula, shaded by exquisite elms, are two or three ancient houses and several modern villas. A carriage-road leads around Town River Bay to Quincy station, by Hough's Neck and Mount Wollaston, in about three miles; and a short ferry crosses to Quincy Point, whence stages run to Quincy.

There are some interesting bits of history connected with this sequestered locality, beginning away back in 1751, when the peninsula of Shed's Neck was laid out in squares and streets (Bern, Hanover, Hague, Zurich, Mannheim, etc.), and arranged "for a town, to be called Germantown." The property soon passed into other hands, and was colonized by German and French Protestant families, brought over from the Palatinate by Joseph Crellius. Here were Hardwigs and Brieslers and Stubings and Schrontenbachs, and many others, who engaged in making glass, being protected by the General Court, as a monopoly. But the enterprise was not remunerative, and in a few years most of the exiled Teutons went away. Their directors were Gen. Joseph Palmer, from English Devonshire, who had a famous mansion and garden at Germantown, with rich furniture, and a celebrated picture by Copley. So genial and delightful was the hospitality of this estate, that it came to be known in the adjacent countryside as "Friendship Hall." Its master became an American general in the Revolution, and advanced such large sums from his private purse, to help the patriot arms, that financial ruin ensued, and he was driven from his home a bankrupt. His brother-in-law, fellow-immigrant, and partner was Judge Richard Cranch, ancestor of the poet-artist Christopher P. Cranch. At Germantown, under such inspiration, the gallant privateersman, Capt. Tucker, prepared fire-ships to send down into the British fleet in 1776; and many another enterprise was set on foot, in defiance of King George and his Parliament.

In the tranquil period which succeeded the Revolutionary War, the fish business became an important industry at Quincy Point. About fifty years ago Germantown was widely famous for this sea-harvesting, and the half amphibious homes of its dozen captains were surrounded with fish-flakes. Among these honest mariners dwelt the eccentric old Lieut. Pennell, who once drove to Boston in a sleigh, on the Fourth of July; and cut up many other queer pranks, to the great edification of his neighbors.

A few years later Germantown became a notable whaling-port, whence the *Creole, Cambrian, Ontario,* and other vessels sailed on their long voyages. Ship-building began at Quincy Point in 1696, when the ketch *Unity* was launched, and has been an important industry there ever since. Between 1854 and 1870 Deacon Thomas's celebrated yard at Quincy Point turned out a score of large ships, some of them of over two thousand tons, besides numerous smaller craft. Here, too, were built the *Triumphant*, the *Modoc*, and other famous vessels of the last decade. Mr. Quincy gives the following description of the launching of the *Massachusetts*, as far back as the year 1789: "The hills around Germantown, and the boats which covered the harbor and river, were filled with spectators from Boston and the neighboring country. Both English and French naval commanders, at that time visiting Boston in national ships, expressed their admiration of the model of this vessel; and it was afterwards pronounced, by naval commanders at Batavia and Canton, as perfect as the then state of the art would permit." She was a frigate-built merchantman, of a thousand tons and thirty-six guns, and at Canton was sold to the Portuguese Government.

To the northward of Germantown, across Rock-Island Cove, is Hough's Neck, which was granted, in 1637, to Atherton Hough, of Boston; and a road was built out on it in 1673. It is a pleasant peninsula, about two miles long, with marshes and uplands, and two or three semi-attached islets. The road from Quincy hither is in a primitive condition of roughness and crookedness, and adds to the isolation of this secluded bay-side park. The outer beaches are lined with cheerful little summer-houses, close to the high-tide line, and commanding a pleasant view over Quincy Bay and its islands, the terraced cottages of Hull, and the inner lines of Nantasket.

Sailors' Snug Harbor, Germantown.

The Great-Hill House is small, but not without many partisans among the Norfolk-county people, who greatly prize their summer visits to "Mears's." The Neck ends at Great Hill, a round and swelling grassy dome, ninety-four feet high, with a very broad and charming view over the harbor and outer sea. Near the Willow House is a long floating pier, where a landing may be made at any tide; and farther out is the bar which leads to the thunderous shore of Nut Island.

Near the point where Hough's Neck joins the mainland, rises Mount Wollaston, on which stands a mansion of the Adams family. It was in the year 1625 that Capt. Wollaston ("a man of pretie parts," as the Pilgrims called him) landed on this shore, near the hill which still bears his name, bringing thirty or forty indentured servants, and a ship-load of goods for trading. But his serfs would not, or could not, work successfully on a domain which in the eternal councils had been pre-empted for freemen; and so it happened that, a year later, the captain took ship again, and sailed away to Virginia. A few of his men remained, and soon came under the happy despotism of Morton. Of all the dwellers in ancient times by these blue waters, the most singular and picturesque was that merry and rollicking scholar and adventurer, Thomas Morton, of Clifford's Inn, London, who signed himself Gentleman, with a large G. He came over in the year 1622; and when Wollaston's colony broke up, four years later, he induced the motley remnants of that praiseless band to revolt, and depose the worthy captain's deputy, and choose himself as their head. Then began wild saturnalia of lawless revels. May-pole dancings, and the quaint and extravagant mummeries of the Middle Ages, of which he, self-styled "mine host of Ma-re-Mount and Abbot of Misrule," was the soul and inspiration. This boisterous and easy-going demagogue soon drew to his forest Arcadia all the loose and dissolute individuals along the coast, and led away many sober laborers from the adjacent colonies, to become companions of his phenomenal society, free from the restraints of the grim little Israels to the north and south. Hither they came, — runaways in stolen shallops, from the outer coasts, deserting sailors, and wondering Indians in their bark canoes, — and joined the ceaseless carnival. The natives took more kindly to Morton, who supplied them freely with guns and ammunition and whiskey, than to his prudent and sedate neighbors, and found more delight in his festive gatherings than in the conventicles of Plymouth and Cape Ann. He thus narrates, in his *New English Canaan*, the charms of the Alsatia of the West: —

"And when I had more seriously considered of the beuty of the place, with all her faire indowments, I did not thinke that in all the known world it could be paralel'd. For so many goodly groues of trees; dainty fine round rising hillucks; delicate faire large plaines. sweete cristall fountaines, and cleare running streames, that twine in fine meanders through the meads, making so sweete a murmering noise to heare, as would even lull the sences with delight a sleepe, so pleasantly doe they glide upon the pebble stones, jetting most jocundly where they doe meete; and hand in hand runne downe to Neptune's Court, to pay the yearely tribute, which they owe to him as soveraigne Lord of all the springs. Contained within the volume of the Land, Fowles in abundance, Fish in multitude, and discovered besides; Millions of Turtle-doves one the greene boughes: which sate pecking, of the full ripe pleasant grapes, that were supported by the lusty trees, whose fruitfull loade did cause the armes to bend, which here and there dispersed (you might see) Lillies and of the Daphnean tree which made the Land to mee seeme paradice, for in mine eie, 'twas Natures Master-peece: Her chiefest Magazine of all where lives her store: if this Land be not rich, then is the whole worlde poore."

Having found such a paradise, he ordained for it games and pastimes of rare ingenuity, whereof let him at length discourse: "The inhabitants of Pasonagessit (having translated the name of their habitation from that ancient Salvage name to Mar-re Mount; and being resolved to have the new name confirmed for a memorial to after ages) did devise amongst themselves to have it performed in a solemne manner with Revels, & merriment after the old English custome: prepared to sett up a Maypole upon the festivall day of Philip and Jacob; & therefore brewed a barrell of excellent beare, & provided a case of bottles, to be spent, with other good cheare, for all commers of that day. And because they would have it in a compleat forme, they had prepared a song fitting to the time and present occation. And upon Mayday they brought the Maypole to the place appointed, with drumes, gunnes, pistols, and other fitting instruments, for that purpose; and there erected it with the help of Salvages, that came thether of purpose to see the manner of our Revels. A goodly pine tree of 80 foote longe, was reared up. with a peare of buckshorns nayled one, somewhat neare unto the top of it: where it stood as a faire sea marke for directions; how to finde out the way to mine Host of Ma-re Mount. . . . There was likewise a merry song made, which (to make their Revels more fashionable) was sung with a Corus, every man bearing his part; which they per-

Sailors' Snug Harbor.

formed in a daunce, hand in hand about the Maypole. whiles one of the Company sung, and filled out the good liquor like ganimedes and Iupiter.''

But Morton's lot, unfortunately for him, was not cast among the happy-go-lucky colonists of Virginia; and his Pilgrim neighbors were keen observers of the profane revels at the Mount. The public sense of New England quickly took offence; and the opprobrious title of Mount Dagon was given to his habitat, after which it obviously became the duty of the chosen people to exterminate the intruding Philistines. Standish marched from Plymouth (in 1628), with eight Roundhead warriors, and seized the Mount, sending its lord a prisoner to England; and Endicott also led the Salem train-band hither, and cut down the odious May-pole. To pay the cost of this Pilgrim raid, assessments were levied on Salem, Hull, Portsmouth, and the Isles of Shoals. A year later Morton returned: but was speedily sent back to England, and saw the burning of Merry-Mount from the ship in which he was being borne away. In 1643 he came back once more to his paradise by Boston Harbor, broken in fortune, and oppressed by weight of years. The grim Puritans speedily seized him, and vainly ordered a fine of a hundred pounds to be collected from him. He fled to Agamenticus (now York), in Maine, where he presently died. This strange episode in New-England history forms the theme of Motley's charming romance of "Merry-Mount," and also one of Hawthorne's "Twice-told Tales."

As Morton himself ruefully wrote, " The setting up of his Maypole was a lamentable spectacle to the precise separatists: that lived at new Plimmouth. They termed it an Idoll; yea they called it the Calf of Horeb; and stood at defiance with the place, naming it Mount Dagon; threatening to make it a woefull mount and not a merry mount."

But Massachusetts was destined to find Mount Wollaston once more a rankling thorn in her side. In 1634 Anne Hutchinson came hither, from England, and preached the pernicious doctrines of Antinomianism (whatever that may have been) so ably and subtly that she won over Sir Harry Vane and many other Puritan magnates. At Mount Wollaston her brother-in-law and adherent, John Wheelwright, a classmate and friend of Oliver Cromwell at Cambridge University, preached a famous sermon, for which the orthodox Boston magistrates decreed him guilty of "contempt and sedition." He was exiled from the colony, and went north into the wilderness, where he founded Exeter. Anne Hutchinson also was banished. She sailed down the harbor to Mount Wollaston, and thence removed to the Dutch country, near New Amsterdam, where she was slain by the Indians. Her adherents, Underhill, Oliver, Rainsford, Aspinwall, and many others, were disarmed of "guns, swords, pistols, powder, shot, or match;" and some of them were exiled from the colony. William Coddington and Sir Harry Vane came to the Mount on Fast Day, 1636, and heard Wheelwright's inflammatory sermon. Coddington was a crown magistrate, who immigrated with Winthrop, and built the first brick house in Boston. He was a large landholder at Mount Wollaston. Having been banished from Boston for his Antinomianism, he fled southward, and founded Rhode Island, of which he was governor for seven years.

In itself this harbor-side hill has many charms, of which let the golden pen of John Lothrop Motley speak: " Merry-Mount — for by that cheerful title, most grating to the ears of the Plymouth people, was the place now designated — was as agreeable a place for an exile's residence as could have been found in the bay. In the centre of a half-moon, the two horns of which curved outward to the sea, forming a broad and sheltered basin, was a singularly shaped, long, elevated mound, rising some fifty feet above the level of the tide. It was a natural knoll of gravel, resembling in its uniformity an artificial embankment; and, although fringed about its base and its sides by white pines and red cedars, it was in its centre entirely bare of wood, and presented a bold front to the sea, which was separated from it only by a narrow strip of marsh. Beyond this cliff, upon the right, as you looked from the hill towards the ocean, was the broad mouth of Wessaguscus River; upon the left, a slender creek wound its tortuous way through a considerable extent of salt-marsh to the sea. Beyond the creek and the marsh was a line of prettily indented coast, with the picturesque promontory of Squantum bending sharply towards the ocean, near which, on the landward side, was a large, wooded, island-like hummock, called Massachusetts or the Arrow Head, the residence, previously to the plague, of Chickatabot, sagamore of the adjacent territory called the Massachusetts Fields. Many gently swelling hills rose, one upon the other, beyond, thickly crowned with white oak, hickory, and ash, whose gigantic but still leafless tracery was clearly defined upon the sombre background of the shadowy pine forests, which closed the view towards Shawmut and completely shut out that peninsula. On the inland side, the eye was delighted with a soft and beautiful panorama. As the region had long been inhabited, at previous epochs, by the Indians, there were many open clearings; and the underbrush and thicket having been, according to their custom, constantly burned, the tall oaks and chestnuts grew everywhere in unencumbered magnificence, and decorated a sylvan scene, of rolling hills, wide expanses, and woody dells, more tranquil and less savage than could have been looked for in the wilderness. Seaward from the Mount the view was enchanting. Round islands, tufted with ancient trees, and looking like broken links from the chain of hills around, seemed to float far out upon the waves, till they were one beyond another lost in the blue distance; while a low but beautifully broken line of coast fringed the purple expanse of the surrounding ocean, and completed the wilderness picture, fresh from the hand of Nature."

Sailors' Snug Harbor.

From William Tyng, its second owner, Mount Wollaston passed in due succession to his great-grandson, John Quincy, who built a house there, in which he lived until his death in 1767. This gentleman was a faithful servant of the people, and the name of the town of Quincy stands as his memorial. The transient connection of another noble family with this locality was attested by John Adams, who erected a granite monument to the memory of his ancestor, bearing these words: "In memory of Henry Adams, who took his flight from the Dragon persecution in Devonshire, in England, and alighted with eight sons, near Mount Wollaston." The crest of the Mount is now occupied by the mansion of the present John Quincy Adams, a leader of the Democratic party in Massachusetts; and a great number of forest-trees have been planted on the slopes during the past forty years, restoring to this historic hill much of its ancient appearance of wild and sylvan beauty.

On a high hill in Quincy stands the villa of Charles Francis Adams, Jr., with a view described by a Southern visitor as including "out yonder the indented ocean, hungering around naked stone islets, or lapping long stretches of acrid marsh." At the foot of the hill is the stately old mansion (built by the Vassall family about the year 1717) where President John Adams died, and John Quincy Adams lived, and from which both of them were buried, the former in 1826, and the latter in 1848. Here Charles Francis Adams now dwells. Nearer the Bay are other villas of the same patrician family. The houses in which the two Presidents, John Adams and John Quincy Adams, were born, still stand in the south part of the village, and are used as tenements. The remains of these statesmen are buried in the portico of the Stone Temple, or Unitarian church, whose gilded cupola is visible from the harbor-hills. Elsewhere in the town is the old house of John Hancock, the famous Revolutionary patriot. Nor were these the only magnates of the locality. For many years (about the middle of the last century) there lived here a Boston-born lad named Henry Hope, whose mother was a woman of Quincy. On attaining manhood he left the shelter of the Blue Hills, and went across the sea to Amsterdam, where he became the head of a banking-house second only to that of the Rothschilds. He lent vast sums to Spain and Holland, and Russia borrowed $35,000,000 from him. The palace which he built at Haarlem was afterwards the home of Louis Bonaparte.

Among the other children of Quincy were Freeman Hunt, the founder of the famous "Merchants' Magazine;" Whitney, the author; Mrs. Ware, a well-known poet of the first half of this century; and many a notable Adams and Quincy.

The large white building near the shore, north of Mount Wollaston, was built in 1865, under the care of A. H. Rice, James L. Little, and others, as a National Sailors' Home, for sailors of the navy, disabled by wounds, sickness, or old age. It possesses all the modern conveniences and many little luxuries, and has been very successful. Near to the Home is the ancestral estate of the late Josiah Quincy, close to the harbor, and from its venerable colonial windows giving prospects over the out-bound and in-bound fleets. The house was built in 1770, in a domain of five hundred acres of woodland and meadow, purchased from the original Indian proprietors by Edmund Quincy in 1635. Here dwell old-time manners and virtues, and the stately memories of the days of Washington and Lafayette.

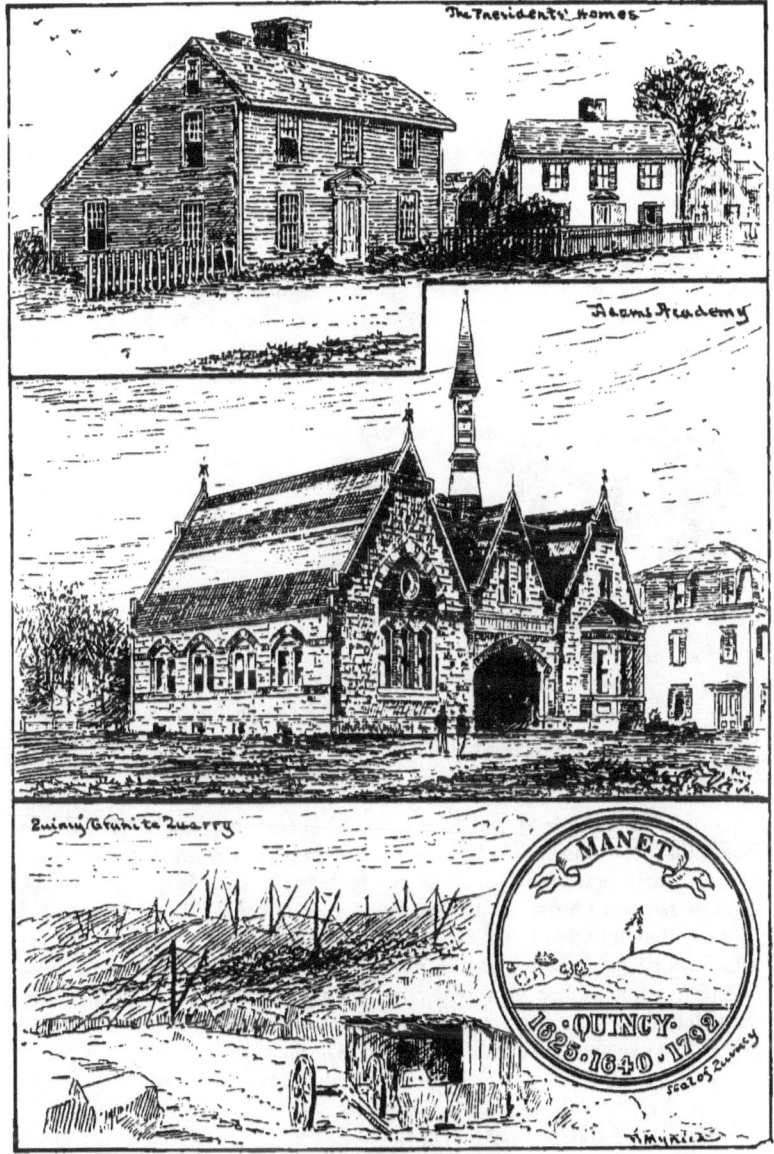

BIRTHPLACES OF JOHN ADAMS AND JOHN QUINCY ADAMS; ADAMS ACADEMY; GRANITE QUARRY. — QUINCY.

Quincy, the chief of the half-dozen villages among these "fair round hillocks and delicious fair plains," with its handsome Adams Academy, new public library, great brick hotel, and newspaper, is near the centre of the town, on the Old-Colony Railway, and about half an hour's ride from Boston. The quality of its citizens is shown on the soldiers' monument in the adjacent cemetery, which tells of forty-one men who died of battle-wounds, twenty in rebel prisons, and fifty-two of disease contracted in the service, out of a contingent of eight hundred and forty-seven men sent into the national armies by Quincy.

A little way back, and very conspicuous from the harbor, is the pretty modern village of Wollaston Heights, on the domain granted in 1636 to Rev. John Wilson, the first minister of Boston, who was a native of royal Windsor, and a fellow of King's College, Cambridge. The shapely hill was graced with a single house in 1869; but now it has two churches, a large hotel, and several score of pretty little villas, commanding charming sea-views.

Near Sailors' Snug Harbor.

The Blue Hills of Quincy and Milton lie to the westward of the village, covering perhaps twenty square miles, and culminating in a magnificent and far-viewing dome-shaped height, six hundred and thirty-five feet above the sea. Scientific men say that this range is older than the Alps or Pyrenees, according to the evidences of geology. It does not appear in history, however, until the year 1007, when the Norse vikings from Greenland saw the distant woody ridges from their galleys cruising off the coast. When Capt. John Smith, that wonderful combination of crusading knight, fearless sea-king, and romantic explorer, first examined our New-England coasts in 1614, he named the high hills over Boston Harbor the *Massachusetts Mount*, in reference to the rich and powerful Indian tribe which dwelt at its foot. But Prince Charles afterward ordained that the name *Cheviot Hills* should be applied thereto, thus initiating the fashion for English names, which was ever afterward filially followed on the shores of the harbor. On these heights often stood the eagle-eyed Indians of whom Morton spoke, saying, "They have tould us of a shipp at Sea, which they have seene, sooner by one hower, yea two howers sayle, than any English man that stood by." According to Edward Everett this land of mountains and lakes was the hunting-park of the Bay tribe.

When Lord Harris was serving in Gage's British army he wrote home hat " The country is most beautifully tumbled about in hills and valleys, rocks and woods, interspersed with straggling villages, with here and there a spire peeping over the trees, and the country of the most charming green that delighted eye ever gazed on."

The Blue Hills are composed largely of granite, or sienite; and Ruskin himself praises the intense purity of such a geological region, claiming also that "the inhabitants of granite countries have a force and healthiness of character about them that clearly distinguishes them from the inhabitants of less pure districts." About eighty years ago the granite-quarries were opened, from which tireless toilers have taken the stone for Bunker-hill Monument, the Custom Houses at Boston, New Orleans, Mobile, Savannah, Portland, San Francisco, Providence, and many other famous public buildings, monuments, and fortresses. Here was built (in 1826) the first railway in America, a line three miles long, on which cars laden with granite were drawn by horses down to the wharf on the Neponset River.

The Blue Hills are very conspicuous from all parts of the harbor and the sea beyond, their regular outlines giving them the appearance of a group of vast domes of unequal sizes. It would be an exaggeration to say that they sustained such a relation to the harbor as Vesuvius does to the Bay of Naples, yet some such idea endeavors to assert itself. The color of the range has been likened to that of the Blue Ridge in Virginia. There is remarkable beauty in these western watch-towers, still lifting their roadless solitudes and tangled forests high above the thronged towns, and looking so wild and untouched that one would hardly be surprised to hear that Massachusee wigwams and tall red hunters were to be found among their inner glens. From the hill-tops of Hull, from the plains of Winthrop, from many of the islands, these gracious summits close the view down the level floor of waters with fine effect. The coloring of the range is richly varied, under changing conditions of sunshine and cloudy sky, from turquoise to sapphire, and then to dappled purple, and then to a formidable sable, when heavy storms lower over them. During his long residence in Europe John Adams once said, "If there is a Bostonian who ever sailed from his own harbor for distant lands, or returned to it from them, without feelings at the sight of the Blue Hills, which he is unable to express, his heart is differently constituted from mine." A few such dry remarks are all that our literature shows about these picturesque little mountains, which, as Charles Francis Adams has justly said, present "lights and shadows making a picture worthy of the pencil of Rembrandt or Claude." They are ignored alike in the songs of our poets, and on the canvases of our artists. Aldrich lived among them for years, but did not find or feign a local legend; Norton's studio faced them, and failed to catch their tints. It is reserved for the twentieth century to do for the Blue Hills what Irving and Cole have done for the Catskills, enshrined in literature and art.

The double-headed peninsula of Squantum projects into the harbor at the mouth of the Neponset, and terminates in a long and bold bluff ninety-nine feet high, overlooking Nantasket Roads and the inner harbor, and occupied by a line of handsome summer-houses. At one end, near Thompson's Island, is the once famous Old Squantum House, which is now a private domain, pertaining to the family of Gen. B. F. Butler. There are some beautiful bits of scenery on this plateau, and on the winding road which leads across the western lowlands to Atlantic station. At one time Squantum bade fair to become a popular summer-resort; but the recent construction of the great Boston sewer across its front has brought armies of laborers here, and makes its present condition the reverse of æsthetic.

The origin of the name of this locality is uncertain. There is an old and puerile tradition that an Indian squaw once threw herself from the cliff into the sea, and the people named the locality *Squaw Tumble*.

Better reasons there are for believing it to have been named in honor of Tisquanto, the Indian chief who first befriended the Pilgrims. Its metropolitan importance in long-past ages is vividly set forth in Edward Everett's classic prose: "The fair domain of our namesake tribe extended from the broad, smooth floor of Nantasket, where the whispering ripple, as it runs up the beach, scarcely effaces the footprints of the smart little sandpipers, all round to the cold gray ledges of Nahant, on which the mountain-waves of the Atlantic, broken and tired with their tempestuous, weltering march through seventy degrees of longitude, conflicting with all the winds of heaven, sink down upon their adamantine bed like weary Titans after battling with the gods, and, lulled by the moaning dirges of their voiceful caves, roll and rock themselves heavily to sleep. Some 'old men of Massachusetts' affirmed that in the interior they extended as far west as Pocontacook. They hunted small game in the Blue Hills, and on their snow-shoes they followed the deer to Wachusett. They passed in their bark canoes

The Profile, Squantum.

through Mother Brook into Charles River; the falls of Nonantum and the head-waters of the Mystic were favorite resorts; they ranged even to the Nashua. Their war-parties met the Tarratines on the Shawshine and Merrimac. But they loved especially the fair headland of Squantum: the centre of their power was Neponset Falls."

Chickataubut was the sachem of the Massachusetts tribes, which held the country from the Charles River to Weymouth, and once could put 3,000 warriors into the field. Most of these were swept off by the great pestilence of 1613; and the chieftain retired to these seashore fields with the feeble remnant of his clan. He received Winthrop and the Boston colonists with stately courtesy, and gave them many valuable presents. He sought them out, at the shabby little village on Shawmut, coming up in some state, with his chiefs and women, and sitting at Winthrop's own table. There is a tradition that, in 1669, he gathered an army of 700 warriors, and marched westward across the colony to the Hudson River, and besieged the great tribal fortress of his hereditary enemies, the Mohawks. The attack was unsuccessful, and the Massachusees retreated rapidly towards Stockbridge. But the fierce Mohawks snared them in an ambush among the Berkshire Hills, and destroyed nearly the entire command, after a long and pitiless battle. Chickataubut and 58 of his sagamores were slain on the field; and the green plains of Squantum saw them no more. Their broad corn-fields were occupied by the immigrating Puritans. The feeble remnant of the tribe came under the government of Chickataubut's brother, Cutshamequin, who led it up the Neponset valley, from whence the Apostle Eliot induced them to go to Ponkapog, on the western slope of the Blue Hills. Here they slowly faded away, and the last pure-blooded Massachusee Indian died in the present century.

In the fall of 1621 the Plymouth Pilgrims became curious about the Massachusees, and ordered Miles Standish "to goe amongst them; partly to see the countrey, partly to make peace with them, and partly to procure their trucke." So the doughty captain took nine men, and Tisquanto the interpreter, and sailed away at midnight. Through the darkness the little shallop bravely held its way up the coast, rounded Point Allerton, and reached the bottom of the Bay, at Squantum. Here the Pilgrims landed at daylight, and found a pile of fresh lobsters on the beach, which they carried under the Chapel Cliff, and breakfasted upon. Afterwards sentries were placed on the Chapel, and Standish and his men found Obbatinewat, the Massachusee sachem. He was persuaded to acknowledge the English authority, though with the dimmest possible idea of what that was; and then the militant missionaries marched inland.

Morton, the delightful Munchausen of ante-Puritan days, proclaims that "Chalke stones there are near Squanto's Chapell, shewed me by a

Salvage." Again, Motley makes him say, "Over at Squanto's chapel yonder, is a fountain of a most remarkable power; for its waters cause a deep sleep of forty-eight hours to those who drink forty-eight ounces at a draught, and so on proportionably." As a reason for this property, he suggests that "the Puritans of Plymouth have buried their oldest and most soporific sermons within the grave of their honored and red-legged friend Squantum, who lies buried there. But, whatever be the cause, the fact is unquestionable. The great Powahs were accustomed to go thither to drink of the fountain, and when filled with its inspiration they would astonish their disciples with the multitude and magnificence of their visions."

Captain Miles Standish.

Morton says that, during his government of Merry-Mount, "Sir Christopher Gardiner (a Knight, that had bin a traveller, both by Sea and Land; a good judicious gentleman in the Mathematticks, and other Sciences usefull for Plantations, Kimistry, &c. and also being a practicall Enginer) came into those parts, intending discovery." This mysterious individual was one of the most interesting of that group of strange men who came hither, apart from the Puritans, and perhaps as parts of a hostile Church-of-England conspiracy, designing to rear a new feudal state on the ruins of the Roundhead colony. In his fascinating romance of "Merry-Mount," Motley places Sir Christopher's home just north of Squantum, at the head of a beautiful cove. He also speaks of him as being the same person (under another name) as the renowned Sir Fulk de Gorges, a knight of Malta, hero of many naval battles with Turkish fleets and Dalmatian pirates, captain of Venetian free-companies, a gallant adventurer in Spain, and a close ally of Sir Ferdinando Gorges in his schemes for renewing the triumphs of Cortez and Pizarro on the coasts of New England. But the Puritans made short work of this brilliant and ambitious monk-soldier, who was branded in their colonial records, as "a person unmeete to inhabit here." Gov. Hutchinson, in his History of Massachusetts (written 120 years ago), thus despatches the unfortunate knight: "In the same ship [in 1631] Sir Christopher Gardner was sent home under confinement. He was a Knight of the Sepulchre, but concealed his true character, and came over last year,

under pretence of separating himself from the world, and living a life of
retirement and devotion. He offered to join to several of the churches,
but he was suspected to be an immoral man, and not received. He had
a comely young woman which travelled with him. He called her his cousin.
For some miscarriages in Massachusetts, he fled to the Indians. They
carried him to Plymouth, having first used him pretty roughly. From
thence he was sent to Boston. He joined afterwards with Gorges, Mason
& others in complaints against the colony." In his "Rhyme of Sir Christopher," Longfellow is equally censorious: —

> "It was Sir Christopher Gardiner,
> Knight of the Holy Sepulchre,
> From Merry England over the sea,
> Who stepped upon this continent
> As if his august presence lent
> A glory to the colony.
>
> "But a double life was the life he led;
> And, while professing to be in search
> Of a godly course, and willing, he said,
> Nay, anxious, to join the Puritan Church,
> He made of all this but small account,
> And passed his idle hours instead
> With roystering Morton of Merry Mount,
> That pettifogger from Furnival's Inn,
> Lord of misrule, riot, and sin,
> Who looked on the wine when it was red."

The first white proprietor of Squantum was the canny Scot, Thompson,
who dwelt upon, and gave his name to, the adjacent island. It was afterwards the domain of Roger Ludlow, "a pious gentleman of good family;"
next, of Mr. Newberry, the ancestor of a celebrated geologist of this
century; and then of John Glover, who established a tannery here, and
had large herds of cattle grazing on the hills. The rocky pile of Musquantum Chapel (whose projecting ledges form a remarkable profile of the
human face) was a favorite landmark as early as 1632. This locality has
notable natural attractions, and has been termed by Charles Francis Adams,
"a miniature Nahant, deep within the recesses of the harbor." In 1716
Squantum was set apart for a hospital, to receive the sick from vessels
entering the Bay. But Dorchester, Milton, and Braintree protested against
it, and the scheme was abandoned. Sixty years later the promontory was
cannonaded by British vessels, and an unfortunate militiaman was killed, on
Moon Island, by a shot.

The Pilgrim Feasts of Squantum were in ancient times celebrated with
great enthusiasm, late in August of each year, and attracted many notables,

and great crowds of the yeomanry. In 1812 the Feast was attended by Gov. Strong, Lieut.-Gov. Phillips, Commodore Bainbridge, and many other eminent men, besides a number of Southern gentlemen; and the cutter "Washington" anchored off the Point, and fired salutes from her artillery. These annual rejoicings were in honor of the Pilgrim Fathers, who doubtless would have been drearily scandalized at their hearty merry-makings. The easy access from the town rendered the feasts very attractive to the solid old merchants of Boston, who could drive hither in seven miles, over the pleasant Dorchester roads, or sail across from Long Wharf. At present the easiest land-route to Squantum is from Atlantic, a station on the Old-Colony Railway, just outside of Boston; and in summer public carriages connect with the trains, and run out to the boarding-houses on the cliff, crossing the plain where the Boston Jockey Club established, in 1812, the first race-course in Massachusetts. Here, also, the old-fashioned musters were held, when the Norfolk-County brigade assembled on training-days, and went through their rural evolutions, enveloped by a host of temporary sutlers and merry-making boys. Farther on the road runs across marshy lowlands, with the Farm Meadows on the left, running almost to Commercial Point. Beyond is the fine ridge of Squantum, haunted by legions of Massachusee ghosts, and beautified by many noble old trees.

Moon Island is now no longer an island, having been joined to Squantum by a substantial artificial isthmus, in connection with the new Boston sewer, whose reservoir has been built here. For two and a half centuries it was the most conspicuous object in this part of the harbor, with its high and grassy bluff rising boldly over Quincy Bay, and dotted with grazing cattle. But now it has become the scape-goat, on which the ills of Boston are to be laid, to be borne off thence into the wilderness of the sea.

Sailors' Snug Harbor.

KING'S HANDBOOK OF BOSTON HARBOR 109

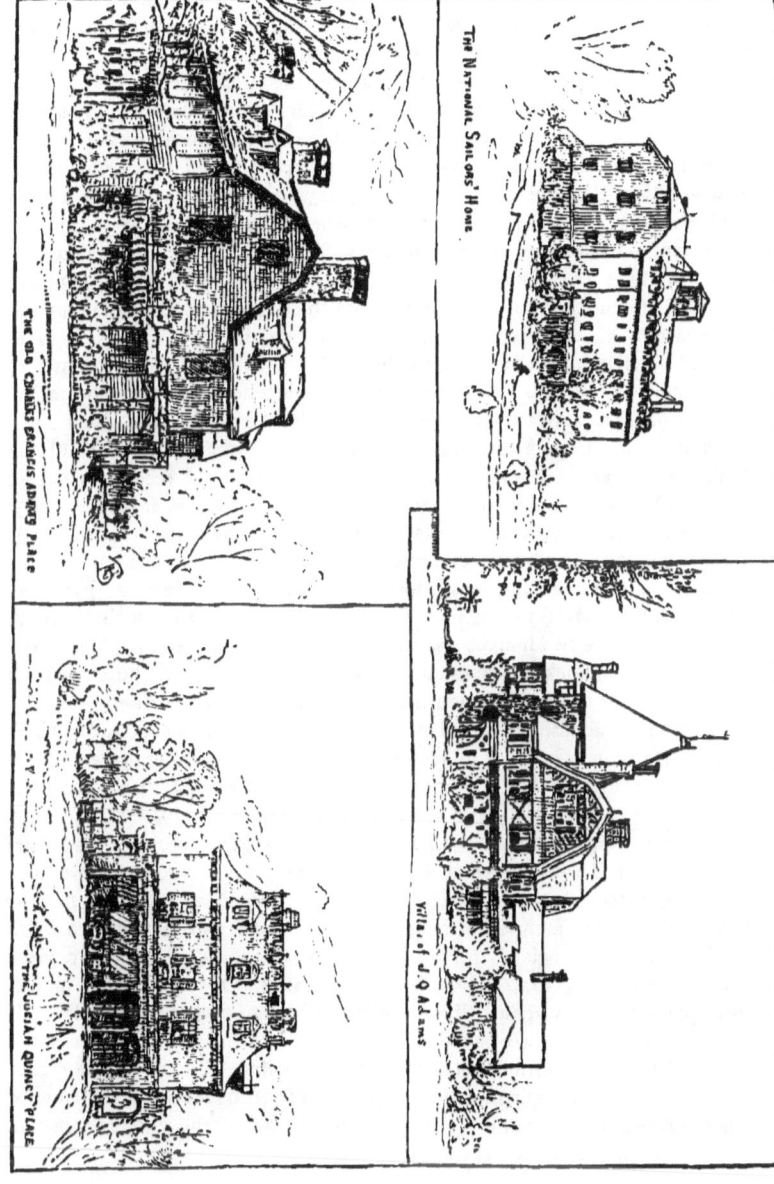

FAMOUS HOUSES IN QUINCY.

A prominent Boston antiquary, who has made a careful study of the ancient resorts and relics of the Massachusetts aborigines, and has examined the shores of the harbor from Nahant around to the South Shore, is of the opinion that the chief home of Chickataubut, the great sachem, was on the southwest corner of Squantum, between Mr. Burckhardt's barn and his house, where there is a beautifully situated and very abundant cold spring, welling out from under the roots of an old tree, and running off into Quincy Bay, opposite Mount Wollaston. Near this spring have been found many Indian implements and weapons, and large shell-heaps, indicative of a permanent settlement, and there are more and larger signs of ancient occupation here than anywhere else about the bay. Nevertheless, there is a very ancient tradition among the people of Quincy that the wigwam of Chickataubut and the palace of his dusky court were established on the very picturesque tree-covered knoll which rises just to the south of the road from Atlantic to Squantum, out on the marshes. From this legend the locality bears the name of *Massachusetts Hummock*, or *Sachem's Hummock*.

Half a mile from Massachusetts Hummock, on the south shore of the Neponset River, is a rocky, savin-covered hillock, until recently occupied by Carl Ditmar's powder works, and now the seat of a less savory industry. Charles Francis Adams, Jr., thinks that this pretty mound, which commands a fine view down the Neponset and out into the harbor, was the home of Sir Christopher Gardiner, the mysterious knight who came into these parts before Winthrop arrived in Boston. The famous Massachusetts fields lay south and west of these two hummocks, and were (as they still are) notable for their fertility. The hillocks were usually chosen as residences in those days, on account of their defensibility and their shelter against bad weather.

In a very elaborate historical monograph of recent publication, Mr. C. F. Adams, Jr., shows Gardiner to have been probably a relative of Queen Mary's Lord Chancellor, Stephen Gardyner, Bishop of Winchester; a veteran of twenty-six years of wars and adventures in France, Italy, Germany, and Turkey; a Roman-Catholic, and a knight of the Papal order of *Cavalieri della Milizia Aureata;* and a secret agent of John Gorges and the anti-Puritan grantees of Massachusetts. He came into these parts six months before Boston was founded, attended by a concubine, and leaving two wives in England, and remained in New England nearly three years, giving great trouble to its magistrates. As Mr. Adams says, "He stands out in picturesque incongruity against the monotonous background of colonial life. It is somewhat as if one were suddenly to come across the portrait of a cavalier by Vandyke in the vestibule of a New England village church. As he passes across the stage, and mingles with the prosaic life of the seaboard settlements, when the seaboard was still the frontier, there is about the man a suggestion of the Spaniard and the Jesuit."

Old Dorchester.

NEPONSET, HARRISON SQUARE, SAVIN HILL, AND THE GREAT SEWER.— CITY POINT.

TO the northward of the Neponset River, the shores of the harbor for several miles lie in the ancient town of Dorchester, which was settled in 1630, and annexed to Boston in 1869. It is now one of the loveliest of suburbs, with several villages among its graceful hills, and many of the noble rural estates for which the environs of Boston are celebrated. Here town and country meet, in happy union, amid a diversity of natural scenery, which affords rare opportunities for generous landscape gardening. Gray old colonial churches and mansions stand side by side with last year's growth of Queen-Anne cottages; and from a score of hill-tops the wide harbor is seen outspread, stretching to the far-away sea. A region so fair and favored, and inhabited by the genuine old Puritan stock (we have seen its steeple-crowned fathers landing at Hull, away back in 1630), must needs have been a nursery of noble men. Among its eminent natives was John Lothrop Motley, who grew up in the love of the sea and its heroes, and was by this inspiration moved to write the most bewitching historical romance of Boston Harbor, and the most vivid and picturesque history of the sea-kings of Holland. Here, too, was born Edward Everett, the silver-tongued orator and statesman, many of whose finest passages were lighted up by the poetry of the adjacent hills and waters. From his own simple and pathetic words, let us recall a mournful picture of the neighborhood. In his youth he often heard of the last Massachusee Indian, who lived in a lonely wigwam on Stoughton Pond, "and used to come down, once or twice a year, to the seaside; hovered a day or two about Squantum; caught a few fish at the Lower Mills; strolled off into the woods, and with plaintive wailings cut away the bushes from an ancient mound, which, as he thought, covered the ashes of his fathers; and then went back, a silent, broken, melancholy man, — the last of a perished race."

Near the mouth of the Neponset River, which flows down from the heights of Sharon and Walpole, is the brisk village of Neponset, once a hopeful outport of Boston, with a very respectable commerce, and now a comfortable suburb. The memorials of antiquity abound in and about this retired corner of Boston, and up through the delightful valley of the

Neponset. On Pine Neck occurred an exciting hunt, 240 years ago, when a huge bear was slain here by Goodman Minot, after alarming the whole countryside. Once a vindictive Indian visited this stalwart hunter's house, in his absence, when there were but two children and a servant-girl on the premises. He fired at the maid, but missed her; and she returned the shot, wounding him in the shoulder. He then tried to break in at the window, and was hotly enough received with a shovelful of burning coals, dashed into his face, upon which, bleeding and fatally scorched, he fled to the woods, where his body was found the next day. The General Court presented the maid with a silver bracelet, bearing this inscription, "*She slew the Narragansett hunter.*" The same old Minot House stood until 1875, when it was destroyed. On Pierce's Hill, near by, is the Pierce mansion, built in 1640, with a museum of Dorchestrian antiquities, and now owned by the seventh generation of the family which founded it. Other neighboring localities are regarded with reverent interest by the local antiquaries.

Commercial Point, which the Indians called *Tenean*, projects into the harbor to the northward, near the mouth of the Neponset River, and has deep-water channels up to its wharves. It was occupied in 1633 by John Holland, who sent out vessels hence in the cod-fishery, for twenty years. During the Provincial era fortifications were erected here; and in 1774 "the greate gun" was carried away, probably to keep it from the British soldiers. In the War of 1812 also, it was fortified, and had the camp of the militia from the western counties, when called out by Gov. Strong, in 1814, to defend our coasts. After its long march from the rendezvous at New Salem, the regiment of farmers found a pleasant resting-place by the Bayside through the fair October weather. One of the commands encamped here was the victim of a singular piratical attack; for on a certain occasion, when ordered to parade before the State House, it neglected to set guards, and on returning from Boston found that people from vessels in the harbor had completely stripped the camp, taking even the tents.

The commercial and shipping business founded here in 1807, proving unsuccessful, was replaced, six years later, by a pottery, bakery, and hotel; but the locality was nearly deserted, and presented a sad scene of desolation and decay. In 1831 a new life was infused into it, when Dorchester capitalists formed a company for prosecuting the fisheries of cod and whales, and six ships and nearly a score of schooners were owned and sailed from the Point. Crowds of hardy mariners then thronged its wharves, spun South-Sea yarns in its tavern, and distressed the Dorchester farmers with their rollicking pranks. For some reason the business did not prosper; and the last ships of the fleet were laden with Argonauts and lumber, and sent around the Horn to California. The next occupants were a firm who erected a huge

KING'S HANDBOOK OF BOSTON HARBOR. 113

Corner Residence of A. A. Nickerson.

Residence of Mr. Young, Architect.

SAVIN HILL, FROM CRESCENT AVENUE.

building for making heavy iron-castings, and carried on a large business here for several years. They then sold the property to the Boston Gas Company, its present owners, whose works are destined to be of great magnitude and importance. The comfortable new club-house of the Dorchester Yacht Club is on one side of the Point. The characteristic American hopefulness has several times seen this dreary old Commercial Point the centre of a coming metropolis; and once the Old-Colony muse predicted its future majesty, in a resounding poem, beginning with these lines: —

> "Where DORCHESTER her lucid bosom swells,
> Counts her young navies, and the storm repels;
> High on the Mount, amid the fragrant air,
> Hope stood sublime, and waved her auburn hair;
> Calmed with her rosy smile the tossing deep,
> And with sweet accents charmed the winds to sleep."

Close to Commercial Point is the pleasant upland of Harrison Square, occupied by a quiet and nobly shaded collection of pretty houses and villas, islanded between the rushing current of the Old-Colony Railway and the harbor, and crossed by several commodious streets. This Arcadian village was once famous for its stanch Abolitionists, who were always free with their money for the good cause of liberty.

A little farther to the northward, nearly insulated by two coves, is the picturesque rocky height of Savin Hill, deriving its name from the evergreen shrubs along the upper slopes. The road which runs around its base is lined with pretty villas, commanding views of the adjacent waters, through the abundant foliage of their grounds. There is a small beach on one side, and toward the harbor projects the peninsula of Fox Point. Until the formidable southerly advance of the town began, Savin Hill (although within 3½ miles of the State House) was a delightful semi-marine paradise, where a few favored gentlemen dwelt in peaceful luxury, with their yachts and horses. But now the city has pre-empted the thirteen acres of picturesque, rocky, and thicketed wild land on the crest for a park; three or four summer boarding-houses have been opened among the villas; and the manifold noises of the metropolis are slowly approaching from the crowded northern streets.

The pleasant highland north-west of Savin Hill is Jones's Hill, recently opened to settlement, and commanding a superb view of the harbor. To the south is Meeting-House Hill, crowned by a church and other public buildings. This was the headquarters and parade-ground of the American right wing during the siege of Boston, in 1775. Farther inland is Mount Bowdoin, at whose foot lived the patrician Bowdoin family, affluent in statesmen and philanthropists. The storied plains and hills of Dorchester cover all the

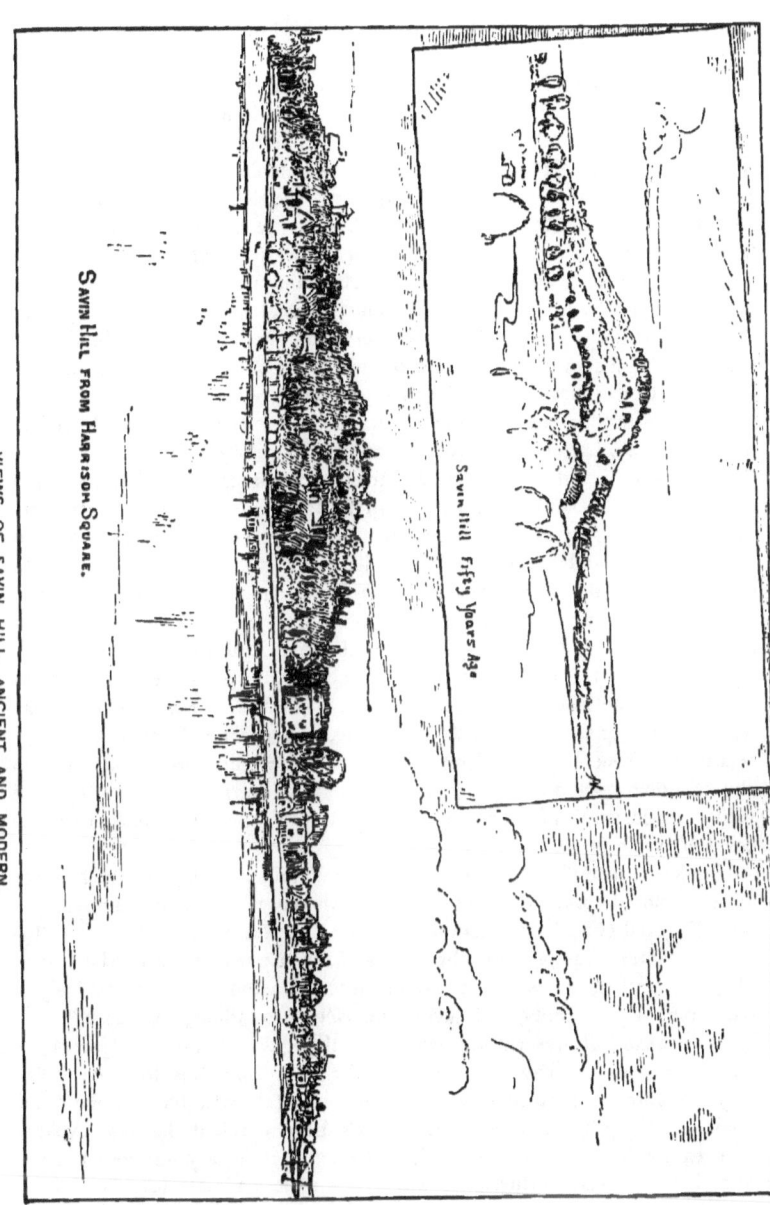

VIEWS OF SAVIN HILL, ANCIENT AND MODERN.

intervening reaches, now rapidly filling with the overflowing population of Boston.

Hutchinson says, in his venerable history, that the capital of the Indians in this region was "on a small hill, or rising upland, in the midst of a body of salt marsh in Dorchester;" and Young thinks that this must have been Savin Hill. The Dorchestrians have an inscrutable joke about Capt. John Smith having landed here, while exploring the New-England coast. In 1633 a fort was built on the crest of the hill, at the expense of Dorchester. The engineer in charge — "straight as an arrow, well-nigh as brown as the Indians whom he fought, in leather breeches and peaked hat, with a heavy sword hanging by his side" — was Capt. John Mason, who had fought in the Netherlands under Fairfax, and afterwards crushed the hostile Pequot tribe in Connecticut. The home of this famous Puritan soldier was on Fox Point, where he lived for many years. Several great guns were mounted on the fort, overlooking the approaches to the harbor of Dorchester. The main battery was probably at the flat rock on the south side of the hill, to command the Neponset River. It was thought that the chief commerce of the settlement would enter that way, since Dorchester was then the chief town of Massachusetts. After the colony changed front to the northward, and the Castle was built, the fort on Savin Hill fell into ruins. Among the ancient residents of Savin Hill was the ambitious and hot-headed Deputy-Gov. Roger Ludlow, a man well off in this world's goods, and a rigid Puritan, as befitted Gov. Endicott's brother-in-law. Being disappointed at not receiving the chief magistracy, he went away to Connecticut, and then to Virginia, where he died. His neighbor was Thomas Hawkins, the fearless old sea-dog, who chartered several war-vessels to the Frenchman La Tour. Afterwards he built the famous 400-ton ship *Seafort*, "set out with great ornament of carving and painting, and with much strength of ordnance," all which naval splendor was lost on the coast of Spain in 1645.

Since the little Gibraltar of Dorchester was dismantled, its site has not appeared in history. In 1824 Lafayette visited the summer camp of the New-England Guards at Savin Hill, which Levasseur, his secretary, called "a very picturesque place on the shores of the sea, where, during the season of good weather, the volunteer companies of Boston come successively to pass some days in tents, and devote themselves to military exercises."

The beautiful description which Motley gave of Boston Harbor, as Blackstone saw it, may well apply to the view from this hill-top: "The Bay was spread out at his feet in a broad semicircle, with its extreme headlands vanishing in the hazy distance, while beyond rolled the vast expanse of ocean, with no spot of habitable earth between those outermost barriers and that far-distant fatherland, which the exile had left forever. Not

solitary sail whitened those purple waves; and saving the wing of the sea-
gull, which now and then flashed in the sunshine, or gleamed across the
dimness of the eastern horizon, the solitude was at the moment unbroken
by a single movement of animated nature. An intense and breathless
silence enwrapped the scene with a vast and mystic veil. The Bay presented a spectacle of great beauty. It was not that the outlines of the
coast around it were broken into those jagged and cloud-like masses, that
picturesque and startling scenery, while precipitous crag, infinite abyss, and
roaring surge unite to awaken stern and sublime emotions: on the contrary,
the gentle loveliness of this trans-Atlantic scene inspired a soothing melancholy, more congenial to the contemplative character of its solitary occu-
pant. The bay, secluded within its forest-crowned hills, decorated with its

The Excursion-Steamboat in 1818.

necklace of emerald islands, with its dark blue waters gilded with the rays
of the western sun, and its shadowy forests of unknown antiquity expand-
ing into infinite depths around, was an image of fresh and virgin beauty,
a fitting type of a new world, unadorned by art, unploughed by industry,
unscathed by war, wearing none of the thousand priceless jewels of civilization, and unpolluted by its thousand crimes — springing, as it were, from
the bosom of the ocean, cool, dripping, sparkling, and fresh from the hand
of its Creator. On the left, as the pilgrim sat with his face to the east, the
outlines of the coast were comparatively low, but broken into gentle and
pleasing forms. . . . A chain of thickly-wooded islets stretched across,
from shore to shore, with but one or two narrow channels between, presenting a picturesque and effectual barrier to the boisterous storms of ocean.
They seemed like naiads, these islets lifting above the billows their gentle
heads, crowned with the budding garlands of the spring, and circling hand

in hand, like protective deities about the scene. On the south rose, in the immediate distance, that long, boldly broken, purple-colored ridge called the Massachusetts, or Mount Arrow Head, by the natives, and by the first English discoverer baptized the Cheviot Hills."

A little way north-east of Savin Hill is Old-Harbor Point, which, after ages of neglect, has recently become a centre of great activity, on account of the works of the great sewer, the *Cloaca Maxima* of Boston, whose works have been constructed on a scale of magnitude and munificence worthy of ancient Rome or modern London. On this Point are two enormous Leavitt and two Worthington engines, with tanks into which the accumulations of many miles of intercepting sewers are discharged, their outflow being pumped up thereinto by the engines, and freed from floating substances and heavy drift, after which the sewage is sent off through the tunnel under Dorchester Bay to Squantum and Moon Island. Handsome stone buildings have been erected here, of great magnitude and imposing proportions. The entire cost of the works on the Point has exceeded $1,000,000. It has for many years been a source of inconvenience and danger to Boston, that her sewers emptied into the streams, bays, and docks of the city, and poisoned the air; their contents being left on the flats at low tide, and driven back around the town by the flood tide. The new intercepting sewers surround the margin of the city, below the level of the existing sewers, and conduct their contents to a still lower main sewer, down which they flow to Old-Harbor Point, where they are pumped up forty feet, and the fluid part passes through the tunnel to Moon Island and the sea. This colossal work has been for some years in successful operation. Its cost has exceeded $6,000,000.

The tunnel under Dorchester Bay is nearly a mile and a half long, and contains 5,000,000 bricks and 8,000 barrels of cement. All of it was cut through solid slate and conglomerate rock, with great difficulty and danger, at a depth of over 150 feet below the sea level, and with an internal diameter of $7\frac{1}{2}$ feet. In the centre of the bay an island has been formed of the *débris* from the tunnel, heaped around the central shaft, whence tunnels were cut eastward and westward, to meet those being driven from the shafts on the mainland. The great five-acre reservoir on Moon Island cost upwards of $800,000. It was constructed by the Cape Ann Granite Company, by digging out the northern part of the grassy hill, stoning and cementing it inside, and defending it by a ponderous sea-wall on the outside. It has four compartments with a capacity of 25,000,000 gallons. The sewage is stored here during the time of one tide, and poured into the harbor about two hours after the ebb-tide has fairly begun. According to the experiments carefully made by the engineers, the receding tide carries it eastward between Long and Rainsford Islands, and between Gallop's and

Gallop's and George's Islands, and throws it against the Brewsters, and thence into the open sea. Fancy the consternation of the lobsters!

Farther to the northward, across Old Harbor, rise the crowded heights of South Boston, now an important section of the Massachusetts metropolis. There were a large number of Indians living on this now populous peninsula until the time of the great pestilence, when so many died that they were left on the ground unburied, and the survivors fled in profound terror. For many decades after the settlement of this region by the whites, great numbers of Indians used to congregate here on a certain day of each year, and hold a commemorative feast, in which all the articles eaten were products of the sea. The locality was at the south end of the present K Street. The Indians called this handsome peninsula by the name of *Mattapan* or *Mattapannock;* and after Dorchester was settled, in 1630, it was a common pasture, abounding in rich grass and diversified by clumps of trees. In 1660 the first building was erected, by Deacon James Blake; and in 1775 there were nine houses here, the finest of which was the mansion of the Fosters, one of whom designed the present State seal. On the night of March 4, 1776, Gen. Thomas occupied the heights, with 2,000 Continental soldiers and 400 carts of fascines and intrenching tools, his men being forbidden to speak above a whisper. The moon shone brightly, and by morning two formidable forts appeared on the hill; and Lord Howe exclaimed in dismay, "The rebels have done more in one night than my whole army would have done in a month." The British positions in Boston were commanded at all points by the guns on the heights; and Washington was so sure that an attack would be made, that he had the entire militia force of Massachusetts called into his camps, and concentrated his floating batteries and boats at Cambridge, ready to carry 4,000 soldiers to land on Boston Common, and fall upon the British garrison, while his best forces should be engaged on the heights. 2,400 regulars were sent to the Castle, under Earl Percy, to storm the new batteries; and this chosen force would probably have been well-nigh exterminated but that a strong gale sprang up and made it impossible for them to land. The British generals, finding it inconvenient to exist in a town so commanded by hostile batteries, made haste to get away; and the right wing of the American army, posted on Dorchester Heights, watched their departure with great joy.

In 1814 new defensive works were constructed here, and several regiments of militia went into barracks to protect them. One night a false alarm was caused, by boats burning blue lights in the harbor. The garrison formed hastily in the darkness, and more than a third of the soldiers fled incontinently into Dorchester. Thirty years later a large town had risen here, with famous ship-yards, one of which launched twenty-seven ships within ten years. Among the chief industries of the present time is the manufacture of iron, in which South Boston has but two or three rivals in America.

In 1803, foreseeing the future magnitude of Boston, Messrs. Tudor, Green, and Mason bought most of the peninsula as a speculation. The ensuing annexation movement was resisted by Dorchester, but without success; and in 1804 the territory became a part of Boston, and its land rose to a tenfold value. There were then 19 voters here; in 1840 there were 6,176 inhabitants; in 1855, 16,612; and now there are upwards of 60,000.

The low promontory of City Point, the most easterly part of South Boston, is the paradise of yachtsmen. Here scores (and sometimes hundreds) of pleasure-boats of all classes are to be seen, — in winter hauled up in yards and on wharves, covered with canvas, and partly dismantled; and in summer, straining at their cables in the blue waters off-shore, graceful, dainty, and apparently full of bounding life and pride. More than a dozen yacht-clubs have moorings here, including vessels from ports scores of miles away. Here, too, are the yards of the shipwrights who make these fair little ladies of the sea, carrying out in careful lines and exquisite decorations the pet theories of the sportsman, or the costly vagaries of the millionnaire. On shore there are half a dozen taverns, frequented by these amateur mariners and their sailors; and a seaside theatre, much patronized on summer evenings, and within half an hour of Boston Common by horse-cars. That portion of South Boston which lies to the eastward of Q Street is to be laid out by the city as a water-front esplanade, together with more than twenty acres of the adjacent flats, which, when filled and graded, will form the City-Point Battery, where the people may come to enjoy the music of the band, the pleasant sight of the ships and islands in the harbor, and the delicious and bracing sea-winds. Even now thousands of people come hither on a warm day, to be refreshed by the views and the salty coolness, or, perchance, to enjoy the sea-baths in the spacious bath-houses which have been built here.

Among the yachts are sloops, schooners, steam-launches, and many convenient and swift little cat-boats. They lie at their moorings, in fairly deep water, and quite out of danger, because large vessels rarely enter this part of the harbor. Another marked advantage of this locality is its comparative vicinity to the lower roads and the sea, enabling the yachts to reach blue water much more quickly than from the inner wharves of the port. The club-houses of the Boston and South Boston Yacht-Clubs are at City Point. During the summer a small sailboat and skipper may be hired, at the public landings, for 75 cents an hour; and rowboats cost about thirty cents an hour. By these means, the upper harbor and Dorchester Bay can be explored, even to the far-reaching and quiet expanses

HOUSE OF THE BOSTON YACHT-CLUB, CITY POINT.

of Quincy Bay, seldom vexed by even the most adventurous of the keels of commerce.

This bustling haven of summer-pleasurers was once the remotest and most solitary corner of Boston. In those ancient days the adjacent hills often re-echoed the roaring of the eighteen-pounders of that oddest of military corps, the Sea Fencibles, — a coast-guard composed of the ship-masters who were left stranded in Boston by the war and blockade of 1812. In their blue short-jackets and white trousers, with anchor-emblazoned glazed hats, these jolly tars would march to City Point, with unsteady rolling gait, and there fire their big guns at floating targets. The soldiers carried boarding-pikes and cutlasses, and yearned for a chance to use their primitive weapons against the hated Britishers. The valorous sea-dogs are now all in their graves, and the American commerce which they loved so well is buried with them. But the great flotilla of pleasure-boats off City Point bears witness that the old maritime spirit is still strong in New-England men.

Captain John Smith.

East Boston (Noddle's Island).

MAVERICK. — BATTLE-DAYS. — YANKEE CLIPPERS. — BREED'S ISLAND.

A MILE and a half north of South Boston, across the inner harbor (at whose western end rise the wharves and hills of Boston), is the Island Ward of East Boston, covering more than a square mile, and connected with the city by three steam-ferries, and with the mainland on the north by several bridges. This locality was for over two centuries known as Noddle's Island, from William Noddle, who was probably sent out by Brereton, and settled upon it in 1629, before Boston was founded. This pioneer was a bachelor, and the name is extinct. Sir William Brereton received an early grant of it; but the first conspicuous settler was Samuel Maverick, Gent., who erected a small fortified mansion, with artillery to defend it, and was in comfortable possession and authority long before Winthrop's fleet entered the Bay. The Puritans, coming later, allowed Maverick to remain here, on payment yearly of "a fatt weather, a fatt hogg, or XLs. in money;" although it is most likely that he was an adherent of the Gorges government, together with Walford, Blackstone, and Morton. He certainly lived under the stigmas of being an Episcopalian and a Royalist, and met with annoying persecutions from the Boston authorities. Maverick was the first New-England slaveholder, when Capt. Pierce brought negroes hither from the Tortugas, in 1638, and sold them in Boston. In 1645, after La Tour's terrible enemy, D'Aulnay, had stormed the fort at St. John, and sailed away with his plate and treasures, leaving Madame La Tour dead of a broken heart, the unhappy chieftain came to Maverick's little castle, where he spent the dreary winter. Not long afterwards the godly brethren of Boston made new encroachments on the rights of their prelatical neighbor, and he found himself forced to depart from the fair island-home. Some years later he died at New Amsterdam.

During their time of suffering from persecution, about 1660-70, the Baptists of Boston used to meet here, under the title of "The Church of Jesus Christ worshipping at Noddle's Island in New England." The poor fellows labored under all sorts of disadvantages in town; but in this insular sanctuary their worship was undisturbed, until the slow liberalization of Massachusetts gave them opportunity to enter Boston as accepted Christian brethren. A century later the comfortable Williams mansion was the pride of the island; and Putnam, Knox, Lincoln, and the clergy of Boston made frequent visits here. The house was graced by six comely daughters, whose harpsichord was the forerunner of musical Boston; and the hills on the island gave pasturage to 43 horses and 223 cattle. After this house was burned, in the skirmish of 1775, Washington gave Mr. Williams one of the Continental barracks at Cambridge, which he moved down to the island, and remodelled into a new mansion. During the siege of Boston a score of young ladies left the beleaguered town, and took refuge on Noddle's Island, perhaps in this well-known house of Williams. One of these was especially dear to William Tudor, the judge-advocate-general of the American army; and he used to visit her frequently, passing from Cambridge to Chelsea, where he undressed, and tied his clothing in a bundle, fastened upon his head; after which he swam to the island, resumed his garments, and called upon the fair lady. The result of these Hellespontic wooings was a happy marriage, whence came three sons and two daughters, in later days patricians of the good Commonwealth.

Passing abruptly from love to war, we find that on this same island was fought the second battle of the Revolution, and the first in which the American artillery was used. On May 27, 1775, Gen. John Stark and 300 men were sent to clear out the live stock on Noddle's Island; and after they had driven 400 sheep inland from Breed's Island, they engaged the British marines on Noddle's, but were driven back when large re-enforcements of regulars crossed from Boston. In the mean time Gen. Gage sent a schooner armed with sixteen small guns, and eleven barges full of marines, up Chelsea Creek, to cut off the raiders; while Putnam came to their relief with 300 men and two guns. The fight lasted all night; but, although fresh troops poured over from Boston, the Americans forced the crew of the schooner to abandon her and flee, and drove back the other vessels. They took the artillery from the captured vessel, and then burnt her, and retired to the mainland, having inflicted severe loss on the British forces. Lord Percy was immensely disgusted at this affair, and wrote home to his father: "The rebels have lately amused themselves with burning the houses on an island just under the admiral's nose; and a schooner, with four carriage-guns and some swivels, which he sent to drive them off, unfortunately got ashore, and the rebels burned her." Philip Freneau, the poet of the Revolution, makes Gen. Gage speak thus, at this time, referring to the partial famine caused by the American raids on the islands: —

"Three weeks, ye gods! nay, three long years it seems,
Since *roast beef* I have touched, except in dreams.
In sleep, choice dishes to my view repair:
Waking, I gape, and champ the empty air.

> Come, let us plan some object, ere we sleep,
> And drink destruction to the rebel sheep.
> On neighboring isles uncounted cattle stray,
> Fat beeves and swine, — an ill-defended prey:
> These are fit visions for my noon-day dish."

In 1780 there were many sick men on the French fleet in the harbor, and barracks were erected on the island for hospitals. The poor fellows christened their gloomy quarters *L'Ile de France;* but small comfort did they find in that, with dead soldiers being borne to the burying-ground every hour. The mortality was serious, and many a good Gaulish veteran was laid to his eternal rest on the hills of Noddle's Island. After the British forces evacuated Boston the island was strongly fortified.

The same works were renewed and and strengthened in 1812, under the name of Fort Strong, having been re-erected by various patriotic societies, and guilds of tradesmen and mechanics, each of which marched to the place on their appointed days. After the removal of the barracks in 1833, the walls of the fort were allowed to waste away. In 1819 Lieuts. White and Finch of the United-States Navy fought a duel here; and the former was killed, according to the code of honor.

The growth of the city of East Boston on these historic pastures of Noddle's Island has been at once rapid and solid. In 1833 there were 8 inhabitants here; in 1835, 600; in 1847, 6,500; in 1880, close upon 30,000. The island is now covered with paved streets, bordered by a surprising number of trees, and the houses of a great industrial and maritime community. The population of the island is about equal to that of Mobile, Savannah, Memphis, Trenton, Utica, or Wheeling.

Some of the finest ships that ever sailed were constructed here by Donald McKay, vessels beautifully finished and furnished, and built for great speed. The *Flying Cloud*, 1,700 tons, made the passage to San Francisco in 89 days, being the quickest ever known. The *Sovereign of the Seas*, 2,400 tons, was the longest and sharpest clipper ever built, and once made a run of 430 geographical miles in 24 hours. She earned $200,000 in less than a year. The *Empress of the Seas* held high rank among the famous clippers of the same epoch. The *Great Republic* was the largest wooden sailing-ship ever built. Her 4,556 tons included 1,500,000 feet of hard pine, 336 tons of iron, and an immense amount of white oak. She sometimes made 19 knots an hour, under full sail; and went from New York to San Francisco in 91 days. Between 1848 and 1858 more than 170 vessels were built at East Boston; of which 99 exceeded 1,000 tons each, and 9 were above 2,000 tons. These were the famous racers, which swept around Cape Horn, and up through the South Seas, crowded with the Argonauts in search of El Dorado. Others belonged to the Liverpool packet-line, and

made regular trips across the Atlantic for many years, exciting the keen and jealous admiration of our British cousins.

The Atlantic Works, on this island, have built iron steamships for Russia, Egypt, Paraguay, China, and the East Indies: the monitors *Nantucket* and *Casco;* the turrets of several other iron-clads; the engines for many American frigates; and entire fleets of ferry-boats and tugs. Other neighboring shipyards and works have done their share in creating that famous American marine which once was the wonder of all-maritime nations.

Extensive and well-matured plans are in process of elaboration, by which the broad flats to the eastward will be converted into docks of the first magnitude, capable of accommodating the largest ocean-steamships, and easily approached from the deep-water channels. What with the great wharves of the Cunard and other lines; the elevators, ship-yards, and marginal railways; and the Grand-Junction wharves, East Boston is the most important part of the Puritan city, in a commercial point of view.

Breed's Island, north-east of East Boston, was first known as *Susanna Island*, in honor of the daughter of Sir William Brereton, to whom it was granted (in 1628) by John Gorges. The Puritans found the practical name of *Hog Island* more to their taste, and thus it remained for more than a century. Late in the last century it was named *Belle Isle* by Russell, who owned it; but the old name clung tenaciously, and is still sometimes heard. In 1687 Judge Sewall, in the presence of numerous chosen witnesses, took possession of Hog Island, by the ancient rite of "taking Livery and seised of the Iland by Turf and Twigg and the House." Here he built a wharf and planted various kinds of trees, and kept a large flock of sheep. He held the domain for many years, making divers improvements, and deriving a fair revenue therefrom. About the year 1800 the island was bought by John Breed, a wealthy English gentleman, who had been well-nigh heartbroken by the death of his betrothed bride, near the time appointed for the wedding, and afterwards sought only to bury himself from the world. Here he had a rich hay-farm, with a score of workmen, an overseer, and a housekeeper. He built the house whose remains are now visible on the south slope of the hill,—a singular stone structure, 200 feet long and one story high, with terraced gardens in front of it, and nurseries in which nectarines, apricots, and other fruits were cultivated. But in time death carried off this peaceful agricultural hermit, and his domain passed to other uses. It is now being rapidly taken up as a seaside settlement; and upon the long and lofty ridge many pretty cottages have already been erected, each with its view of sea or harbor, or rugged hills of Essex.

Rural and Puritan Winthrop.

SUNNYSIDE, COTTAGE PARK, CRYSTAL BAY, AND OCEAN SPRAY. POINT SHIRLEY.

UT from the main, east and south, and forming the northern shelter of Boston Harbor, runs the peninsular town of Winthrop. It is beautifully diversified with hills and meadows, isthmuses and coves; and, although but 989 acres in area, it has eight miles of beach. The thousand inhabitants of this sea-girt corporation are served by an odd little narrow-gauge railway, diverging from the Boston, Revere Beach and Lynn Railway at Winthrop Junction, and running hourly trains down over the marshes to Great Head and Point Shirley, stopping at every street. A branch line leaves the Eastern Railroad, back of Revere Beach, and runs down into Winthrop, heading toward Point Shirley.

The chief village stands on the pleasant high ground nearly midway between the sea and the harbor, and commands fine views in either direction, on one side to Nahant and Marblehead, and over the open ocean; and on the other to the fortified islands and the Blue Hills of Milton. It is a pretty New-England hamlet, without a touch of suburbanism, and as rural and

A Fisherman's Home, Point Shirley.

simple as if it were inwalled by the distant hills of Berkshire or Aroostook. Two or three country stores, a bleak town-hall, two comfortable wooden churches, a few dignified and emparked mansions, half a dozen residences of village magnates, and several score of neat and embowered houses of the yeomanry, — these elements compose the familiar picture, the same here as in hundreds of other places in these six Yankee sovereignties. Within short cannon-shot of the State House, and overlooking the great channel of commerce and its procession of ships, remains a village in which Judd's Margaret might find herself at home. The ghost of Gov. Winthrop, flying from Irish-Italian-Portuguese Boston, may rest here, on his son's summer farm, and say, "What! and grown so little in a quarter of a millennium!" It is still remarkably free from the foreign element, and consequently enjoys almost a complete immunity from pauperism and crime. Liquor is legally banished from its borders, a fact to which the delightful peacefulness and decorum of the beach villages may be attributed. Bibulous roisterers find a woefully dry country south-east of Revere Beach, and make no second visits there.

To the south of the village, overlooking the harbor, and surrounded by plantations of small trees, is the stately old mansion which was formerly occupied by Mr. C. L. Bartlett, the well-known shipping-merchant of Boston. Hence his chivalrous son rode lightly away to enter the Federal army in 1861 ; and hither he was brought back three years later, wounded almost to death, and with barely strength to write, as he felt the pure air of the Bay replace the malaria of Virginia, " This being at home is delicious; comfort and rest." In 1853 the great Italian patriot, Garibaldi, who came to Boston in command of a ship from South America, was entertained for some time as a guest at this place; and thirteen years later, when Gen. W. F. Bartlett, the merchant's son, was in Italy, he received an invitation to Caprera, where he made a pleasant visit with the Garibaldi family. The lad, with whom the grand Latin patriot had rambled along the shores of Winthrop, had now become a veteran general officer, full of deep and terrible experiences. In four years the college-boy had risen from the ranks to the command of a division; had suffered several grievous wounds and gloomy captivity; and returned home, broken by hardship, and under the shadow of approaching death. These verses are from the poem which Whittier wrote, after the young hero's death : —

> "Mourn, Essex, on thy sea-blown shore,
> Thy beautiful and brave,
> Whose failing hand the olive bore,
> Whose dying lips forgave!
>
> "As Galahad pure, as Merlin sage,
> What worthier knight was found
> To grace in Arthur's golden age
> The fabled Table Round?"

After the death of the gallant young general, the Bayard of the army, the estate passed into other hands. Farther toward the city, on a picturesque point projecting into the harbor, stands the fine old mansion occupied for so many years by the eminent educator, George B. Emerson, and often visited by Agassiz and other scholars. The trees which shade the avenues and grounds were planted by his own hand, and greatly beautify the place.

The quaint old farmhouse which still stands on Shirley Street is said to have been the home of Deane Winthrop, the sixth son of Gov. Winthrop. It was built probably as early as 1649; and here the honorable governor and other colonial magnates, including also Chief-Justice Sewall, made many summer visits. Here Deane died, in the year 1704, having

The Old Deane Winthrop House, near Ocean Spray.

lived hereabouts for forty years. He was the founder of the town of Groton, which he named for the home of his family in England. A little way beyond this ancient house, and over Ocean Spray, is the noble headland of Grover's Cliff, whose 180 acres of rolling pasture-land were for many years owned by the corporation of Boston. In 1867 the city council ordered the construction of a new and magnificent hospital for the insane, on this estate; but the mayor vetoed it, being opposed to such a large outlay of money, and also objecting to the establishment of a public institution on an exposed headland. The subsequent erection of the State Asylum at Danvers rendered it unnecessary; and the land staid in possession of the city until 1883, when it was sold at auction. It is now known as Winthrop Highlands, and has two summer-hotels, the Argyle and Aloha, and many cottages and villas. A noble seashore drive runs from Beachmont across the Highlands to Point Shirley.

Winthrop is rich in summer resorts, on her sea-swept shores. Ocean

Spray and Point Shirley are the chief ones, but Crystal Bay and Sunny Side and Harbor Avenue each has its advocates and *habitués*. Sunny Side is a little group of summer cottages, with boat-house, wharf, and still-water beach, fronting southward on the harbor, near Snake Island and its wide *entourage* of flats. This colony of sequestered houses is usually occupied of late years by the Vokes family, so famous in the annals of British and American comedy.

Cottage Park is another cluster of cottages fronting on the harbor, and mainly occupied by summer visitors from the city. It is on a bluff, just inshore from Apple Island, and sheltered from easterly storms by the trees of the old Bartlett estate. There is a small pier here, with bath-houses, arbors, and other appurtenances. The view across the harbor to the Blue Hills is full of impressive beauty; while on the right, three miles distant, appear the massed houses and many spires of Boston. In this prosperous

little summer village stands the Cottage-Park House, a large boarding-house, where the cottagers can get their meals. From this point, the view extends southward, over the graceful elms of Apple Island, and out through the opalescent air, by many a historic islet and promontory; and westward, to where the red sun sets behind Boston.—

> "Like eye of God aglare
> O'er evening city with its boom of sin."

These pretty pleasure-houses are but the formal successors of the summer wigwams of the red men who were once lords of the soil, stalwart hunters and fishers, and gallant archers. The Indians who dwelt on this side of the harbor were of the Pawtucket tribe, whose domains reached as far as Concord and Portsmouth. The head of the clan at Chelsea (Winnisimmet) was Sagamore John, who died in 1633, with many of his people. The Winthrop peninsula, surrounded with fishing-grounds, appears to have been a favorite resort of the red men; and many remains of their wigwam villages have been found upon it. One of the first edicts published by the

Puritans at Boston established a game-preserve here, saying: "That noe pson wtsoeuer shall shoote att fowle vpon Pullen Poynte or Noddles Island, but the s^d places shalbe reserved for John Perkins to take fowle wth netts." In 1635 the peninsula became a common, for pasturage; and Boston caused a house and cattle-yard to be built at the Point. The territory appears to have been occupied subsequently by farms, owned by non-resident proprietors, who kept here servants and tenants. In the summer they sometimes came down from Boston, to enjoy the sea-air, and relief from the turmoil of the town, which then had four or five thousand inhabitants. Deane Winthrop had an estate of 120 acres at Pulling Point, and here "he was wont to set up a bush when he saw a ship coming in." Capt. Gibbons also had a place near by; and once (in 1643) his wife and family, on their way down from Boston to the Point, were terribly frightened on meeting La Tour's French ship. Slavery flourished here in those ancient times; and

Great Head, Winthrop.

the negro burying-ground in the north part of the town had many quaint monuments. Connected with the Bill mansion, on Lincoln Street (now over two centuries old), were several sable slaves; and their bills of sale are still preserved. There is a legend that one of these negroes buried his acquisitions, — a tea-kettle overflowing with silver coin, — and died without revealing its whereabouts. This is the Captain Kidd's treasure of Winthrop, and has stimulated no end of delving on its pleasant headlands.

Very slender are the threads of history and tradition which connect the green hills of this country town with the outer world. She rests quietly on the shores, watching the grand promenade of the commercial fleets, the dainty quadrilles of the yachts, and the Terpsichorean achievements of the breathless steam-tugs, which, with their iron hands clasped upon those of the *Mary Jane* of Liverpool, or the *Gypsy Maid* of Baltimore, guide her, in a stately gliding minuet, down the mazy channels, to the outer sea;

and return, up the blue floor of waves, leading some other thousand-ton beauty, the *Empress of the Seas* perchance, or the *Saucy Sally* of Kennebunk, or *La Reina Margherita* of Genoa. Meanwhile Winthrop placidly observes the scene, the fair wall-flower of the harbor.

One of the most attractive summer villages on the Massachusetts coast is this prettily-named district of Ocean Spray, in the town of Winthrop, with its beach gently curving between two high cliffs, the bright wide sea in front and the level salt-marshes behind. The line of beach rests at one end on Great Head, and at the other on Grover's Cliff and the unbroken green slopes of the city estate. The view includes the aristocratic peninsula of Nahant, with its villas and cliffs, about four miles distant across the Bay, and reaching far out into the water; and on the right front are the ragged and picturesque Brewster islands, off the mouth of Boston Harbor. The surf is usually light, and bathing is quite safe; but during easterly and northerly gales there is a tremendous pounding along the entire line of beach, and the waves leap fifty feet high over the adjacent bars of Great Head and the sea-walls of Deer Island. There are usually a few yachts anchored off the beach, in which the Spray villagers cruise through the narrow seas toward the North Shore.

Up to the year 1875 the site of this village was a barren waste of gravel and coast grass, whose only product was the seaweed washed up on the beach, and whose value did not exceed $40 an acre. In 1875 Dr. Samuel Ingalls bought forty acres of the Wheeler heirs; laid it out in building-lots and avenues; and sold many of the former at auction, at 1½ to 2 cents a foot. During a single year these prices were quadrupled; and then the fourteen acres bordering on Capt. John Tewksbury's beach, adjacent, were put upon the market. There are now several scores of cottages at Ocean Spray, mostly of a more attractive order of architecture than is usually found in beach-houses; and in some cases they are spacious and substantial villas, occupied throughout most of the year. The arid gravel which surrounds them has been covered with loam, and laborious attempts at gardening have been rewarded with some measure of success. The local summer society is peculiarly homogeneous and mildly evangelical, with every evening devoted to some form of associated pleasure, musicales, square dances, or chapel-going, and ending early, so that by ten o'clock nearly all the house-lamps are out, and the resonant music of the low surf breaking on the beach is almost the only sound that is heard. Ocean Spray, and particularly the part outside the hotels, is a place for rational enjoyment and plenty of rest. The spirit of Winthrop, the first lord of the manor, seems to brood over it still.

It seems somewhat enigmatical that this should be a favorite summer-house for actors: yet such is the case, and the merry pranks of the Vokeses,

Nat. C. Goodwin, and other stage celebrities, are often rehearsed among these beauties of nature. At the north end of the beach is The Shirley, a comfortable summer-hotel of modern construction and accommodations, and very close to the edge of the surf. Near the Shirley is the pretty little building of the Casino, adapted and used for dancing and amateur theatricals, and the scene of temperate gayeties throughout the livelong summer. The Winthrop-Beach House is another hotel at this point. Near the southern end is the Great-Head Hotel, an airy and well-built structure, close alongside the railway.

On Main Street is the seat of one of Boston's fairest charities, the Seashore Home for sick and destitute children, transferred here from Plymouth, in

Boston, from Winthrop Great Head.

1878; and every season taking two or three hundred poor children from the hot and unhealthy streets of Boston, and placing them in pure air and good influences. It is a very noble and satisfactory work, and the only regret is that the resources of the institution are not sufficient to care for a vastly greater number of these innocents. The seventh chapter of Book IV. of Michelet's "The Sea" (*La Mer*) should be read as a preliminary to visiting this beautiful charity; for it describes the foundation of the first seaside hospital for children, which was done by the majestic old city of Florence, but little more than twenty years ago.

Great Head, or Green Hill, about half a mile south of Ocean Spray, is a symmetrical curving eminence, 100 feet high, from whose summit very extensive views are given over the adjacent bays and shores, and out on the open sea. The railroad passes around one side of it, over the beach; and on the other is the fine carriage-road to Point Shirley, following the curves of the harbor. Within five years a pretty summer village has grown up around Great Head, and a planked walk projects into Crystal Bay, for the convenience of the mariners of the new local yacht-club. The new construction is securely enrailed, and is the Brighton Pier of this quiet resort, where the transient citizens may "loaf, and invite their souls," and feel the sea all around and beneath them, without fear of *mal du mer*. This placid sea off Winthrop is indeed capable of profound agitations, and many a ship has been dashed in pieces against the heads hereaway. In the great March storm of 1878 four vessels were driven ashore at Ocean Spray and Great Head; one of them being the brig *Katahdin*, bound from Portland to Matanzas, and wrecked while trying to make Boston Harbor. Many people came down from the neighboring cities to see these helpless victims of the gale, beaten by the foaming sea.

Winthrop may be likened in its outline to a rose, rising from the blue sea, and opening toward Middlesex County. Curving gracefully from south-east to south, over a mile long, and generally but a few score feet in width, the stem of this fair Puritan rose of Winthrop ends in the nodulous expansion of Point Shirley, with its tombs of dead enterprises, and the long level of Gut Plain. The locality was relatively much more important in ancient times than now, and is often mentioned in the chronicles of the fathers. One of the first appearances of the name was in September, 1631, when "Willm" Bateman was left on shore of Pullen Poynte, being very sicke and weake." Those with him were forced to return home to Plymouth, leaving him what provisions they had. On returning two days later they found him dead, about a stone's-throw from where they left him, at about high-water mark. "Soe the jury psents that he dyed by God's visitaçon." In 1634 William Wood thus described the region: "The opposite shore is called *Pullin-point*, because that is the usuall Channel. Boats used to passe thorow into the Bay; and the Tyde being very strong, they are constrayned to goe ashore and hale their Boats by the sealing, or roades, whereupon it was called *Pullen-point*."

In the diary of the Rev. Noadiah Russell we find this entry, in September, 1682: "Being on Tuesday at night a snowy stormy night Mr. Horton master of a ship was coming up to Boston but by reason of ye violence of ye storm and ye boysterousness of ye sea was forct to run on shore at Pullens Poynt where ye ship was staved to peices 3 men drowned ye rest got on shore on an Island but by reason of ye coldness of ye weather and their want of clothing, 3 or 4 more of them died so that 6 or 7 lost their lives, after break of ye day they knew where they were and went to a house yt was on the Island."

The *Boston News-Letter* of Sept. 13, 1753, thus announced how the new fishing-station here, founded by capitalists in the town, was opened: "On Saturday last His Excellency the Governour [Shirley] did the Proprietors of *Pulling-Point* the Honour of dining with them at said Point, where a very elegant Entertainment was prepar'd for him; he was attended thither by the Proprietors, and a Number of Gentlemen of Distinction from the Town; he was saluted with fifteen Guns from *Castle William* as he went down, and the same Number when he return'd; and was receiv'd at the Point with all the Demonstrations of Joy that so new a settlement was capable of. His Excellency express'd great Satisfaction on finding so considerable an Addition to that valuable Branch of Trade, the COD-FISHERY,

Old Mansion, Point Shirley.

and hoped the Gentlemen concern'd would meet with such success as to make them ample Amends for so noble an Undertaking. The Proprietors, after having leave from his Excellency, gave it the name of *Point Shirley*." The events connected with its christening made this an aristocratic summer resort, where several of the best families of Boston had villas. Among these was Governor John Hancock's summer home; and there is still preserved a letter of Edmund Quincy, sent by Mr. Otis to Mrs. Hancock, and conveying friendly messages to other families. This letter was sent "*via* Apple Island;" most of the peninsula being then covered with forests, except at the Point, where there were 25 or 30 houses, several stores, and a church. The proprietors spent so much on their villas, that they could not properly equip the fisheries; and so their hopes of erecting a new Gloucester here were disappointed. But the place made a good camp-ground in 1759, when Bagley's Massachusetts regiment lay here nine days before embarking for Louisburg. In 1764, when small-pox was devastating the Province, an inoculating hospital was opened at Point Shirley by the Boston doctors, aided by Dr. Barnett of New Jersey. It was given out that the locality then had many comfortable and decent houses to accommodate patients. The Point saw a gloomy sight in November, 1775, when British boats landed here with 300 aged persons, women, and children, sent out of the besieged town of Boston.

In May, 1776, when the Continental privateers *Franklin* and *Lady Washington* were stealing out of Boston, through Shirley Gut, the former grounded, and could not be moved. Here the two vessels were attacked by a flotilla of boats from the British fleet outside, and a furious battle was fought amid the whirling eddies of the strait. The man-of-war barges fired grape and langrage, and were answered by the cannon of the *Franklin*, loaded with musket-balls, and the swivels of the *Lady*. Pikemen defended the decks, from behind high boarding nettings, and upset two of the barges with boat-hooks. After a half-hour of very close and deadly work, the attacking party retreated, and the saucy little cruisers were left free to make sail and escape to sea. The next morning two children, playing on the Winthrop shore, found there an overturned British barge, and the dead body of a royal marine, with a spear-wound in his side. He was buried just to the eastward of the old Bartlett mansion; and Captain Mugford, the commander of the *Franklin*, who was slain during the fight, received a stately military funeral at Marblehead.

He had richly earned it; for, without what he had given to the American army, Gen. Gage could have driven Washington's half-armed militiamen into the Berkshire Hills. While the frigate *Lively* lay in Marblehead harbor, some months before, Mugford was impressed as one of her crew, and remained on board until released in answer to the supplications of his wife. During his service on the *Lively*, he heard the sailors talking of a great powder-ship soon expected from England; and so, without waiting for a commission, he put to sea in a fishing-smack, and cruised up and down the bay in search of her. At last the coveted vessel hove in sight, and the innocent-looking fisherman sailed up alongside. Suddenly the scene changed, when Mugford made fast to the towering British ship, released his gallant comrades from their hiding-place in the cabin, boarded the hostile deck with a rush, and carried her away as a prize, within sight of His Majesty's fleet off the light-house. She was called the *Hope*, and her cargo of powder and arms became more than a hope for the Continental army.

A rude fortification was erected on the hill, during the Revolution, to defend the entrance by Shirley Gut. During the War of 1812 the frigate *Constitution* once stole out to sea through this narrow strait, escaping the British blockaders that were hovering off the harbor.

About the year 1830 Sturgis & Parker established the salt-business here, and erected several large buildings. To this the contemporary poet-laureate of the lower harbor thus delicately alludes: —

> "Point Shirley, to forget, oh muse,
> Indeed would be a fault,
> Which STURGIS never would excuse,
> Who manufactures salt."

In subsequent years the Point was the seat of the extensive works of the Revere Copper Company, whose abandoned buildings still remain, with their tall brick chimneys. On the little mound above are queer old houses, rickety and spider-haunted, but with evident remains of old-time dignity. Perhaps these were the villas of the Provincial era,

A Lobsterman's Cabin, Point Shirley.

of the Hancocks and their friends, where the fair Puritan ladies discussed the fashions of the time of King George II., and watched the Provincial fleets sailing out against Louisburg, or Quebec, or the Spanish Main, with their husbands and sweethearts on board. The poor old houses are disconsolate enough now, looking down on the industrial Pompeii of the copper-works, and out on the calm blue waters beyond, monuments of pathetic dilapidation. Harborward from the gloomy and silent buildings of the Revere Copper Company is a rude colony of fishermen, most of whom, as the numerous nets bear witness, are engaged in the pursuit of lobsters. In and about their cabins are many very quaint and interesting scenes, connected with the lives and avocations of the toilers of the sea. Several of their homes and outbuildings are the cabins and upper works of defunct steamships which have been burnt on Apple Island; and the state-room which sheltered a Knickerbocker princess or a Beacon-Hill Hypatia may now give protection to the domestic animals or the dripping nets of a Point-Shirley lobsterman.

Occasionally a premonitory flutter of activity animates the Point. Some one is going to make it a freighting-point for ocean-steamships, with a standard-gauge track connecting it to the Eastern Railroad; some one else is going to start the wheels of industry in the half-dismantled copperworks; or a great company will run fast excursion-steamers a dozen times daily from Boston to this wharf, to rival the glories of Nantasket. But these halcyon days never come, and again the amphibious residents resume their lives of calm serenity.

Taft's Hotel, or the Point Shirley House, close to the strait which separates Deer Island from the Point, has been conducted by the famous caterer Taft for more than a quarter of a century, and is the most celebrated resort for *gourmets* in all New England, if not in America. Through all these passing decades, thousands of the most prominent men of Eastern Massachusetts, with their guests, and *bon-vivants*

from all parts of the Union, have enjoyed the delights of this wonderful and inexhaustible larder. Oftentimes as many as threescore distinct species of fish and game are kept here in stock at once, the birds being numbered by thousands. It is *au règle* for the Boston gentleman to drive, with his visitor from the South or West, over the short and pleasant road to Point Shirley, and there, with great pride, to test the bewildering variety of dainty dishes which Taft has on his *menu*, from the rich turbot and Spanish mackerel, the mullet and Mexican bonetta, to the paper-shell clams, grass frogs, and soft-shell crabs — from Illinois grouse and Erie ducks to Delaware rail and reed-birds, Jersey willets, a great variety of snipe and plover, and humming-birds served in nut-shells. Many cosmopolitan and globe-trotting gentlemen have stated their conviction, that, while Delmonico's may justly claim the palm of excellence in other respects, there is no place in the world where a fish and game dinner is served so successfully as at Taft's. Here the famous Atlantic Club used to meet, with Holmes and Lowell, Emerson and Longfellow, and other choice spirits, at its board; and the chiefs of the literary Boston of to-day are familiar with this favored locality. Many another group of hungering (and thirsting) patricians has found happiness here, — conclaves of financiers, re-unions of veteran officers, detachments from the city clubs, and political councils often seeking, for the time, no more formidable task than the time-honored (and difficult) one of throwing stones from the Point on to Deer Island.

We have followed the coast of Boston Harbor, from the finger-tip of Hull, along wave-swept Nantasket, past quaint old Hingham and Weymouth, and historic Quincy and Dorchester, by the eastern wards of Boston, and down to the northern peninsula, gathering here and there a bit of picturesque history, a half-forgotten legend, a gem from the rich treasures of Motley or Everett or Thoreau or Longfellow. It now remains to sail down among and through the islands, and so on out to sea : —

> "When the pink sails at sunset faded out,
> Far, far, north-east, when, outward-bound, the fleet
> Left home and love behind, and steered away."

Castle Island and Fort Independence.

THE OLD PURITAN STRONGHOLD. — PROVINCIAL AND BRITISH GARRISONS. — THE VIRGIN FORTRESS.

FROWNING over the channel, 2½ miles from Boston, and 900 yards from South Boston, rise the batteries of Castle Island. As far back as 1853 Dr. J. V. C. Smith predicted that in time a solid mass of buildings, the homes of 300,000 people, would extend on reclaimed land out to Thompson's Island. The present Fort Independence is a handsome and substantial stone structure, erected since 1835, on the site of Castle William. It has five sides, each of which is commanded by projecting bastions and flank defences, with large howitzers in the casemates and 15-inch Rodman guns on the barbettes. The accuracy and enormous power of the latter have been tested by firing at targets on the outer point of Thompson's Island. In the casemates which overlook the ship-channel is a long line of the heaviest guns, with a formidable battery of 10-inch smooth-bores on the barbette above, protected from a raking fire from down the harbor by very thick traverses. There are several outworks, also, with grim-looking armaments, and long lines of ponderous guns on the parade-ground, with pyramids of black cannon-balls beside them. Probably the officer who commands the defences of Boston would object to a more technical account of the number and calibers of the cannon here, which might fall into the hands of some Chilian or Canadian admiral, and forever frighten hostile vessels from the front of the city.

Several inclined planes and stone stairways lead from the enclosed pentagonal parade-ground to the top of the rampart, whence very charming views are afforded, especially across the islands to the eastward. Beneath, and opening toward the parade, are the cavernous quarters of the garrison, the storehouses, bakeries, ordnance-rooms, and other adjuncts of a fortress. Back of the fort, and just outside its picturesque old gate, are two stately elms; and a line of chestnut and elm trees leads thence to the southward, towards the row of pretty brown cottages which were once used for the officers' quarters. The rich greensward affords pasturage for a few luxurious cows and a sinecured horse, who approach the infrequent visitors to the island with a kindly interest, born of uneventful lives. In 1804 the Secretary of War wrote to Capt. Freeman, who commanded here for many long years, "I have no objection to two cows being kept for the use of the garrison; but I cannot conceive there will be any use for a horse on Castle Island." The cows stay on, though the garrison is forever gone; and the nobler animal which so puzzled Secretary Dearborn, eighty years ago, still grazes along the *glacis*. Near these fragrant pastures, the thick grass tangles itself around the mouldering wheels of a battery of 30-pound Parrott guns, which, in times now growing ancient, thundered their fatal warnings among the hills of Virginia. The low and broad-based white building near the head of the western wharf was the home of the commanders of the fort, where Arnold, De Russey, Hayes, Best, and other well-known officers, had their headquarters, and dispensed a courtly hospitality, after the manner of the old army traditions. The architecture of the house, with its surrounding verandas, seems to indicate that it was planned by some veteran from the far Southern posts, — from Pensacola perhaps, or Mobile; and the pathetic little forget-me-nots, whose clustering blue-and-gold stars gleam in the weedy and neglected garden, may be mementoes of the fair ladies of the Hayes family, whose father, a gray old general, passed hence to the eternal soldiers' home. Near the west front of the fort is the cemetery, with the graves of soldiers who have died within thirty years, most of them marked with tablets bearing the melancholy word, UNKNOWN. There are also two or three forgotten graves of Massachusetts volunteers, on which no Decoration-day flowers are laid; and the battered old tombstone of Edward Pursley, who died here in 1767. Farther out, on the south point of the island, is the large building of the hospital, through which these veterans made their last march. One of the quaint old epitaphs in the garrison cemetery (now lost) read thus: "*Here lies the body of John* ——, *aged 50, A faithful soldier, and a desperate good Gardener.*"

In the 250 years during which this island has been the main bulwark of the port, there have happened many strange things, many quaint occurrences, and many tragic episodes, at a few of which we may glance in passing. The fortress had its birth in the very dawn of the history of the Bay colony, even before Cromwell bore witness to the virtues of religious faith and dry powder. Fort Hill, in Boston, was adorned with a battery as early as 1632; but the cautious Puritans thought it would be better to hold an enemy at bay (if need came) farther down the harbor, out of gunshot of the sacred First Church. After Winthrop and his councillors had been half frozen at Hull, looking for a place to build "ffortyficaçons," they allowed the question to rest until about midsummer of 1634, when Governor Dudley and his Council, with "divers Ministers and others," visited Castle Island, and, in the rich beauty of a July afternoon, voted that it was exactly the place for a fortress. Two platforms and a small earthwork were erected, under the supervision of Roger Ludlow of Dorchester; the General Court resolving soon afterwards that "The ffort att Castle Iland, nowe begun, shalbe fully pfected, the ordnance mounted, evry other thing aboute it ffinished, before any other ffortificaçon be further proceeded in." Captain Simpkins, of the Ancient and Honorable Artillery Company, became the first commander of the Castle, and was succeeded by Gibbons and Morris. In 1635 one of the Castle officers was Thomas Beecher, who had come over as master of the *Talbot*, in Winthrop's fleet. Among his descendants is Henry Ward Beecher. Lieut. Morris was deposed and banished from Massachusetts in 1638, because he supported the hated Antinomian heresy of Mrs. Hutchinson. He had also caused great scandal by his

Main Gate, Fort Independence.

adherence to the flag of England, whose cross was deemed heathenish by the Puritans. The St. George's cross was left out of the colors of the Boston train-bands, as savoring of Popery; but remained on the Castle standard, to avoid trouble with England. Sewall wrote, "I was and am in great exercise about the Cross to be put into the Colours, and afraid if I should have a hand in't, whether it may not hinder my Entrance into the Holy Land." Other zealous Puritans even made way with the Castle flag, and the masters of the ships in the harbor raised great complaints thereat. Harry Vane, who was then governor, feared that if these honest sailors returned to England, reporting that there was no standard on the defences of Boston, the colonists would be denounced as rebels: wherefore he ordered that the royal colors should be displayed at the Castle. This, as the ingenious Rev. John Cotton pointed out, could not be construed as an approval by Boston of the detested and idolatrous cross, in view of the fact that the Castle pertained to the king. But no English flag could be found in the town, and the governor was obliged to accept one offered by the captain of a ship. Many years later, after our Sir Harry Vane had been immortalized in one of Milton's noblest sonnets, he led the Republican party in the English Parliament, headed the Solemn League and Covenant, rivalled and was imprisoned by Oliver Cromwell, and on the restoration of the Stuart monarchy received the crown of martyrdom for freedom, meeting his death like a very gallant knight and gentleman.

In 1635 three cannon (one of which belonged to Deputy-Gov. Bellingham) were carried down on lighters to the Castle; and the garrison soon showed that they intended to be recognized in the harbor, by firing on the ship *St. Patrick*, and forcing her to strike her colors. A gentle hint was not always enough, for about this time the pinnace of one Anderson stood out three shots before she would heave to. The English sea-captains found it hard to comply with the etiquette of this mud fort, which demanded as much respectful notice as if it had been South-Sea Castle or the Tower of London. In 1637 three ships from Ipswich, England, sailed up the harbor, bearing 360 passengers. One of them refused to anchor in front of the Castle, and the vigilant gunner tried to fire a shot across her bows. The cannon was badly aimed, for the ball struck the vessel, and killed a passenger in the shrouds. The governor and his inquest decided that this unhappy immigrant "came to his death by the Providence of God," — a verdict which must have excited great admiration among the colonial Dogberries.

It was rather bold and deadly work for obscure transatlantic artillerists to be doing. At any rate, the General Court thought it hardly worthwhile to spend money in keeping this hornets' nest in repair; and so it was abandoned the next year. Several citizens, however, kept the works in order voluntarily. aided by small grants, until 1643, when the ordnance and ammunition were removed to Cambridge, Charlestown, and Ipswich, and the island passed into Capt. Gibbons's hands, by lease. When La Tour's French frigate, the *Clement*, sailed up the harbor a few weeks later, and fired a salute, there was no one at the Castle to answer it; and no one to oppose her, had the intent been hostile. This evident danger aroused the citizens, and in 1644 delegates from Boston and the five adjacent towns petitioned the General Court to restore the Castle and garrison. Their prayer was refused (even then the country members voted on principle against Boston measures); and with great difficulty the six towns got permission to build a fort here at their own expense, on condition, furthermore, that the work so built should belong (not to the contributing towns, but) to the Colony.

A singular report was carried abroad to England before 1650, and printed there, that "eighteen Turkish men-of-war had attacked and burned Charlestown, killing 40 of its citizens, and holding the remainder for ransom." Those were the days when the Moslem corsairs swept the seas: and in many a smoky English forecastle the sailors drearily sang the ballad which begins, —

> "Oh, I have got a ship in the north country,
> She goes by the name of the Bold Galatee;
> But I am afraid she will be taken by that Turkish galley
>   As she sails along the Lowlands,
>   Lowlands low;
>   As she sails along the Lowlands low."

Boston was not to be surprised by such a phenomenal attack of the gallant Asiatics, or even by the nearer French or Dutch naval guerillas. In order that the *Allah il Allah* or the *Angelus* should not sound from the site of the godly First Church, the castle was restored, and well garnished with black British guns. The new commander was Lieut. Davenport; and his instructions bore warrant to examine all vessels coming in; to allow trading-ships to enter and depart freely; and to send half his garrison (of twenty men) to town each Sunday, to attend divine worship. He was ordered, "the Lord having furnished him with able gifts," to take care of the garrison as his own family; and had a third of the island for himself, and a tenth for the gunner. The town tried to induce ten families to settle on the island, in the hope of thus having a permanent and resident group of militiamen under the walls of the defences.

During the civil war in England a ship arrived at Boston from one of the Royalist ports, and was straightway attacked and captured by a parliamentary vessel from London. The Castle opened fire on the latter, for an infraction of the peace; and the Londoner's guns returned the cannonade. Finally, however, she yielded; and the unfortunate Royalist ship, wrested from her possession, was made a prize by the Massachusetts authorities. The commander of the fort was ordered "not to permit any more ships to fight in the harbor, without Licence from Authority." The delicious quaintness of this colonial edict must have profoundly affected the belligerent naval parties, for we hear of no further engagements about Boston during the civil war. Perhaps, however, the sea-dogs of king or parliament could not afford to get the necessary license. Without this, they must keep as quiet as fishing-boats; for, in 1645, the Legislature ordered the "cheife millitary officer of the trayne band of the towne of Boston" to arm and garrison his batteries, and "If any shipps wthin yor harbor shall quarrell, & shoote one at another, whereby the people or howses may be endangered, you shall use your endevor and Power to stay and suppresse such attempts, & to bring such shipp or shipps under comãnd." At the same time, the Legislature " not taking it well, yt ye Castle is & hath binn so long neglected by ye sevll tounes yt undertooke the finishing thereof," ordered Boston to complete the Castle gates within a fortnight, on penalty of a heavy fine. £150 were appropriated for the works, and £280 for yearly pay for the garrison, which consisted of a captain and ten men in winter, and ten additional soldiers during the rest of the year. Three years later this force suffered a reduction; and it was appointed that "uppon an alarum given by the Castle, viz., by shootinge off two great guns, & fireing of a beacon, and hoysting & lowering the flag, or anny two of the sd signes," a re-enforcement of forty men should instantly be sent down from Boston.

In 1651 the Legislature passed this order: "Forasmuch as this Courte conceives the old English colours now used by the Parliament of England to be a necessary badge of distinction betwext the English & other nations in all places of the world, till the state of England shall alter the same, which we much desire, we being of the same nation, hath therfore ordered, that the capt. of the Castle shall presently advaunce the afforesaid colours of England uppon the Castle uppon all necessary occasions." Davenport, the cross-hater, was sorely galled at this order, but perforce obeyed it. He was a grim old Puritan, who came across the sea two years before Winthrop's colony; and had been so delighted with Endicott's act in cutting out the cross of St. George from the English flag, that he named his daughter *Truecross*. His equipment now included two boats, a drum, six murtherers, and two muskets and pikes for each soldier. The works were thus described by a contemporary: "There was a small Castle built with brick walls, and had three rooms in it; a dwelling Room below, a lodging Room over it, the Gun room over that, wherein stood six very good Saker Guns, and over it upon the Top Three lesser Guns." And in 1654 it was written in *The Wonder-Working Providence*, that "The Castle is built on the North-East of the Island, upon a rising hill, very advantageous to make many shots at such ships as shall offer to enter the Harbor without their good leave and liking, the Commander of it is one Captain *Davenport*, a man approved for his faithfulness, courage, and skill, the Master Cannoneer is an active Ingineer; also this Castle hath cost about £4,000, yet are not this poor pilgrim people weary of maintaining it in good repair, it is of very good use to awe any insolent persons that putting confidence in their ship and sails, shall offer any injury to the people, or contemn the Government, they have certain signals of alarums, which suddenly spread through the whole country. Thus are these people with great diligence provided for these daies of war, hoping the day is at hand wherein the Lord will give

Casemate Battery and Southern Face, Fort Independence.

Antichrist the double of all her doings, and therefore they have nursed up in their Artillery garden some who have since been used, as instruments to begin the work."

Soon afterward Boston sent a great bell down to the Castle, probably for use in alarming the bay-villages. It was one of the bells which a Yankee sea-rover captured on a ship bound for New France or New Spain, and had been destined for the tower of a Roman-Catholic church. It appears that some reminiscence of the Inquisition must have come with this melodious gift; and so, about this time, we find tokens that the little colonial Gibraltar began to be used for sinister purposes. In 1661 the General Court ordered "Nicholas Upshall to be imprisoned at Castle I for drawing Quakers here. None to speak to or see him but his own family." Probably other heretics against the State religion were interned in the little block-houses on the island, and held on the rack of the east winds.

In 1665 a flash of lightning killed Capt. Davenport, as he lay on his bed, alongside the powder-magazine. Another grim Roundhead soldier, Capt. Roger Clap, was put in command of the Castle, and held it for 21 years, resigning then, rather than carry out an odious order of Sir Edmund Andros. He would have none but pious men in his garrison; and "in his time it might be seen that Religious and well disposed men might take upon them the calling of a souldier, without danger of hurting their morals or their good name." The garrison now consisted of several officers, with 20 soldiers from Boston, 12 each from Charlestown and Dorchester, and 10 from Roxbury. Clap demanded that the port-holes should be repaired; and that the platform should have additional supports, since it sustained six guns, each of 3,000 pounds weight, and also, on training-days, crowds of people. He also complained that he had endeavored to stop the leaks into the rooms, but in a short time they would again be in the same condition as before; that in the frequent hard rains he and his wife had been driven from their beds because they were so wet with rain, and had to leave their small house for the Castle for shelter in dark stormy nights, and "sometimes in snow above my wife's knees." She certainly expressed a reasonable desire that she might live in such quarters, "that in the cold winter she may not go so far out of dores to bed, if the Court will be pleased to show us the favor." Edward Everett says that "When the great Dutch admiral De Ruyter, the year [1665] after that famous *Annus Mirabilis*, immortalized by Dryden, having swept the coast of Africa, had been ordered to the West Indies, 'intending,' says Capt. Clap, not a whit daunted at the thought, 'to visit us,' the Captain adds, with honest exultation, ' Our battery was also repaired, wherein are seven good guns.'"

In 1673, "having considered the awful hand of God in the destruction of the Castle by fier," the General Court ordered it rebuilt: and the next year came one of the earliest official junketings in Boston Harbor, when "Itt is ordered, that the whole Court on the morrow morning goe to the Castle to view it, as it is now finisht, & see how the countrys money is layde out thereupon, & that on the countrys charge; which was donn." They had been aided in the expense of construction by a singular dispensation of judicial Providence. It seems that Governor Bellingham, a victim of occasional mental derangement, died in 1672, leaving a large property for charitable purposes. But his will was somewhat incoherent; and therefore, after heated discussions, the General Court cut the Gordian knot by devoting the entire estate to rebuilding the Castle-Island fort. To increase this fund, and maintain repairs, every vessel above the size of twelve tons was obliged to pay a shilling a ton for each voyage to Boston, to be applied to the fortifications. £160 a year had been granted for the Castle, with which the captain must pay himself, the gunner, and the three soldiers of the garrison; but the contributing towns paid chiefly in shoes and corn: and Clap gloomily wrote that "had not your petitioner through God's goodness some estate of his own, he might sometime be put into straits, and so he is also like to be to get wood to burn on this cold island, and other things he wants which cost him a great deal of money in a year."

In 1676 Edward Randolph thus described the fort: "Three miles from Boston, upon a small island, there is a castle of stone lately built, and in good repair, with four bastions, and mounted with 38 guns, 16 whole culverins, commodiously seated upon a rising ground sixty paces from the waterside, under which at high-water mark is a small stone battery of six guns. The present commander is one Captain Clap, an old man; his salary £50 per annum. There belong to it six gunners, each £10 per annum." Clap went off duty in 1686, and was succeeded rapidly by Winthrop, Savage, Pipon, and Fairweather. In the same year the gunner, Supply Clap, was killed, on the island, and buried to the mournful sound of minute-guns.

In Drake's "Captain Nelson," we read that "The Castle, as it was then and still is called, was a regular and well-built work of stone, with bastions at each of its four angles, and a formidable array of cannon on its walls. All vessels were required to lower their colors in passing; and such as were outward bound to exhibit a pass, signed by the governor, before they could proceed to sea. As the captain of the Castle was expected to enforce exact obedience to these regulations, the approach to Stamboul was not more strictly guarded." This is not the only mention of Castle Island in the pages of romance; for when Lydia Maria Child wrote "The Rebels," full sixty years ago, she located here one of its most exciting scenes, the burial of the treasure-chest, an episode quite in the vein of "The Mysteries of Udolpho."

To return to the quaint old-time records: In January, 1686, according to Sewall's diary, it was "extream cold, so that the Harbour frozen up, and to the Castle. This day so cold that the Sacramental Bread is frozen pretty hard, and rattles sadly as broken into the Plates." Later in the year President Dudley was received with a salute of 25 guns, as he sailed by in a royal frigate. After 1691 the lieutenant-governors became *ex-officio* commanders of the Castle, which was for a few years known as Fort William and Mary. As soon as the Boston people heard of the landing of the Prince of Orange in England, in 1689, and his marching against the tyrannical and papistical King James, they rose in arms against Sir Edmund Andros, James's representative, and seized his forts at Boston. 5,000 armed New-Englanders paraded in the town, and soon captured the Castle and its garrison of regulars, and also the royal frigate *Rose* in the harbor. Andros was imprisoned at the Castle, with the chief officers of his government; one of whom, Commissioner Palmer, wrote here, while the pleasant spring days enlivened the harbor, his famous "Impartial Account of the State of New England." Andros did not take his captivity kindly, but often tried to escape. Disguised as a woman, he passed two lines of sentinels; but the outer guard recognized military boots under his skirts, and haled him back. Again, his servant made the sentry very drunk; and Sir Edmund left the Castle, and got as far as Rhode Island, whence he was returned to captivity once more. For eight months the noble baronet languished on the island, under Puritan guards, regretfully remembering the days when he was one of the freest and merriest officers of Prince Rupert's bold dragoons. Years later he became governor of Virginia, where the cavaliers endured his sabre-knot *régime* for many years; and he founded William and Mary College for their elevation.

After the unhappy knights and gentlemen of England had been set free, quiet reigned in the little fort for some years. But in 1696 the apprehensions of a French naval attack caused the committee on defences to order new batteries and bastions at Castle Island; and they had a number of ships moored in the harbor, "in line of battle, to annoy the king's enemies in case of an attack." Finally, in 1701, all the old Colonial works on Castle Island were removed, and a scientific fortification of brick was commenced. The slab over the portal bore the following inscription (in Latin): "In the thirteenth year of William III., most invincible king of Great Britain, France, and Ireland, this fortification (called Castle William — *Wilhelmi Castellum* — from his name) was undertaken; and was finished in the second year of the reign of the most serene Anne, Queen of Great Britain, France, and Ireland, and in the year of Our Lord 1703. Built by the Tribune William Wolfgang Römer, chief military engineer to their Royal Majesties in North America." Boston committees supervised the new constructions, and with difficulty kept peace between Römer and the colonial officers. Even Sewall himself was obliged to go down to the island, and tell "the young men that if any intemperate language proceeded from Col. Römer, t'was not intended to countenance that, or encourage their imitation; but observe his direction in things wherein he was skilful and ordered to govern the work." A considerable part of the cost of the Castle was borne by the British Government, whose officers had therefore a right to name the new outworks, the Crown, Rose, Royal, and Elizabeth Bastions. Some part of the wall of Römer's fort still remains, hidden under the granite ashlar of the present works. New troubles soon arose; for Sewall reports, in August, 1703: "It is said the Colors must be spread at the Castle every Lord's Day in honor of it. Yesterday was first practised. If a ship come in on the Lord's Day, Colors must be taken down. I am afraid the Lord's Day will fare none the better for this new pretended honor." And a year later he added: "1704. Lord's day, April 23. There is great firing at the town, ships, Castle, upon account of it being the Coronation day, which gives offence to many. Down Sabbath, up St. George!" In 1709, when a delegation of Mohawk Indians came to Boston, on their way to England, they were shown over the Castle, with high military ceremony. At this time, and for many years, Capt. John Larrabee was in charge of the works. In 1711 the alarm was sounded from the Castle, and re-echoed by drums beating to arms in Boston streets. But the incoming fleet was friendly, and the batteries soon saluted the fifteen great frigates and five veteran regiments (of Marlborough's army) which Lord Bolingbroke had sent from England to conquer Canada. In 1725 another and larger party of Indians were sent here as captives; but they very ingeniously evaded the sentinels, and escaped from the island. A few years later the annual trainings were held on the island; and the brave militiamen received copious refreshments of biscuits, cheese, and punch. In 1740 the ice in the inner harbor was unbroken for weeks, and many people drove down to the island over the firm and level surface of ice.

When Gov. Burnett came to assume his jurisdiction over Massachusetts, in 1728, the Castle gave him a resounding salute; and Mather Byles (perhaps in view of the fact that the new executive was the son of the famous Bishop of Salisbury) wrote a stately poem, in which we find the following Cowperian lines: —

> "And thou, O BOSTON, Mistress of the Towns,
> Whom the pleas'd Bay, with am'rous arms, surrounds,
> Let thy warm transports blaze in num'rous fires,
> And beaming Glories glitter on thy Spires."

Boston watched her little fortress with tender care, and the subject came up in almost every town-meeting. In 1735 the report went out that the mortar had deteriorated so much that the walls were crumbling; and the engineers erected a new battery at the eastern end of the island. Five years later the guns were carefully re-mounted. In 1744 the town rejoiced at the arrival of twenty 42-pounders and two mortars, sent from England for the Castle. These guns were taken out on the Provincial fleet the next year, and did grand service in the bombardment of the French fortress of

Louisbourg. There they were managed by Gridley, who had been one of the chief engineers of the Castle, and hammered down the Grand Battery and the King's Bastion, and poured their heavy missiles into the heart of the great Catholic fortress. A year later the island batteries saluted the entering ships of Sir William Pepperell and Admiral Warren, returning victorious from the siege of "the Dunkirk of America, whose sombre towers rose like giants over the northern seas." Another year passed; and hundreds of citizens were seen upon the island, repairing and building fortifications, while 6,400 rural militia crowded the streets and Common of Boston. A grand armada of 16 ships-of-the-line and 95 frigates, with an army on board, had been sent by France to destroy the spoilers of Louisbourg.

> "For this Admiral d'Anville
> Had sworn by cross and crown
> To ravage with fire and steel
> Our helpless Boston town."

Longfellow tells, in his "Ballad of the French Fleet," how their plans came to nought. But, had they escaped the perils of the sea, what could our little Yankee forts have done against so vast an embattled host? Yet in 1750 Capt. Peter Goelet, of New York, reported that "The Harbour is defended by a Strong Castle of a Hundred Guns, Built upon An Island where the Shipping must pass by and within hale. Its Situation is Extraordenary as it Commands on Every Side and is Well Built and kept in Exceeding Good Order."

John Phillips, whose father, grandfather, and great-grandfather were New-England divines, held the position of chaplain of the Castle from 1746 to 1759. Sir William Pepperell and Gov. Pownall had the keys of command during a part of that time; and Chaplain Phillips was made resident commander from 1759 to 1770, being the last Massachusetts Provincial officer in charge of the island. The defences were composed of a star-fort on the high ground, a long water-battery near the channel, and two block-houses at the ends of the island. Some of the best American artillerists in the Revolution received their first lessons here. The Massachusetts soldiers in garrison generally numbered about fifty men, and were quartered in the citadel; while in the spacious barracks outside, the veterans of Shirley and Pepperell were kept in 1753, the Royal Americans in 1758, Irving's Provincials in 1765, and several companies of Royal Artillery in 1766-67. When Gov. Pownall arrived at the seat of his government, the conqueror of Louisburg, who was also the senior councillor, held the command of Castle William. Sir William Pepperell, in presenting to the governor the key of this fortress, observed that the Castle was the key of the Province. His Excellency replied, " Sir, the interest of the Province is in your heart: I shall, therefore, always be glad to see the key of it in your hands."

In 1761 the remnants of the Acadian people were shipped to Massachusetts, to be scattered among the Bay towns. But the vessels were brought to off Castle William, and held there, under its batteries, while the General Court debated as to what to do with these mournful exiles. At last it was resolved that they should not be allowed to land, and the transports were sent to sea again.

Between 1760 and 1770 there were two imposing funerals here, when Sir Thomas Adams, commander of the *Boston* frigate, and the daughter of Governor Sir Francis Bernard, were buried. When Fort Independence was built, the workmen discovered their corpses, enclosed in elaborate coffins, under arches of masonry. They were carried to the south point, and re-buried; but, as no one then knew of their history, they were placed among the graves of the common soldiers, and all trace of the spot has been lost.

In 1764 the barracks of Castle William, then accommodating 480 men, were opened for inoculated patients, during the raging of the small-pox. 3,000 persons were inoculated, and several doctors were in residence at the castle. Four years later the Royal commissioners fled from angry Boston, and took refuge here. Near the West Head, at this time, stood a block-house, wherein the officers dwelt: while the older block-house, where many of the soldiers were quartered, was on the most southerly point. Shirley's battery was a strong detached work on East Head, commanding Shirley Gut. For six years the post was held by British garrisons. At the time of the Tea-Party the cannon were kept loaded: and Copley, the celebrated artist, visited the island in unsuccessful endeavor to mediate between the townspeople and the Royal officials. In September, 1770, a Royal order reached Gov. Hutchinson, in virtue of which he was obliged to give up the castle to Col. Dalrymple, who was stationed at Boston with the Fourteenth and Twenty-ninth Regiments.

After the Boston Massacre the citizens demanded that the Royal troops be taken out of the town, and they were accordingly quartered at the Castle. The soldiers found consolation in singing the following, and other verses of animosity: —

> "Our fleet and our army, they soon will arrive;
> Then to a bleak island you shall not us drive.
> In every house you shall have three or four,
> And, if that will not please you, you shall have half a score.
> Derry down, down, hey derry down."

Soon afterwards the Twenty-ninth went to New Jersey, and the Fourteenth sailed to the West Indies. A few years later, when the Fourth,

Fifth, Thirty-eighth, and Forty-third British Regiments lay on Boston Common, and the Welsh Fusileers held Fort Hill, the Castle was garrisoned by Col. Leslie's Sixty-fourth Regiment, and contained nearly all the Royal stores and powder from New York. The troops that raided on Salem were embarked here; and frequent scouting-parties landed at City Point, destroying the buildings on the peninsula, and carrying off detached American pickets. In March, 1776, the Castle batteries were trained on the adjacent heights of South Boston, and poured a hot fire upon the new American forts there. But the Continental troops, sheltered by Gridley's admirable intrenchments, replied fearlessly; devoting most of their shot, however, to the British lines nearer the town. These were the liveliest days the island ever saw; and its guns, directed against the people whom they were meant to protect, roared hotly over the rebel bay. When the town was evacuated, the garrison burned the barracks, blew up the magazine, and otherwise devastated the island. Washington sent Col. John Trumbull down, as soon as possible, to take possession of the burning Castle, and save what he could from the general wreck. (Trumbull was then fresh from Harvard College, and in later years he perpetuated his memories of the Revolution in the huge paintings now in the Rotunda at Washington.) The Continental troops restored the works almost immediately, under the command of Lieut.-Col. Paul Revere; and when the French frigate *Hermione*, 36, sailed up the harbor in 1779, bearing the Marquis de Lafayette, Castle William gave her a good republican salute. In 1778 Gridley renewed the works, under the direction of Congress; he being then chief engineer of the Continental army. The rubbish was removed, as far as possible; and an epaulement arose on the site of the Shirley bastion, armed with disabled guns left here, to which new trunnions had been added. When the British frigate *Somerset* was wrecked on Cape Cod, in 1778, her armament of 21 handsome 32-pounders was saved, and mounted on the Castle. The garrison during much of the Revolution consisted of an invalid corps, and the barracks were used as a station for recruits. When Washington visited Boston in 1789, the batteries here made grand salutes. A contemporary picture shows the island as a high embrasured bluff, with several plain buildings on and about it, a pier running out toward the channel, and a preternaturally long flag. At this time there were 150 cannon on the island, most of which had been abandoned by the British when they fled from Boston. The first salute fired here by a British frigate in honor of the American flag was in 1791, when H.B.M.S. *Alligator* sailed up the harbor, and discharged thirteen guns when passing the Castle, which were returned by the artillerists on the island. The commander of the *Alligator* was Sir Isaac Coffin, a native of Boston, who afterwards became a famous British admiral. In 1799 the Duke of Rochefoucauld-Liancourt reported that he had been informed by Gen. Knox, late Secretary of War, that Congress had appropriated $100,000 to fortify these islands, but that the State of Massachusetts had forbidden the prosecution of the work. From 1785 until 1805 the criminals of the State were confined on the island. Among these was Stephen Burroughs, one of the quaintest of rascals; none of the county jails being thought strong enough to hold him. There were at first 16 prisoners here, many of them hardened and desperate criminals. Burroughs quickly effected his escape, with seven companions, by digging through the wall of the casemate, and carrying off the Castle boat and the sentry who should have guarded it. They were all re-captured on shore, and received 100 lashes each. At a later day, when there were 45 prisoners in the bombproof, he formed a plan to overpower the garrison, overawe the town

Castle William in the Last Century.

with the artillery of the fort, capture and heavily arm the best vessel in the harbor, and sail away to some foreign land, after blowing up the Castle. Burroughs attacked and dispersed the main guard single-handed; but his fellow-convicts feared to follow him, and the brave fellow was stricken down, ironed, and lashed. He remained in duress until the year 1788.

From 1799-1801 the Castle was used as a place of captivity for soldiers and sailors of France, with which power we were then at war. Sometimes there were as many as 250 of these merry fellows here at once, especially after the capture of the war-vessel *Berceau;* but the garrison found no such difficulty with them as with the truculent criminals of Massachusetts.

In 1798 Massachusetts ceded Castle Island to the United States; and when President John Adams visited the island, a year later, the little fortress was christened Fort Independence. Four years afterwards a new barbette fort was finished here, with bastions named Winthrop, Shirley, Hancock, Adams, and Dearborn; the constructing engineer having been Lieut.-Col. Tousard, 2d Artillery, who was succeeded by Col. Foncin, formerly governor of the French colony of Cayenne. Ten years later Gen. Dearborn put the island in posture of defence, under apprehension of a British naval attack, and fully garrisoned the fort and outworks.

During the War of 1812 Fort Independence was occupied by details of Massachusetts militia, largely from Dorchester and adjacent towns, whose discipline was rapidly perfected amid these grim and warlike environments. The commanders of the post between 1808 and 1828 were Gen. Moses Porter, a veteran of Bunker Hill and of Washington's campaigns; Gen. John P. Boyd, who had commanded 10,000 Indian cavalry at Madras, and led a brigade at Tippecanoe and in the war in Upper Canada; Gen. James Miller, who fought so gallantly at Lundy's Lane; William Gates, who afterwards captured Osceola, and led the Cherokees from Georgia to the Indian Territory; Col. Isaac Lane, a veteran of many battles; Col. Nathan Towson, the famous artillerist who defended Fort George and Fort Erie so well; Col. Abraham Eustis, who led the light artillery in the attack on Toronto; Gen. John R. Fenwick, a South-Carolinian, badly wounded at Queenstown Heights; and Gen. W. K. Armistead of Virginia, who commanded in the famous Seminole campaigns of Florida. Among the subordinates in the garrison were Col. J. Snelling, from whom a fort in Minnesota was named; Samuel Cooper, who became adjutant-general of the rebel army in 1861; and B. L. E. Bonneville, the Tennesseean officer whose journal of a journey across the Rocky Mountains was edited by Washington Irving.

On the lonely shores of City Point, occasional duels took place, as when Rand and Miller met there in mortal combat. The officers at the fort saw them, and sent a barge to stop the fight; but, before it reached the shore, Rand was shot through the heart, leaped high in the air, and fell dead. The island itself was the scene of several duels; and on the *glacis* still stands the marble monument of Lieut. Massie of the Light Artillery, who was slain in this manner (in 1817) when but 21 years of age. The pathetic little memorial bears this couplet: —

> *Here Honour comes, a Pilgrim gray,*
> *To Deck the turf, that wraps his clay.*

In the quiet years succeeding the War of 1812, a small garrison remained here, whose most interesting member was private Rochford, a veteran of Wolfe's Canadian campaigns and a British soldier at Bunker Hill, who drifted hither in his white old age, and had a home given him on the island. He was the minstrel of the post, continually composing songs of war and adventure, which he sang to groups of his comrades, sunning themselves on the quiet parade-ground. Occasionally there was a flurry of excitement, as when (in 1806) a band of Sacs and Foxes, Osages and Pawnees, were received here with military honors; or when Gov. Strong visited this alien stronghold in his sovereign State; or at the unfortunate times when soldiers guilty of high crimes were executed in presence of the assembled troops.

In 1818 the sentries on guard at the Castle at early dawn raised a general alarm, and turned out the guard post-haste, alleging that they had seen the sea-serpent swimming swiftly by the island, in the faint light of early morning. There were several of these sentinels; and their concurrent testimony convinced Col. Harris, the commandant of the fort, that they had really seen the famous monster of the seas, as he avouched to Amos Lawrence.

Col. John Montresor, of the Royal Engineers, spent many months and £10,000 of the King's good money on Castle Island in 1770-72, building barracks and other works, some of which remained for many years. At that time the island was defended by 210 pieces of artillery, of which 46 were 42-pounders. Montresor found much reluctance among the Bostonians as to helping him, and philosophically recorded that they in like manner treated Col. Romer, whom William III. sent out many years before. One of the Puritan burghers rose up and said, "Mud walls and prayer make sufficient defences for this colony;" and Romer rejoined, "But a stone wall with good guns and ammunition make no bad defence." So he went on and finished his island castle, and for many years it was regarded as the strongest fortress in British America.

There was no such opposition when the United States began to refortify the island in 1833; and for nearly twenty years swarms of workmen were engaged here, constructing the present handsome fortress. Its massive casemates were each divided by movable board partitions into two sections, the gun-room and the squad-room; the former composing a series of connecting artificial caverns called the gun-gallery, inhabited by monstrous guns, and looking out on the channel. The squad-rooms look out on the parade-ground, and were the barracks of the garrison, each one being arranged for the occupancy of ten soldiers. In 1851 the United-States engineers finished their work, and left the island · and a garrison was forthwith stationed in the fine new fortress. Its commander was Brevet-Major George H. Thomas, captain in the Third Artillery, a gallant young Virginian officer who had won great renown in Ringgold's Battery during the Mexican war. In after-years he became a major-general in the United-States Army, victor in the battle of Nashville, and one of the foremost leaders in the war for the Union. In the quiet old days at Castle Island his post-adjutant was Lieut. Chauncey McKeever (son of brave old Commodore Isaac McKeever), who was brevetted brigadier-general for meritorious services against the Southern rebels.

One hardly looks for births on such a narrow scrap of sea-girt earth, inhabited by rough soldiers, and useful only as a gigantic gun-carriage to protect the cities peacefully clustering on the amphitheatre of hills to the westward. Yet here was born Professor Henry Laurence Eustis of Harvard. a classmate of James Russell Lowell, George B. Loring. William W. Story, and Judge Devens, and afterwards at West Point with Grant and Halleck. He graduated first in this great class of conquering heroes; and though he laid aside his uniform, and spent a dozen years in building up the Scientific School of Harvard University, when the long roll of the civil war resounded across the Union, the Castle-born warrior hunted up his old sword, and went South as colonel of the 10th Massachusetts Infantry. In the infernal battle at Salem Heights, Va., he held his command firm as a rock in front of the enemy until their supports came up, and the colonel of the 122d New York cried out, "Git out of here. you 10th Massachusetts fellers! you've fit long enough." After his valiant service in the field, Eustis returned to his duties at Cambridge, where he died a year or two since. His father, who was stationed at the Castle at the time of his birth, was a nephew of Gov. Eustis, and rose to a generalship in the old regular army, being promoted upward through the lines of the Fourth Artillery.

Since 1883 a fierce contention has been waged between Massachusetts antiquaries and War-Department officials on the question whether the works on Castle Island were at one time named Fort Adams. The papers of the West-Point Military and Philosophical Society bear witness that such was the case; but the silence of local historians as to the matter gives reason for the Boston Dryasdusts to look upon the report with grave doubting.

The old brazen bell, with its Scandinavian inscriptions, that from time immemorial had been kept at the Castle. was brought up to the city in 1884, and deposited in the museum of the Bostonian Society, where it aroused forthwith a rancorous contest between the antiquaries, some of whom pointed confidently to it as proof of the ancient Norsemen's discovery of the harbor, while others regarded it as once the property of a comparatively modern Swedish ship, the *Patriot*.

It was well that this bit of antiquity had been carried to a safer haven; for not long afterward the fort was invaded by sacrilegious thieves, who crawled through a casemate, and removed such trifles as they could most easily carry away. So brilliant was their success, that these bold adventurers essayed a similar foray at Fort Winthrop; but here they were attacked in the rear and surrounded by the garrison of one man, and haled away to captivity in a Boston dungeon

For fifty years this was one of the quietest garrisons on the long coast-line of the United States. New armaments were brought on from time to time; the troops in the barracks gave place, according to army rotation, to companies ordered hither from the forts along the Gulf or among the Sierras; and the ancient walls were replaced by the new works which now occupy the ground. But, when the Secession War broke out, Gov. Andrew reported that the Boston forts were "entirely unmanned," and asked authority to put a State regiment into them. A little later he ordered the 4th Battalion of Massachusetts Infantry on the island. The post was commanded by Major Stevenson, who became a general, and was killed in the Wilderness. Among the bright young fellows who entered the school of war at Fort Independence, were Barstow, who died at Newbern; Abbott, killed in the Wilderness, when major of the 20th; Robeson and Mudge, who died at Gettysburg; and Russell, Hallowell, and Crowninshield, each of whom won a colonelcy in the field. Another private soldier in the 4th was W. F. Bartlett, a student at Harvard, who wrote thus of his experience at the fort: —

"I have learned more military than I could have learned in a year at the armory or from books.... I value the knowledge acquired in the last month more highly than all the Greek and Latin I have learned in the last year." In after-years this gallant youth became a general in the national forces, and won the proud title of "the Bayard of the North." The 4th Battalion subsequently became the 13th Massachusetts Infantry. When Banks was driven back down the Valley of Virginia by Stonewall Jackson, and a wild panic ran through the North, the garrison of Fort Independence was sent away to the front, a detachment of Boston volunteers taking its place. Early in the year 1863 the island was made a headquarters for recruits, which the General Government was demanding of Massachusetts in larger and larger quotas, as if the Bay State were a fountain of sword-bearers. When the draft-riots broke out in Boston, the garrison was hurried into the city to aid in the protection of property. At the end of 1863 the fort contained 107 cannon, including 40 24- and 32-pounders in barbette, and 54 guns of the same grade, and 21 large columbiads, in casemates.

The municipal authorities have, within the last four or five years, endeavored to get the National Government to cede to them the island, with the intent to add it to the system of city parks. Being joined by a projected causeway to the Marine Park at City Point, a noble sea-fronting driveway and pleasure-ground were to have been instituted here, free to all comers. But the United-States authorities refused their consent, maintaining the necessity of retaining the island ready for occupancy as a military post on the inner line of defence, saying that "the knowledge that the interior waters of the harbor were swept by fire from the batteries would much diminish the probability of an attempt being made by an enemy's vessels to run by the exterior line." During this discussion it appeared that the present works here cost $2,000,000, and that the fortress covers 5.30 acres; the exterior batteries and glacis, 10.69 acres; and the rest of the island 5.61 acres. In the spring of 1888 Congressman P. A. Collins secured the passage of a joint resolution authorizing the city to extend its driveway and promenades around the island, without prejudice to the fortifications. But President Cleveland vetoed the bill, saying, "It is quite plain that the occupancy of this island as a place of pleasure and recreation, as contemplated under this resolution, would be entirely inconsistent with military or defensive uses. I do not regard the control reserved in the resolution to the secretary of war over such excavations, fillings, and structures upon the island as may be proposed, as of much importance. When a park is established there, the island is no longer a defence in time of war. I am now advised by the secretary of war, the chief of engineers, and the lieutenant-general of the army, in quite positive terms, that the resolution under consideration should not, for reasons fully stated by them, become operative. I deem the opinions of these officers abundant justification for my disapproval of the resolution, without further statement of objections."

According to the plans of the Boston Park Commissioners, the fortifications on the island were to have been left undisturbed, the main public uses of the place being confined to the construction of a broad driveway and promenade around the outside of the walls and along the edge of the shore and the sea-wall. These improvements would increase the military efficiency of the post, rather than detract from it, since it would then be much easier to convey troops and supplies to the fortress in time of need. To the thronging myriads of Bostonians the proposed promenades would have been a rich blessing, giving them access to one of the finest view-points in the harbor, whence the lower bay and the open sea are outspread in the field of easy vision. It is to be hoped that the national authorities may, before many years, regard the petition of their good city of Boston with more favor, and (under proper restrictions) let the people become the protectors and beneficiaries of the noble old battle island, with its picturesque and heroic memories. The Puritan city should find in her quaint and sea-beaten virgin fortress an interest akin to that felt by Edinburgh for its Castle, or London for its Tower, so that every eye would kindle with interest when looking upon its gray and lonely walls. And this new value would appear when the people were allowed to become more familiar with it, and the legends of the locality become familiar, touched and adorned by the bright fancy of battalions of Boston authors, and made even more vivid by the historical paintings of Boston artists. Away off in the twentieth century, when the United States of America is summoning all its power for defence against the united kingdoms of Europe, the 5th Alaska Infantry, and the 27th

Yucatan, and the 9th Manitoba, may encamp on the island, and regard the ivy-draped walls with such reverence as the Iberian and Thracian legionaries, called in from the Roman frontiers, felt when looking upon the Capitoline Hill. And in the remoter days, when all the battle-flags are furled, the Castle may remain as a picturesque and venerated memorial of an ancient barbaric age, like the ruined abbeys in the green valleys of England to-day.

Fort Independence was evacuated in the year 1879, in pursuance of Gen. Hancock's policy of concentrating his garrisons, so that better discipline and drill might be maintained in larger posts. The parade-ground and quarters at Fort Warren are commodious; and the troops were transferred to that point, where they may become familiar with the position which is the key to the harbor. The Castle is now defended only by Ordnance-Sergeant Maguire and a fort-keeper, who find quite enough to do in warning off unauthorized visitors from the closely adjacent shores of South Boston. A few laborers are kept at work, repairing the damages of envious time, sodding the ramparts, etc.; and they toil on, day after day, in a shamefaced and somnolent way, as if half-aware how alien from nineteenth-century life is this patching of mediæval walls. But the tompions of the great guns are kept well-oiled; and in the magazine are cartridge-bags of powder (with grains as large as walnuts), and piles of sabots, and cannon-balls and shells of mammoth proportions. If the *Inflexible*, or the *La Galissonière*, or the *Italia* can shed such fiery raindrops from their mailed sides, they must be the works of gods, rather than of men.

This fortress, which the old fishermen and pilots still call "The Castle," is the most ancient military post in the United States, continuously occupied for defensive purposes; and its records (up to 1803) fill a huge folio volume, whose pages are closely written over in the delicate clerkly hand of fourscore years ago. This very interesting chronicle was deposited by Gen. Benham (in 1875) in the care of the New-England Historic-Genealogical Society, and has furnished some of the incidents herein set forth. Probably this is the oldest virgin fortress in the world. Important as its position is, and often as hostile flags and armaments have been within sight of its walls, the fort has never been besieged, and has never surrendered to an alien summons. One after another, new flags have succeeded each other on its tall banner-staff, — the crossless flag of Endicott, the cross of St. George, the crown-emblazoned red cross on a white field, the pine-tree flag, the white ensign of Massachusetts, and the broad banner of the United States; but their halyards have been drawn by no hostile hands. What other fortress can show so stainless a record for two hundred and fifty years?

How short is the distance between the Old World and the New, when, in a half-hour, one may pass from the intense modern activities of State Street, or the dull decorum of the Back-Bay residence-quarter, to this lonely and deserted fortress, with the fresh east wind rustling the long grass on its parapets, and undisturbed birds flying in and out of the gloomy casemates! Under these gray walls (modern indeed, but laid in the mould of antiquity) you may dream of St. Jean d'Acre, of the wars of the Holy League, of the storming of Quebec, — or you may read Sir Walter Scott, or Charles Lever, or the noble old "Chronicle of a Drum." If the day is drowsy, you may hear strange sounds, — the psalm-chanting of the ancient Puritan garrison; the martial tread of Sir Edmund Andros, pacing up and down the narrow parade-ground; the plaintive songs of the Acadian exiles; the resounding oaths of the British officers; the reverberating thunder of Washington's bombardment of Boston; the nasal twang of companies of Yankee "trainers;" the crash of the *Shannon's* fatal broadsides; and the reveille of the assembling Massachusetts volunteers in the last war. Then the great bells in the neighboring city peal out the noon-hour; an excursion-boat rushes by, with its band playing favorite airs from "Olivette," or "The Merry War;" the swell from an in-bound British steamship breaks along the strand; and you are aroused from mediæval dreams, to take part in the new life which is stirring in the world of to-day.

Governor's Island and Fort Winthrop.

JOHN WINTHROP AND HIS CHILDREN. — THE GREAT FORTRESS. — THE CITADEL.

THIS high green island is very conspicuous in all views of the upper harbor, and lies within two miles of Long Wharf, and less than a mile from Fort Independence. It is occupied by the strongest earthwork in Massachusetts, at present ungarrisoned, but heavily armed. In ancient times the place was much more visited than now, when the frowning defences of a military post have supplanted the homes of summer rest. The locality was first known as Conant's Island, probably in honor of Roger Conant, some time a conspicuous citizen of Hull. After the Colony granted it to John Winthrop, the head of the infant State, in 1632, it was called Governor's Island, and its annual rent was placed at a hogshead of wine *that should be made thereon;* and afterwards two bushels of the best apples *there growing,* — by which means the sagacious Winthrop secured an exemption until such time as his vineyard or orchard became productive. As to the apples, one bushel was to be given to the governor of the Colony, and another to the legislature: so that he thus secured for himself one-half of his own tribute. Here, in his famous "Governor's Garden," with his Indian servants, the worthy Puritan chieftain enjoyed many a happy day, and regarded his rising metropolis across the narrow channel with dignity and comfort. Here he doubtless smoked many a sweet and contemplative pipe, amid whose blue wreaths of incense he may have built strange prophetic air-castles along Beacon Hill, as the sun went down behind that august height. In a letter written to his wife, in 1637, he says: "I pray thee send me six or seven leaves of tobacco, dried and powdered;" and so, in common with his great contemporary John Milton, and his doughty Dutch neighbors at New Amsterdam, he found joy in the most un-Puritanic of weeds. The present lord of the island maintains the ancient traditions, both as to devoutness and smoking.

The governor planted here the first apple and pear trees in New England, and made gallant efforts to raise, also, grapes, plums, and other fruits. Many a noble orchard of the Bay towns may show lineal descent from this island-nursery; and the Yankee Pomona can justly claim this as her birthplace and shrine. His Puritanic Excellency found it worth while to erect a small fort, or blockhouse, here; and also had some kind of a house in which to live during parts of the heated season. The hospitality of the place was bestowed freely on visitors and immigrants of distinction. In 1638 Josselyn wrote that there was not an apple or pear tree in all New England, save those on Governor's Island; and described how he had enjoyed the pippins there produced. In 1643 the Huguenot noble, La Tour, who had been driven from his fort at St. John by D'Aulnay, an adventurous relative of Cardinal Richelieu. sailed into Boston Harbor in a ship with 140 Huguenots from La Rochelle, and visited Winthrop on his island, seeking aid against his Catholic enemy. The austere Puritans referred to the Bible to see if they could find any precedent for such action. but found no certain response from that oracle. "On the one hand, it was said that the speech of the Prophet to Jehoshaphat, in 2d Chronicles xix. 2, and the portion of Solomon's Proverbs contained in chap. xxvi. 17th verse, not only discharged them from any obligation, but actually forbade them to assist La Tour; while, on the other hand, it was agreed that it was as lawful for them to give him succor as it was for Joshua to aid the Gibeonites against the rest of the Canaanites, or for Jehoshaphat to aid Jehoram against Moab, in which expedition Elisha was present, and did not reprove the king of Judah." But when they had assured themselves that it would be allowable for them to aid the distressed nobleman, they sent such a fleet that D'Aulnay's forces were quickly scattered.

In Winthrop's first will. he wrote thus: "I give to my son Adam my island called the Governor's Garden, to have to him and his heirs forever; not doubting but he will be dutiful and loving to his mother, and kind to his brethren in letting them partake in such fruits as grow there. I give him also my Indians there, and my boat, and such household as is there." Soon afterwards, and eight years before his death, the governor settled the island on Adam and his heirs, reserving for himself one-third of its fruits. Twenty years later the owners petitioned the General Court to remit its tribute of apples, saying that the product had greatly fallen off. Adam Winthrop was the ancestor of the Cambridge Winthrops, so called because his great grandson, Prof. John Winthrop. was for more than forty years connected with Harvard College, where he achieved great works in science. It was the professor's great grandson, Col. John Winthrop of Louisiana, who owned the island when the United States took possession of it, in 1833.

Margaret Winthrop and her family often dwelt on the island, among its pleasant orchards of apples, pears, and plums, and under its hard-blown grape-vines. Here her sturdy sons made visits, when the cool harbor breezes wooed them from the little town of wood and thatch close by. Of these were John (her stepson). the founder of Ipswich and New London, and governor of Connecticut ; Stephen, who became one of Cromwell's colonels, and member of Parliament from Aberdeen ; Adam, the heir of the island ; Deane, a resident of the present town of Winthrop ; and Samuel, who became deputy-governor of Antigua, and ancestor of Lord Lyons and the Duke of Norfolk, — "and thus the Puritan blood of Margaret Winthrop is found flowing in Old England, after two and a half centuries, in the veins not merely of the highest nobility, but of the leading Roman-Catholic family of the realm."

The colonists had trouble enough with this mountainous guard of the port. Not only did it lure on to its strand the good ship *Friendship*, bound for St. Kitts, in 1631; and hold here for a week a half-dozen good Puritan burghers, in 1635, while an angry sea beat on all its shores; but also, in 1643, terrible voices were heard issuing therefrom, which could not have been the accents of the good governor, and "sparkles" of fire cor-

Fort Winthrop, Governor's Island.

ruscated on its heights. For a brief space the Governor's Garden was regarded as an isle of demons by the superstitious and witch-ridden Bostonese. In 1696, however, the committee on defences ordered the construction of an eight-gun battery on the south-east point, and a ten-gun battery on the south-west point, the cannon to be taken from the works on the town-wharves. French visitors were then expected, and they were to be held at arm's-length down the Bay. Exactly fifty years later new and more formidable fortifications were begun here by Richard Gridley, the chief bombardier in the siege of Louisburg, colonel of the First Massachusetts Regiment, Provincial Grand Master of Masons in America, a Harvard man, editor, lawyer ("the Webster of his day"), mathematician, and military engineer. We cannot learn much of the residents of the island in those days, but at least one hero was cradled there. When David Williams was born on this island, in 1759. it might have been an easy task to cast his horoscope, and predict that the infant whose eyes first rested on a broad rim of blue waters, across lines of redoubts, should become (as he did) a famous and valiant pilot and privateersman. But little is heard of the island thenceforth until 1776, when several British transports were driven ashore here by the furious gale which prevented Lord Percy from being annihilated on Dorchester Heights. It does not appear that the rattling skirmishes and cannonades with which nearly every other island was visited came near this spot, where peace reigned in desolation. In 1793 the Massachusetts Historical Society held a meeting here; James Winthrop, one of its owners, being then a member of the society. Fifteen years later the summit of the island was occupied by Fort Warren, an enclosed star-fort of stone and brick, with brick barracks, officers' quarters, magazine, and guard-house. During the War of 1812 these works were fully garrisoned; but Gen. Dearborn considered this point the key of the harbor, and laid out new defences, inviting the men of Boston to come down with spades, pick-axes, and wheelbarrows, to aid in their construction. The low battery on the southern point of Governor's Island was built several years before the War of 1812, of brick and stone, with a brick guard-house and magazine; and once mounted fifteen cannon. It is a picturesque bit of antique fortification, whose purpose was to sweep the wide flats adjacent, and deliver a level point-blank fire at the hulls of hostile vessels passing in the channel. Later, in the War of 1812, the Sea-Fencibles went on duty to guard the batteries, and mortars were placed in the works. Furnaces stood ready, so that all the shot required for the guns could be heated; and the presumably gallant defenders dreamed fondly of British ships-of-the-line bursting into flames, as these red-hot globes of iron plumped into them from water-line to shrouds. The commanders of the *Shannon* and *Tenedos* must have heard that the irate Sea-Fencibles were dashing their tarry toplights on this gloomy isle, for they kept their ships far out in the offing until the war was over.

During the days of Lieut.-Gov. Thomas L. Winthrop, the island was celebrated for its hospitality; and the Massachusetts Historical Society had meetings on its green mounds, where the venerable antiquaries could discuss the genealogies of Peter Cakebread and Robert Bootefish, and the "three brothers, one of whom landed in Virginia," etc., without alarming the town. Lieut.-Gov. Winthrop, the father of the Hon. Robert C. Winthrop, was not a proprietor of the island, since he was descended from Gov. John of Connecticut; but received the freedom of the estate from his friends and kinsmen, the Cambridge Winthrops.

The fortress which now rambles, apparently without plan, over the high bluffs, was commenced some years before the Secession War, under the direction of Gen. Sylvanus Thayer. The name of Fort Warren was then transferred to the modern work on George's Island; and the new defence here received the name of Fort Winthrop, in honor of the ancient Puritan governor. In 1861 it had received no armament, and had never been occupied as a military post; but when Gen. Schouler inspected the defences late in 1863, he found at Fort Winthrop 25 large Rodman guns, and 11 pieces of other calibres and forms. Various companies of State militia and volunteers garrisoned the post during the civil war, and found it an ineffably dull station.

The island contains seventy acres of land, comparatively low on the east, and rising to a fine commanding height on the west. Here are the great military works, on which vast sums of money have been expended by the Nation. There is little of the delusive symmetry of masonry to be seen; for vast mounds of well-turfed earth cover the entire hill, with ponderous outworks on the bluff to the eastward, mountainous magazines, and skilfully contrived traverses. Here and there long underground passages, arched with masonry, lead from one battery to another, or enter the main stronghold. At the crest of the hill is the citadel, — a massive granite structure, so well curtained by impenetrable earthworks that only its top is visible from the harbor, and entered by a light wooden bridge high above the ground. The lower story, with its roof hung with small stalactites, contains the cistern; the second story is the barracks of the garrison, with rooms opening on an interior court; the third story contains the officers' quarters; and above, on the top, covered by a temporary roof to protect them from the weather, are the immense Parrott rifled guns, which look down on the harbor. On the south of the hill a long stone stairway, so built that it cannot be raked, or carried by a rush, leads to a battery at the water's edge. Among these heavy mounds, lurk scores of powerful 10 and 15 inch guns, well mounted, and peering grimly out on the channel, as if hoping, with a dogged iron patience, that some time their hour may come. Meanwhile Sergt. Roche, gray veteran of Mexican and Southern wars, keeps watch over the fortress, from his quarters in the time-blackened barracks near the eastern end of the island, and hangs the keys of the frowning citadel among the pictures of the saints in his little parlor. A phalanx of fierce black dogs stand guard at the farmhouse by the wharf, and make a securer defence than good-natured Irish-American sentinels could; and on the *glacis*, and up the slopes of the ramparts above, plump cattle graze through the long day, and look wisely out over the thronged harbor.

Bird Island formerly lay close to Governor's Island, toward the northwest; and its site is marked by a spindle, rising over a gravelly shoal. The loss of this bold bluff, around which the narrowed tide swept with scouring force, was reckoned by Professor Gould as one of the worst disasters which has befallen the harbor. The original shape of each of these islands was that of a perfect dome; but the continuous action of the north-east gales and surges for centuries has cut away half of their curves, leaving almost perpendicular cliffs on their north sides: and in this case every thing has been destroyed, and only the low-tide wreck of an island appears.

Bird Island was a spacious tract in the year 1630, as large, according to Professor Gould, as Governor's Island now is. In 1634 a party of men were frozen in, and obliged to stay here all night. A few years later the right to mow grass on the adjacent meadow was granted by the General Court to Thomas Munt. In 1726 the French miscreant, John Battis, with his son, and three Indians, were hung at Charlestown, and then cut down, and carried out, — a ghastly freight, — and buried on Bird Island. Other criminals, pirates, and sea-robbers were put to death, and buried here, or hung in chains, making a ghastly but perhaps salutary spectacle before the wharves and shipping. In 1790 there still remained a handsome grassy islet on this site; but afterwards a great deal of ballast and sand was removed therefrom, as Mayor Quincy complained in 1827. The same thoughtless dilapidations seriously injured Gallop's, Long, the Brewster, and other of the lower islands. But little such help was needed, however, for Wabun, the East Wind, and his allied waves, to batter down the hill of gibbets, and blot it out from the offended Bay.

Sergeant Schwartz, Fort Winthrop.
(Lately retired.)

Thompson's Island and Spectacle Island.

A SCOTTISH WORTHY. — THE BOSTON FARM SCHOOL. — A BOURNE OF DEAD HORSES. — APPLE ISLAND.

THOMPSON'S ISLAND is three miles from Long Wharf, one mile from Castle Island, a mile and a half from Savin Hill, and half a mile from Squantum, to which one may almost wade at very low tide. There are broad flats on the east and south, and deep channels on the north and west. The bar on the south has long been famous for its delicious clams; and many a feast did the old provincial Dorchestrians enjoy on the adjacent shore. It is a narrow island, a mile long, with 157 acres of good and fertile soil, rising into two hills, and indented by a cove. The salt-water pond, which formerly covered part of the lowlands, has been dyked and drained, like a new Haarlem Sea, and its site is now occupied by fertile meadows. On West Head stands a pleasant grove, planted about the year 1840, by the Hon. Theodore Lyman, who also bequeathed $10,000 to the Farm School. The trees which diversify the slopes produce excellent fruits, and the rich soil of the island brings forth notably good crops.

An ancient tradition says, that in 1619 Thompson examined the harbor-islands, in company with Masconomo, the sagamore of Agawam (who made an affidavit to this effect), seeking a proper place to establish his trading-post: and chose the island which still bears his name, because it had a small river and a harbor for boats. In 1620 Miles Standish came hither with William Trevour, a sailor of the *Mayflower*, and named it Island Trevour, reporting, "and then no Natives there inhabiting, neither was there any signe of any that had been there that I could perceive, nor of many, many yeares after." Trevour made affidavit that he took possession in the name of Mr. David Thompson, gentleman, of London; who, indeed, soon afterwards secured a grant of the locality. He had been sent over by Gorges and Mason to superintend their settlement at Portsmouth; and, when Standish went thither to seek supplies for the starving Pilgrims, Thompson returned to Plymouth with him. From thence he and Gorges journeyed to Weymouth, and sailed from that embayed port to Portsmouth. They probably examined the island at this time; for in 1626 Thompson returned, and established here one of the first permanent settlements in the harbor, antedating Boston by several years. It was a trading-post, where the Indians exchanged their beaver-furs and fish for the trinkets of civilization; and the same proprietor had a similar place on the Kennebec. The island was taken possession of as *vacuum domicilium*, to which no man had claim; and its advantages were vicinity to the sea, good anchorage under the lee of Castle Island, and vicinity to the Neponset Indians. Blackstone testified that he knew "ould Mr. Thompson," who chose this place for settlement because "there is a harbor in the island for a boat, which none of the rest of the islands had."

The Scottish island-lord took a deep and kindly interest in his Indian neighbors, concerning whom he had fantastic theories. In conversations with Morton of Merry-Mount, and his mysterious neighbor, Sir Christopher Gardiner, he maintained a belief that they were descended "from the scattered Trojans, after such time as Brutus left Latium." But he drove sharp bargains with the descendants of Priam and Paris, and piled up many a bale of peltries in his little castle of logs. Near by were Morton, and the Wessagusset colonists, and other isolated settlers, the unwitting pioneers of a great company. It was of these that Prince wrote, " To the south-east, near *Thompson's Island*, live some few *Planters more*. These were the *first* Planters of these Parts, having some small *Trade* with the Natives, for *Bever Skins*, which moved them to make their abode in those places, and are found of some help to the new colony."

Thompson was a Scottish gentleman, a traveller and scholar as well, and had been the London agent of Sir Ferdinando Gorges's company, for whose interests he had appeared even before the Privy Council. He died in 1628, leaving his wife and infant son to garrison the island, and to give generous hospitality to the colonists of Boston and Dorchester. After the arrival of the Puritan fleet, the good Episcopalian lady abandoned her snug Atlantis, and sailed away to where she could hear once more the familiar " Let your light so shine " in some distant prelatical realms. In 1634 Massachusetts granted the island to Dorchester, which leased it for twenty pounds a year, the revenue to be applied for a schoolmaster. It has been said that this was "the first public provision made for a free school in the world, by a direct tax or assessment on the inhabitants of a town." Fourteen years later came David's son, John Thompson, demanding his birthright, and bringing affidavits from Trevour, Standish, Blackstone, and Masconomo, to prove his claim. The General Court found his title good, and restored the island to him, giving to Dorchester, in lieu thereof, a thousand acres in the present town of Lunenburg. Six years later the Indian Winnequassam claimed the island, but was decided against by the courts. John Thompson returned to England, and sold his Western estate to two Bristol merchants. The region was well known by these people: for since 1622 ships of Bristol had visited the southern part of Boston Harbor, at the annual fishing-seasons, exchanging guns and ammunition for beaver, martin, and musquash skins. For the next century and a half the island was used for farming, with but a single flurry of excitement, in 1775, when American foragers destroyed the houses, and lit up Quincy Bay with their flames.

In 1834 the proprietors of the Boston Farm School purchased the estate for $6,000; and it was annexed to Boston, with the precious right reserved to the Dorchestrians of digging clams on its banks. A handsome brick building, 106 feet long, with a projection in the centre, was erected, with dining-hall and offices on first floor, schoolrooms on second floor, and dormitories above. In 1835 the Boston Asylum for Indigent Boys was united with the Farm School. There are about 100 boys (of from 8 to 17 years of age) on the island, for whom the school stands *in loco parentis*. Up at sunrise, and busied in practical studies and useful labors, the lads lead a happy and contented life; and their health is efficiently preserved by the

Thompson's Island, from South Boston.

pure air of the Bay and their frequent baths in the sea. Within two or three years a spacious new building has been erected, with gymnasium and work-shops, where the boys may receive a practical mechanical training. Some of the graduates of this school have occupied high and honorable positions in the outer world; and many of them visit the island in after-life to renew their memories of the place once so dear to them. The great catastrophe of the institution is now almost forgotten. It occurred in April, 1842, when a large boat, full of the boys, returning from a fishing-excursion down the harbor, was upset by a sudden squall, and twenty-three of the lads were drowned, besides the boatman and a teacher.

As a well-known citizen said, 40 years ago: "That little island reminds one of the old mythological fable of Latona, who, when she had no place on earth for her to bring forth and rear up her young, had an island created for her own special uses: and something like it exists here;

for when the boys who prowl about our city streets, fatherless, motherless, forlorn, and homeless, are discovered, this little Thompson's Island rises as a refuge for them; and here they are sheltered and educated, until they are fit to go forth into the great world, and battle manfully with it." It should be borne in mind that this is not a reformatory institution, but a home-school for teaching practical farming and the common educational branches to indigent American boys of good character.

Hawthorne once visited the Farm School, and thus reported his experience: "A stroll round the island, examining the products, as wheat in sheaves on the stubble-field; oats somewhat blighted and spoiled; great pumpkins elsewhere; pastures; mowing ground, — all cultivated by the boys. Their residence, a great brick building, painted green, and standing on the summit of a rising ground, exposed to the winds of the bay. Vessels flitting past; great ships with intricacy of rigging and various sails; schooners, sloops, with their one or two broad sheets of canvas; going on different tacks, so that the spectator might think that there was a different wind for each vessel, or that they scudded across the sea spontaneously, whither their own wills led them. The farm boys remain insulated, looking at the passing show, within sight of the city, yet having nothing to do with it; beholding their fellow-creatures skimming by them in winged machines, and steamboats snorting and puffing through the waves. Methinks an island would be the most desirable of all landed property, for it seems like a little world by itself; and the water may answer for the atmosphere that surrounds planets. The boys swinging, two together, standing up, and almost causing the ropes and their bodies to stretch out horizontally. On our departure they ranged themselves on the rails of the fence, and, being dressed in blue, looked not unlike a flock of pigeons."

The views from Thompson's Island are full of variety and beauty, especially from the high ground about the house, and include broad expanses of azure sea, and many a snug little island. The nearest and most conspicuous of these is Spectacle Island, with its busy colony of manipulators of defunct animals, its myriads of spiders, and its unhallowed perfumes. Here is exemplified the commendable Old-World thrift, by which useless refuse is converted into products of value, by the aid of ingenuity and industry.

Spectacle Island covers about sixty acres, its graceful trim bluffs being of about equal size. Sailing down the harbor, after Castle Island is passed, the bold headland of Spectacle is seen on the right, with a large barn on its summit, as the only sign of human occupancy. From other points appear the rendering-works and their chimneys, low down, near the Bridge of the Nose.

As early as the year 1666 Spectacle Island (even then so-called) was, for the most part, owned by the Bill family, who continued to hold it for nearly a century. In 1684 Samuel Bill bought it from the son of Wampatuck, the chief of the Massachusetts Indians, who inherited his father's authority over the fast-diminishing tribe. The deed (now in the possession of Mr. F. J. Ward) begins thus: "By these presents I Do fully, freely, absolutely give, grant, sell, enfeaffe, and convey unto the said Samuel Bill his heyeres

Wreck of the Brig "Grace Lothrop," Point Allerton.

and Assignes forever one certain Island, Scituate in the Massachusetts Bay, commonly known and called by the name of Spectacle Island."

It was at the earliest days covered with trees; and Winthrop relates that a party of thirty men came down here one bright January day, to cut wood. They were overtaken with wind and snow, followed by extreme cold; and so, the harbor freezing, except for a narrow channel, it was with great difficulty that a few found themselves able to get as far towards home as Castle Island, while several were carried through the ice to the Brewsters, where they remained two days, with neither food nor fire, suffering intensely from the extreme cold.

When the tide is low, the aptness of the name *Spectacle* is very evident;

for then the island is seen to consist of two nearly equal parts, connected by a narrow isthmus. Both these parts, anciently called the East and West Spectacles, are high, — the northerly one being a bold bluff, facing the channel. In 1717 a part of the island, "on the cleft or brow of the southerly highland," was sold by Mr. Bill to the town; and here a hospital was built, and used for eighteen years, when it was for some cause removed to Rainsford Island. In 1728, when H. M. S. *Sheerness* lay just off Spectacle Island, the last duel was fought upon Boston Common, and young Phillips killed Woodbridge. At midnight he was put on board the vessel. She sailed at dawn, and his forfeited life was safe from the Puritan gibbet.

When Sir Francis Wheeler's fleet arrived here, after its unsuccessful expedition against Martinique, with yellow-fever on board, Boston wanted Spectacle Island for a quarantine hospital. In 1739 the estate once more belonged to the Bill family, who sold it, in 1742, to Edward Bromfield, a prominent citizen of Boston. For many decades thereafter, excursion-parties from the happy little colonial town used to come hither on summer days, and encamp on the breezy slopes, or prepare their gypsy dinners over driftwood fires on the beach. In 1742 the hay which had been made here was hauled to South Boston on the ice, amid much provincial merriment. But the waters in this direction were not always safe to unarmed excursionists; for very novel dangers haunted the sea. In that famous week of September, 1726, when twenty bears were killed within two miles of Boston, the unfortunate beasts seem to have concluded that they might find more peaceful shelter down the harbor. Two were slain while swimming from Spectacle Island to an adjacent shore; and, a little farther out in the channel, a boat suffered a fierce attack from a large bear, which was beaten off, with great difficulty, by the use of boat-hooks and oars.

As the nineteenth century advanced, Spectacle was more and more favored by summer visitors, until one Woodroffe opened a house of entertainment in 1847. Here the current events were discussed by parties of grave citizens, — the annexation of California, the election of President Taylor, the rise of settlements in the prairie territories, — while the savory dishes of sea-products were in preparation, and the high-flavored punch underwent assimilation.

In 1857 the island was bought, for $15,000, by Nahum Ward, who founded here a large establishment for rendering dead horses, still in possession and full activity. At this time there stood here two brick powder-houses, two dwellings, and a wharf. Many buildings have been erected since, to accommodate the extensive and increasing business. In 1872 the lucrative industry of rendering cattle-bones was introduced; and in 1874 came the rendering of tallow and suet. The tanks are of iron, and all possible precautions are taken to prevent odors from getting abroad in the harbor. Every day the steam-tug and barges pertaining to the company go down from their wharf on Federal Street, laden with dead horses and refuse from slaughter-houses; "which matter," says Mr. Ward, "if it were allowed to remain in the city for three days in summer, would *cause a plague.*" There are 30 men employed on the island, and 13 families dwell there. The vegetable-gardens cover 5 acres, and the mowing-land 37 acres. About 2,000 dead horses are received here yearly, from points within ten miles; and their products are hides, hair, oil, and bones. This, however,

Rocks on the Outer Brewster.

is not a leading feature of the business, the main part of which is connected with cattle-bones and tallow. Other articles of manufacture are glue-stock and neat's-foot oil. Surely this must be one of the Isles of Greece; but even the harbor muse flouts it, thus: —

> "The next, for frolic, once was fam'd,
>   In ancient happy time;
> And long, has Spectacle been nam'd,
>   A name unfit for rhyme."

Apple Island, which is seen on the left, as one sails down the harbor, is nearly three miles from Boston, and just off the shore of Winthrop. It is always noticed among the first, simply because of its rare grace, rising in a gentle slope from the water's edge, — such a perfect shape, crowned with

waving elms fifty or more years old, proud and beautiful, and marking the
island at once as unlike any other. At low water it is for some distance
surrounded by flats, and becomes difficult of access. In very early times
Apple Island belonged to Boston, and was used (like the other islands)
chiefly for pasturage; but having a rich soil, and being well sheltered, it
became in time private property, owned in 1723 by the Hon. Thomas
Hutchinson, father of Gov. Hutchinson, who was the author of the History
of Massachusetts. It passed in 1802, by will, to an English mariner,
who, living in Northumberland and knowing little about it, allowed the
property to decay, and the island to lie idle. About this time Mr. Marsh,
an Englishman, being attracted by its beauty, and perhaps by its fitness as
a home for Britannic insularity, settled there with his family, and became
so attached to the soil that he resolved upon owning it; and, after many
an unsuccessful search, at last (in 1822) found the proprietor of the island,
buying it of him for $550. Black Jack was Marsh's negro servant, well
known about the harbor, and at one time much talked about on account of
his brutal treatment by certain naval officers, who charged him with helping
a sailor to desert. By the exertions of Samuel McCleary, he was enabled
to recover heavy damages from his assailants. Here Marsh lived, contented
and happy, until the age of sixty-six, when he died (in 1833), and was
then, by his own request, buried upon the western slope of his beautiful
island-home. The funeral was attended by many gentlemen from Boston.
Two years later the house was burned, leaving the island again lonely.

The island covers ten acres. It was bought by Boston in 1867, and now
belongs to private citizens. Aside from the irregular athletics and ichthyophagous
picnics of the North-street gladiators, it finds conspicuous use
in the annals of destruction. Here many a famous old ship, by lapse of
years and buffetings of alien seas grown decrepit and useless, has been
hauled up on the beach and burned, in order to get at the metal used in
her construction. There is a kind of pathos in the final sacrifice of these
trusty old vessels, whose keels, no more to plough the yielding waves, are
dragged across the muddy flats, and abandoned to the flames. Dismantled
and forsaken, the flames riot along the venerable hulls, crackling through
the deserted cabins, and throwing out their wild banners from the falling
spars. At such times the island is wrapped in rolling smoke, and glows
like Stromboli, among the waves, while the lower harbor is illuminated by
a baleful light. In a few hours nothing remains but the stock of the junk-merchant.
Among the victims of this lurid shore, burned at the stake in
the name of the copper-market and the iron-trade, have been the famous
old steamships, *James Adger*, destroyed in 1858; the *Baltic*, the last of the
Collins line; and the *Ontario*, one of the immense wooden steamships built
at Newburyport for the transatlantic trade.

Long Island.

THE BATTERY. — AN AZOREAN COLONY. — JOHN NELSON. — WAR MEMORIES.

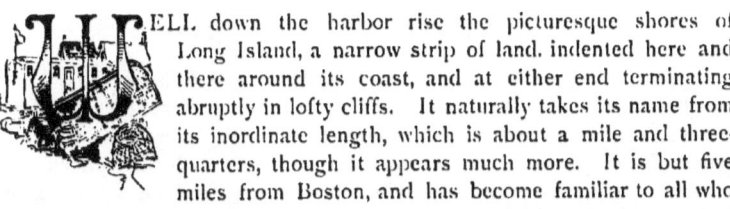ELL down the harbor rise the picturesque shores of Long Island, a narrow strip of land, indented here and there around its coast, and at either end terminating abruptly in lofty cliffs. It naturally takes its name from its inordinate length, which is about a mile and three-quarters, though it appears much more. It is but five miles from Boston, and has become familiar to all who pass, by its municipal buildings, and still more by the light-house, perched upon the very tip of the steepest bluff in the harbor, eighty feet above high-water mark. It bears a clear and brilliant fixed light, visible for fifteen miles at sea. The battery which crowns the cliff, presenting only a range of low green mounds to the view of the passing sailor, is a formidable little work, of modern construction, with walls of great thickness, bombproofs, and other defences, partly separated from the rest of the bluff by a deep dry moat. There are no cannon here now; but it would be a matter of very slight delay to mount a line of heavy guns which could deliver a formidable plunging fire on the ship-channel, and perfectly command the approaches through Broad Sound. The favor with which this insular paradise was at first regarded faded out in time, and by the year 1840 there remained but a single farmhouse. But when the United States wanted to buy Eastern Head, for a light-house, the proprietors discovered that every rod of the soil had a great value; and the Government was obliged to go through a long lawsuit, in order to acquire the 35 acres on the bluff without emptying the Treasury. The national domain extends to the pond on the west; and the weather-beaten old houses near the wharf and around this side of the hill were the shelters of the workmen on the fort. The seaward front of the Head is defended by a handsome sea-wall, whose construction cost $150,000.

The light-house was built in 1819, and is a round white iron tower, attached to a neat little house, which serves the keeper as a home. On two sides it is surrounded by ramparts, which rest upon the very edges of the steep cliff, and, though at present of little service as defence, yet certainly are picturesque, being clad with verdure, and dotted all over with daisies and buttercups, forming by their great mounds and deep embrasures just the most delightful place in the world for a merry game of hide-and-seek. It is pleasant to sit there, and look off across the Bay, beyond all land, until the purple sea is lost in purple sky, watching the tiny yachts and great ships coming in and going out, and the flag-decked steamers, from whose decks distant music floats upward. Or, should one care for a less lofty view, at the base of the cliff is the most charming promenade, over the top of the massive wall, built lest the persistent sea should take to itself the very island. This promenade over the works and at the water's edge is about semi-circular, and, if followed round, brings one to the little pebbly beach and cove on the east side of the island.

Near this point stood a quaint little cluster of huts, inhabited by a colony of olive-skinned Portuguese fishermen, most of whom were from the Azore Islands, and reproduced on this far-away sister of Fayal and San Miguel the customs and sports of their homeland. Many a pretty little Azorean child ran along the grassy slopes of the hills near by, seeking vainly for the oranges and pine-apples, the palms and periwinkles, of his

"Summer isles of Eden lying in dark-purple spheres of sea."

Along the shore the boats were drawn up; and the dark fishermen loitered by the water-side, waiting for time and tide to serve, and calling on Santo Cristo to deliver their out-bound dories from peril or a barren cruise.

In the year 1887 the City of Boston found itself obliged to evict these unfortunate fishermen, in order to reserve the island for municipal purposes. The operations of dispossessing the residents were met with a passive resistance on their part, resulting in many distressing scenes, and calling forth much commiseration among the people at large.

In 1850 the occupants of the island were George Smith, the farmer, and Nicolas Capello, the Portuguese fisherman. The heirs of the latter, and their compatriots, numbered 30 families at the time when the island was depopulated. The control of the Long-Island Company passed into the hands of Thomas J. Dunbar of Boston, about the year 1860; and from his heirs the city acquired the domain, paying about $140,000 for it.

On the little upland south of the fishermen's huts, and near the head of the steamboat-wharf, rises the great new buildings of the City Almshouse, on whose front is the finest and most luxuriant grove in the harbor. Beyond and running south the island becomes lonely and desolate, until it finally ends at South Head, a high bluff rising over the water, serene and quiet, peopled only by the skimming swallows, and keeping its silent guard over Spectacle Island, just across a narrow reach of blue water. The total area of Long Island is about 216 acres; and it is separated from Governor's and Castle Islands by President Roads, and from Deer Island, not quite a mile to the northward, by Broad Sound. Around its southern shore is the

Western (or Back) Way, which is much used by coasting-vessels entering or leaving the port.

The rise, decadence, and fall of Long Island as a home for men might be made an interesting theme by some Gibbon of the adjacent villages. Sedition has harbored here; battle has been waged; martial revels have been celebrated; and love has been made in the old ways. The island first appears in history in the year (1634) in which Wallenstein was slain, at the middle period of the Thirty Years' War; when it was granted, with Deer and Hog Islands, to Boston, in the halcyon days when "these isles abounded with Woods and Water, and Meadow-ground,

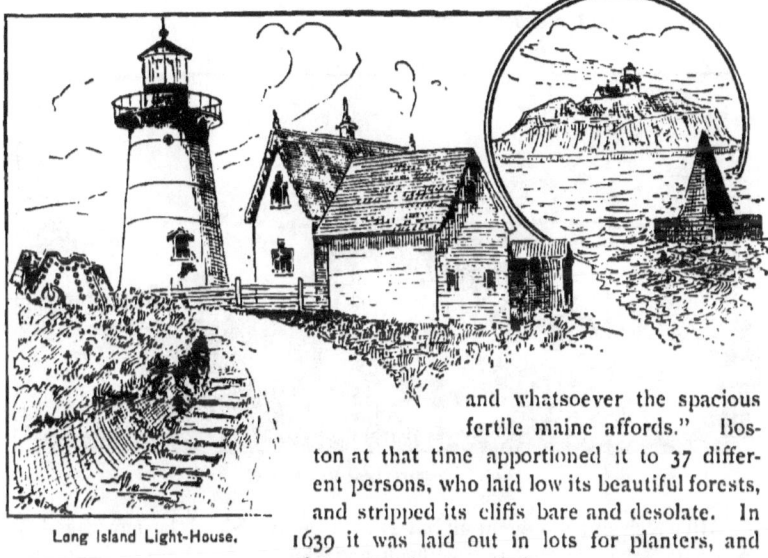

Long Island Light-House.

and whatsoever the spacious fertile maine affords." Boston at that time apportioned it to 37 different persons, who laid low its beautiful forests, and stripped its cliffs bare and desolate. In 1639 it was laid out in lots for planters, and after a time became their own, on the payment of a yearly rent of sixpence an acre, for the benefit of the free school. But this agreement was not always kept; and in 1667 the town gave up the island to the renters, on condition that the back rent should be paid; and so it was, not long after, that Long Island passed firmly into private hands. A manuscript in the Geneva Library, in which a French Huguenot refugee describes his visit to America in 1687, speaks of the "number of very pretty islands that lie in front of Boston, most of them cultivated and inhabited by peasants." The term "peasant" was misapplied; for here on Long Island was the house of John Nelson, the hero of Drake's romance, whom the records call "a young gentleman of Boston, a near relation to Sir Thomas Temple, but an episcopalian, and of a gay, free temper." He it was who headed the

Bostonians in their attack on Sir Edmund Andros and his troops at Fort Hill in 1689. Such a man would have been at least a chevalier in France. In 1692 Nelson, having been captured by the French while on a voyage to the eastward, discovered some secret designs which were being matured against the New-England colonies, and informed the authorities of Massachusetts from his prison at Quebec. For this patriotic act he was sent to Paris, and shut up in the Bastille for a long time, obtaining his release through the intervention of Sir Purbeck Temple. After twelve years of absence, the gallant captain returned to his little kingdom of Long Island, where the Nelson family gave a famous feast to celebrate the liberation of their chief. Fragments of the table-cloth used on this occasion (about the year 1702) are still preserved among his descendants.

Interior of Battery, Long-Island Head.

After Nelson had bought all but 4½ acres of the island, he mortgaged it to certain Salem capitalists, "with all and singular the houses, buildings, barns, orchards, gardens, pastures, ffences, woods, stones, beach, wharffes, liberties, immunities, hereditaments, emoluments," etc. From Nelson's heirs it passed to Charles Apthorp, whose heirs sold their domain, "butted and bounded Northerly, Southerly, Easterly, and Westerly, by the sea," to Barlow Trecothick, Lord Mayor of London, who had married Grizzell Apthorp. In 1791 Trecothick's brother-in-law sold it to James Ivers, whose heirs conveyed it to Thomas Smith of Cohasset in 1847; and two years later it was vested in the Long-Island Company.

In July, 1775, a detachment of 500 Continental soldiers, in 65 whaleboats, landed on Long Island, and took off all the sheep and cattle there, together with 17 British sailors. They were hotly cannonaded by the men-of-war in the harbor, and chased to Squantum by an armed schooner and barges crowded with blue-jackets; but got off safely with their prizes, whose loss was grievously mourned by the hungry officers in Boston. Colonel Pierce thus described the affair in his diary: "Our people go to Long Island, and fetch of all the cretors, and took 13 merceens prisoners."

Two years after the port of Boston was closed, a squadron of British frigates still lingered in the roads, blockading the harbor and insulting the State. John Adams wrote from Philadelphia to John Winthrop, in May, 1776, " Is there no such thing as getting upon Lovell's Island, or George's Island, and driving away the men-of-war which lie in Nantasket Roads?

The Long-Island House (torn down in 1885).

Can nothing be done at Hull or Point Alderton? I am afraid you are as destitute of active and capable engineers as in spirited commanding officers. . . . I never shall be happy until every unfriendly flag is driven out of sight, and the Light House, George's and Lovell's Islands, and the East end of Long Island, are secured." He advocated the construction of galleys, like those of Turkey and Venice, armed with 42-pounders; and added, "A kind of dodging Indian fight might be maintained among the islands in our harbor, between such galleys and the men-of-war."

The efficacious hint was given in June, 1776, when a force of Continentals and militiamen occupied Long Island, and planted several heavy guns on East Head. At the same time another force had taken position at Hull, and upon a concerted signal the newly raised batteries opened hotly on the hostile ships. These, indeed, were not slow at replying; and for a space the lower harbor was wrapped in white cannon-smoke, and its islands reverberated with the crash of opposing broadsides and field-works. Finally, however, after several ships had been hulled. and a destructive shot had torn up the upper works of the flagship, the fleet moved away to sea.

They should have left a frigate off in the bay, to warn incoming British vessels: for several of these, with rich cargoes, sailed unsuspectingly into captivity in this snug little Yankee harbor. Even worse befell a transport full of Highlanders, coming to re-enforce the king's armies in America, even before the fleet had been driven from Boston. The poor Scots were sorely assailed by two Yankee privateers in Massachusetts Bay, but hotly beat them off, and sailed onward toward their desired port. But Capt. Tucker's Marblehead privateer and an armed vessel of Rhode Island took up the chase, the former running in Broad Sound, and the other on the east of Long Island. They found the transport aground; but her guns were served so well that the Rhode-Islander was driven behind the island, and Tucker's spars were shattered, and his sails and his pine-tree flag were riddled. At last the British ship struck her colors, and her rich cargo of military stores became the spoils of the Americans. The commander and 36 men had been slain; and these were buried on Long Island the next day, in a sad and solemn procession, preceded by the Scottish bagpipes, wailing the coronach, and followed by the lamenting women who had accompanied their husbands from the North Country.

When the splendid new line-of-battle ship *Independence* and the famous frigate *Constitution* were blockaded here in 1814, by a strong British squadron, the Massachusetts authorities requested that they should be moved into the lower harbor, so that the enemy could take them away without endangering the city by a bombardment. But stout old Commodore Bainbridge refused to accede. and begged the State to guard the bay for its own sake; asserting, that, in case of an attack, the naval people would defend themselves with all possible vigor, and the town could not help receiving serious damage in the engagement. Among the defences which he strongly advised was a battery of 18-pounders on Long-Island Head, with a garrison at Hull; and there is little doubt that the final adoption of such precautions by the State kept Boston from molestation during the war.

During the first two years of the Secession War, Long Island was alive with soldiers: the State volunteers making ready for the field. or resting here on their return. The Ninth Regiment lay in camp here through May and June, 1861, and then sailed away on transports to Washington; and in the chapters in the regimental history devoted to this period, the following bit of description occurs: "The island was, upon the south side, thickly studded with trees; a beautiful verdure clothed the miniature valleys; and of a summer morning when the sea was calm, and the red glory of a summer sunrise looked down upon the dotted camp-ground, the scene was inexpressibly beautiful. It was a good thought, the selection of Long Island for a military rendezvous, not only for its sanitary merits, but for the security it afforded against desertions. It boasts many fine parade-grounds, walks, and lounges, while beautiful views of the sea and land greet the eye in every direction."

On April 17, 1861, the Third Massachusetts Regiment sailed down the harbor in a steam-transport; and on the same day the Fourth Regiment left the city. Both commands were from the Old Colony, and went to Fortress Monroe by sea. The Third destroyed the navy-yard at Norfolk, and fought the Virginians at Hampton. In July the regiment was brought back, and encamped four days on Long Island, before being mustered out. The Fourth was the first Northern regiment that marched on to "the sacred soil of Virginia." It fought at Big Bethel, and returned to encamp on Long Island with the Third; where for a few days the boys had a chance to rest in security, far from rebel alarms and the hardships of the field. The Long-Island House was the headquarters building in those days; and many a bright young officer solaced his impatience by promenading its long piazzas, while awaiting orders to the fatal front. At the end of the year 1863 there was a camp of over 1,000 conscripts on Long Island, and several full companies of heavy artillery. The post was under the command of Gen. Devens, and the camps stood on the slope between the Portuguese village and the summit beyond the Long-Island House. The troops here suffered extremely from cold; and at times it was found necessary to relieve the sentries every half-hour, just as is done in the Citadel of Quebec on winter nights. An iron discipline had to be maintained here among these unwilling soldiers; and not a few would-be deserters were drowned in the adjacent waters, while trying to gain the mainland.

Portuguese Village, on Long Island.

Since the close of the Rebellion the island has lain fallow, awaiting new changes. The great hotel was run, with varying success, by many different administrations, and sometimes with a goodly number of guests, who enjoyed the pleasant views of the harbor, and the rustling groves in front of the house. The hopeful avenues of the land-company were occupied by only a feeble group of shabby cottages; and the sanguine dreamers who hoped to see here a new island-ward, like East Boston, must wait until the twentieth century, at least, before their prophecies are realized. As a summer resort the locality suffered from its proximity to certain unæsthetic quarters of the town, whose adventurous young men found here a domain where the terror-inspiring helmets of the city-watch seldom intruded. Occasionally a large assemblage of bruisers and plug-uglies visited Long Island, with the intent to have a comfortable prize-fight; but the police-boat, with a detachment of stalwart officers, as often made a dash on the desecrated island, and prevented the consummation of the affair.

The soil of the island is reputed to be very rich; but it has been used mainly for the pasturage of horses and sheep, great numbers of which have revelled on these fenceless plains. There was at one time much talk of converting the island into a marine park, connected with South Boston and the North End by city steamboats, and affording a place of recreation for the people of the most densely crowded wards. Somewhat later the Naval Committee discussed the feasibility of selling the United-States Marine Hospital at Chelsea, and establishing a new one on Long Island. In 1882 the city fathers debated as to the expediency of transferring hither the municipal charities and prisons at South Boston and West Roxbury; and in 1885, having purchased the island, they began the construction of the present spacious brick building, adequate for the housing of 400 paupers.

Lovell's Island and Gallop's Island.

THE LOST FRIGATE MAGNIFIQUE. — THE QUARANTINE HOSPITAL. — NIX'S MATE.

WEST of the Brewster archipelago, and upwards of six miles from the Hub of the Universe, stands Lovell's Island, separated from George's by the main ship-channel, and exposed on its northern side to the full force of the Atlantic, which was found to encroach so greatly upon it, that, in 1843, measures were taken to build there a costly and massive sea-wall. Lovell's is three-quarters of a mile long, and about half that distance in width, and is the flattest of the large islands in the harbor. It was named, probably, for Capt. William Lovell, who lived in Dorchester in 1630; and the first mention of it occurs in the Massachusetts Records in 1636. In 1648 it was granted to Charlestown, "pvided that halfe of the timber and fire wood shall belong to the garrison at the Castle." A part of the island was also given to James Brown, "if he set up a stage and follow a trade of fishing there." Again, in 1654, it was granted to Hull; but at the present time belongs to the Government of the United States, and is used by the Light-House Board. A steep little upland rises beyond the wharf, covered with long, fine grass; and descends towards the north to a long, low point, reaching out into the sea, and called Ram's Head. This was the scene, some sixty years ago, of a dreadful shipwreck, when a vessel from Maine struck upon the rocks at midnight, and, though all its crew and passengers reached the hill-top, at morning not one was found alive, the cold being so intense as to freeze them to death. It was thus vividly described by an ancient poet: —

> "At length they gain'd the sea-beat strand,
>   And rescued from the waves;
>   On Lovell's Island only land,
>   To find more decent graves.
>
> "For ere the tempest, howling night,
>   With horror ceas'd to roar;
>   Each soul had gone with rapid flight,
>   Where sorrow springs no more.

> "Among the rest, a youthful pair,
> Who, from their early youth;
> Had felt of love an equal share,
> Adorn'd with equal truth,

> "Lay prostrate 'mid the dire alarms,
> Had calm resign'd their breath;
> Fast locked within each other's arms,
> Together sunk to death."

The great bowlder, which is still visible on the bluff, and has been for many decades the rendezvous of picnic-parties, became invested with a mournful and romantic interest from the events of that terrible night. Under its unavailing shelter were found the bodies of the young man and woman aforesaid, closely locked in each other's arms. They were on the eve of being married, and had sailed for Boston, to buy there the furniture of their home. Sad fate was theirs, — to die inside the harbor, within cannon-shot of a thousand happy firesides!

In the early days of the Colony, many trees covered Lovell's, and were cut for fire-wood. Upon its southern point stood, until lately, a solitary tree, used for many years as a guide for the pilots of incoming vessels. The island has been found a good pasture for horses, and once was overrun by pretty pink-eyed rabbits. On the wharf are duplicates of the great whistling buoy off the Graves, and the bell-buoy off Harding's Ledge, besides an endless number and variety of others, ready, in emergency, to take the places of those now in different parts of the Bay. A track runs thence to Ram's Head, over which horses draw the great granite blocks used on the sea-wall and breakwater. This was first built at an expense of $90,000; but proved inadequate, and the necessary additions cost the Government some $40,000 more.

Between Lovell's and Deer Island is the channel of Broad Sound, used by small vessels and steamboats bound for the eastern ports, but too shallow for large ships. It is much shorter and less intricate than the main channel, but even here the inevitable dangers of the sea have been fatally predominant. So late as June, 1858, the beautiful new schooner *Prairie Flower*, with a pleasure-party of 47 Salem gentlemen on board, was upset by a squall here, and seven of her passengers were drowned.

The ancient history of Lovell's was not recorded, and only here and there is a passing mention made of it. Away back in the year 1645, the crew of a Portuguese ship in the Roads stole some goats from these islands, upon which the Puritan magistracy rose in wrath, and made a prize of the unfortunate vessel. They did not release her until a good round fine had been screwed out of the captain. During the same year a ketch was wrecked upon the island; although, two years before, the Boston pilots led La Tour's fleet safely out through Broad Sound, past the island, "where no Ships of such burden had gone out before, or not more than one." In August, 1685, a ship came in with small-pox on board, and was ordered by the council "to remove lower to Lovell's Island, and there the Passengers, Ship, and Goods between Decks to be Aired: None to come to Town till further Order." In the latter part of 1782 Admiral Vaubaird's French fleet sailed into Boston Harbor. The immense three-deckers, *Triumphant* and *La Couronne*, and a dozen smaller frigates, passed inward safely; but the *Magnifique*, a stately line-of-battle ship, missed stays off Lovell's Island, and went ashore. There she lay for many years, a noble and melancholy wreck, until time and the winter storms gradually broke her in pieces, or buried her under the sands of the sea. The ship-of-the-line *America* was then being built at Portsmouth, and Congress gave her to the French Government, to recompense it for the lost *Magnifique*. The Boston pilot whose carelessness caused her loss became sexton of the New North Church; and the parish lads annoyed him by chalking on the meeting-house door, —

"Don't you run this ship ashore
As you did the seventy-four."

The treasure-seekers have made many an attempt to secure the riches which they fancy went down with the *Magnifique*. About the year 1840 they found pieces of the very beautiful wood of which she was built; and in 1859 large quantities of lead, copper, and cannon-balls were found. Ten years later the United-States engineers who were widening the channel brought up many oaken timbers of the old French frigate, more than twenty feet below the surface of the ground. The place where she struck, on Man-of-War Bar, is now solid land, above the sweep of high tides.

About six miles from Boston, and between the main channel and Nantasket Roads, rises the high bluff of Gallop's Island, whose Revolutionary fortifications have been replaced by a dainty summer-house, perked jauntily over the channel. Below is the great sea-wall, built since 1868 by the United-States engineers. From this bluff the strange gravelly ridge of Beachy Point stretches many rods to the eastward along the channel, almost submerged at high tide, but bold and conspicuous enough when the ebb tide has lowered the channel.

The first owner of the island, long before 1650, was Capt. John Gallop, then the best pilot in the Bay, who had here a snug farm, with a meadow on Long Island, a sheep-pasture on Nix's Mate, and a house in Boston. He achieved great distinction by piloting in the ship *Griffin* through a new-found channel, when she had on board 200 passengers, including the Rev. John Cotton, the Rev. Thomas Hooker, and other fathers of New England. Shurtleff thinks that this channel was the Black-Rock Passage ; and Savage prefers to consider it the channel leading from the north, between Lovell's and the Great Brewster. Gallop was also distinguished for a naval exploit off Block Island, where he attacked a party of Indians in possession of the shallop of John Oldham (formerly of Hull), slaying several of the savages, and recovering the body of his murdered friend. When the old pilot died, in 1650, he valued the island at £12, and estimated its area at 16 acres.

The richness of the soil made this a favorite location for successive generations of farmers. Even now it produces about seven hundred bushels of vegetables yearly, and ten tons of hay: and its dairy yields milk and butter enough for the local demand. In old times the farmers here supplied the ships in Nantasket Roads with vegetables and milk and pure spring water; and many parties of summer voyagers used to visit these fertile shores, and enjoy the quaint hospitalities of the Snow place.

Gallop's was long owned by gentlemen of Quincy and Hingham, and passed, in 1819, into the possession of Peter Newcomb, who dwelt here for many years. It was purchased from his son by the city of Boston in 1860, for $6,600, and loaned to the United States for a camp-ground. In the latter part of the Secession War there were long lines of barracks on the island, where at times 3,000 recruits were quartered, many of them being professional bounty-jumpers, with $1,500 to $2,000 in each man's pocket. All manner of employments were assigned to these soldiers, to keep them from mischievous idleness; but the sutler was the busiest man on the island, and the happiest. During the winter the recruits suffered terribly from the cold. The island was under the command of Gen. Hendrickson, and had a church and a library. Here the Thirty-eighth Massachusetts Regiment was quartered, on returning from the wars, in 1865. They were veterans of the Louisiana campaigns, and the later battles in the Carolinas; and, as their steamer approached the harbor, one of their number wrote: "The luxuriant banks of the Mississippi, or the historical ones of the Potomac, had no charms compared with the dwarfed shrubbery of Cohasset, of Scituate, of Marshfield, and of Plymouth." Here also the Second Massachusetts Heavy Artillery and the Fifty-fourth (colored) and Sixty-first Infantry Regiments were encamped.

Since 1867 the island has been used as a quarantine hospital, for infectious diseases, — the Quarantine Grounds lying between Gallop's and Deer Islands. Between 1866 and 1881 there were 765 persons placed here,

The Port Physician boarding an Inbound Ship.

afflicted with dangerous contagious diseases, of whom 221 died. Most of these had small-pox or yellow-fever.

There are on the island two hospitals, a dwelling, and other buildings, all of which belong to the city of Boston. The appearance of the place is cheerful and bright, in spite of its mournful destination; and, if any thing could revive the poor sailors whose veins have been filled with fatal poison on the far Spanish Main, it would be the tender care and pure sweet air which awaits them on this cool northern islet. But the record of deaths shows that nothing avails to save, in many cases; and the yearly enlarging cemetery on the island bears witness that poor Jack finds here his last snug harbor, his long repose from a life of unutterable toil and hardship.

Nix's Mate is a large gravelly shoal between Long Island and Gallop's Island, partly bare at low tide, and crowned by a singular and ominous-looking beacon, now perhaps eighty years old. It is a massive piece of copper-riveted masonry, 40 feet square and 12 feet high (with stairs on one side), upon whose top stands a black wooden pyramid, 20 feet high. As early as

1636 this locality was known as Nixes Island, when it was granted to John Gallop; and at a later day it divided with Bird Island the dishonor of being the place of execution for pirates, where the bones of these luckless sea-dogs were exposed in chains and on gibbets. Murderers and burglars were executed on the Common, or down on Boston Neck; but the people whose crimes were perpetrated on the ocean suffered the penalties of the law in sight of its accusing waters.

The usual form of the popular legend of this locality states that Capt. Nix was killed at sea, and that his mate was charged with the crime, and executed on this island, protesting his innocence, and prophesying that the place which witnessed his judicial murder would be washed away by the angry sea. This is certainly not historical, for the present name was applied

Nix's Mate Island, in 1700.

to the place two hundred and fifty years ago, at a time when no man had yet been executed in Massachusetts for murder or piracy. Another form of the legend states that Nix was a freebooter, who sailed into Boston in 1680, his ship well laden with treasures ravished from unarmed ships. Anchoring down the harbor, he and his mate went ashore on the island, on a dark night, and buried several bags of coin; after which, to keep the secret as close as possible, Nix murdered his companion, and buried him also. The continuation of the story is crowded with ghastly circumstances.

There are enough cases of this kind recorded in the sober annals of the colony, without need of invoking tradition. For upwards of a century Massachusetts Bay was infested with freebooters, who plundered passing vessels at will, and were sure of a short shrift and stern retribution when caught. So annoying were these scourges of the coast, that even Winthrop's *Blessing of the Bay*, the first vessel built in the colony, was armed and sent out as a cruiser against them. In 1689 Tom Pound and his ma-

rauding ship were captured by the Boston vessel *Mary*, after a fight, in which the commander of the latter was mortally wounded. Pound was executed, his indictment charging that he, "being under a red flag at the head of the mast, purposely and in defiance of their Majesties' authority, had wilfully and with malice aforethought committed murder and piracy upon the high seas, being instigated thereunto by the Devil." About the same
time Thomas Hawkins, a young man from one of the best Massachusetts families, was executed for the same crime, with nine of his comrades. Fifteen years later John Quelch and five of his men were brought up the Bay, condemned as pirates, escorted by 40 musketeers and two ministers to Bird Island, and there executed. The *News-Letter* said that "notwithstanding all the great labour and pains taken by the Reverend Ministers of the Town of *Boston*, ever since they were first Seized and brought to Town, both before and since their Trial and Condemnation, to instruct, admonish, preach, and pray for them; yet as they led a wicked and vitious life, so to appearance they dyed

Nix's Mate.

very obdurately and impenitently, hardened in their sin. His Excellency intends to send an Express to *England*, with an Account of the whole matter to Her Majesty."

In 1717 Captain Bellamy cruised in the Bay with the formidable pirate-ship *Whidah*, of 23 guns. She was finally decoyed on to Wellfleet bar, and 102 of her crew were drowned. For a hundred years parts of this vessel frequently became visible at low tide, and coins from time to time washed ashore near by. Six of the crew, previously detached into a prize, were taken, and executed at Boston. Well into the eighteenth century the British war-vessel *Sea-Horse* was stationed here for years to repress piracy; and many a long cruise did she make against their haunts. In 1724 John Phillips was the most notorious sea-robber in these waters; but, having impressed some unwilling young men into his service, they revolted, on good opportunity, killed their chief, and carried the vessel into Boston, where certain impenitent men of the crew were hung in gibbets on Bird Island, on whose gloomy shores many a jolly Jack the Rover had preceded them.

A famous sufferer on Nix's Mate was William Fly, who headed the crew of the *Elizabeth* in a mutiny, while on a voyage from Jamaica to Guinea, and threw overboard the captain and mate. Afterwards they changed the name of their vessel to *Fame's Revenge*, and embarked on a piratical cruise along the American coast. But their prisoners rose upon them, placed Fly and three of his men in irons, and ran the *Fame's Revenge* into Boston, where the unfortunate buccaneers were executed. Fly was hung in irons, on Nix's Mate, over the graves of his confederates; and here his bones shook and rattled in the sea-air for many months, as a grim warning to all mariners. The *Boston News-Letter* reported that Fly "advised Masters of Vessels not to be Severe and Barbarous to their Men, which might be a reason why so many turn'd Pirates; the other Two seem'd Penitent, beg'd that others might be warned by 'em."

The Boston merchantmen of those days were hard fellows to tackle. In 1748 Colonel Quincy's ship *Bethell*, 20 guns, bound for the Mediterranean, encountered a Spanish treasure-ship, which surrendered directly, fancying that its antagonist was an English sloop-of-war. The bold Captain Freeman had doubled his crew by dressing up dummies and handspikes with extra coats and hats. The *Bethell* and her prize sailed up Boston Harbor in triumph, and 161 chests of silver and 2 chests of gold were removed from the latter to Colonel Quincy's house. When such well-armed merchantmen fell into the hands of their mutinous crews, they became formidable scourges to commerce. As late as the year 1772, there are notices of pirates on the coast; and Col. Pierce's diary in that year says, "Nov. 22. The Pirates take a scooner and killed the hands."

A writer in the "Memorial History of Boston" resents Lord Macaulay's charge that there were many "old buccaneers living in comfort and credit at New York and Boston." But there were certainly many queer maritime characters in the little colony, such as those of whom Lowell speaks, "Retired sea-captains (true brothers of Chaucer's Ship-man), whose exploits had kindled the imagination of Burke, added a not unpleasant savor of salt to society. They belonged to the old school of Gilbert, Hawkins, Frobisher, and Drake, parcel-soldiers all of them, who had commanded armed ships, and had tales to tell of gallant fights with privateers or pirates, truest representatives of those Vikings, who, if trade in lumber or peltry was dull, would make themselves Dukes of Dublin or Earls of Orkney."

Among the wild rovers of those days was Captain Cromwell, a poor vagabond of a common sailor about Boston in 1636; but ten years later, under a dubious license from Lord Warwick, he captured a fleet of Spanish ships, and brought the whole array into Plymouth, and then to Boston, where honest old Bradford averred that "he scattered a great deal of money, and yet more sin, I fear." He slew one of his men in the street with a rapier-thrust; presented a rich sedan-chair to Governor Winthrop; and then fared away on a three-years' cruise, in which he captured many prizes. Then he returned, to become a solid man of Boston, and presented to the town six great bells, doubtless originally intended for some Spanish-American convent. Between these fearless sea-kings and the freebooters whose bones rattled above Nix's Mate there was a world-wide difference, to be sure. Captain Kidd had been brought into Boston, a captive, and sent thence to London, to be put to death; but the fame of his exploits and gains led many an honest sailor astray, and at last to a dreary death on this surf-beaten shore.

A hundred years ago the island was large enough to be used for pasturing sheep, and its chief bluff bore the name of North-End Point. It is certainly a strange coincidence that Nix's and Bird, the two gibbet-bearers, are the only islands in the harbor to be washed away and blotted out, as if

Lovell's Island and the Brewsters, from Gallop's Island.

kindly Nature refused to endure their presence. A curving shoal runs half a mile south-westward from the Nix's Mate beacon, and would be the most dangerous point in the Bay, were it not for the high black pyramid.

The beacon was erected under the auspices, and at the suggestion, of the Boston Marine Society, and formed the theme of many communications between that organization and the National Government. One of our cuts shows the island as it appeared many years ago, before the last of the aborigines had vanished from the scene. The approximate date when the last Massachusee canoe disappeared cannot be found; but in 1853 Edward Everett narrated the following incident, which is at least *ben trovato:* "A few days ago, as I saw in the newspapers, two light birch-bark canoes appeared in Boston Harbor, containing each a solitary Indian. They seemed as they approached to gaze in silent wonder at the city of the triple hills, rising street above street, and crowned with the dome of the State House, and at the long line of villas stretching far into the background; at the numerous tall vessels outward bound, as they dropped down the channel, and spread their broad wings to the breeze, and those which were returning weather-beaten from the ends of the earth; at the steamers dashing in every direction across the harbor, breathing volumes of smoke from their fiery lungs. They paddled their frail barks with dexterity and speed through this strange, busy, and to them, no doubt, bewildering scene; and having made the circuit of East Boston, the Navy Yard, the city itself, and South Boston, dropped down with the current, and disappeared among the islands."

The Port Physician going out.

Since the second edition of this Handbook was published, the author has discovered that the story of Capt. Nix killing his mate, as detailed on page 190, was a latter-day production of the gifted Irish-American poet, James Jeffrey Roche.

It appears, furthermore, that the destruction of the island was partly due to the carrying off of the greater part of its material by slaters, who opened here a valuable quarry. Joseph Borrowscale has in his possession bills for Nix's-Island slate made out nearly a century ago.

A new version of how the place received its name has recently been brought to the light by the discovery of the fragment of an alleged old letter, which was written somewhere between the years 1700-10. *Se non è vero, è ben trovato.*

"You will minde, Niclass, that when wee war in Lisbone laste yere, you did telle me a marvillose tale about an iland nere Boston, wch had shone the Provedences of God in reveleing the misstakes and crueltys of man. How a Dutch captayne Nyx was kylled at sea, and how hys admirall had takyn hys Mate and Try'd hym and Hanged hym on this iland for the Kyling — and how the Mate did saie, I shal pruve to ye all that I did not Kyl the captaine, for this iland shal wash awaye to show my innosence. And you said the iland is now washing away, to show the Mate was innosent.

"You will minde I did tell you I had herd a verry diferant stories about that iland, and the way yt got hys name, and that I wolde get it write from my gransir, and write it for you. And see, dere Niclass, I have writ it here.

"When my great gransir, Captaine William Perse came to Virginia in 1607, in the ship *Sea Venture*, there was on bord a little Dutch boy, a kind of pouther monkey, and my great gransir liked hym much. This boy, after manie years, came and settled in James Citie in Virginia, where he dy'd verry olde, not manie yeres since. Thys Dirke Stone, for that was hez name, had ben a saylor man all heys life. He had sayled from Englande to Virginia, and to the Barbadoes and to New Englande manie times in the shippes *Bona Nova, Hopewell, Truelove, Frances Bonaventure, Hope, Swan*, and in the *Jewell*. He had served the Hogen Mogens under that famous saylor Andrew Block in a little ship called the *Henroost* (Unrest), and while with Captaine Block he came to your Province, and at the place the Dutch called Voshaven which olde Dirke sayd, meant Fox Harbor. So it happened that when the *Jewell* sayled from London with the flete, which bro't the worshipfool Master Wynthrop to Massachusetts, old Dirke was the Pilot of the *Jewell*. The peopel who came in these shippes did not know where they were to dwelle, and so first the flete went to the place called Nahumkick, near to Voshaven. And by and by they were minded to settle in Shawmut, which you call Boston, and which is in the bay called by the Dutch Voshaven. The shippes went into the bay, and laid nere a place called Nantascot, and cast anker behind an iland. Then the sun went down, and the winde rose and the surf roared on the beches.

"Dirke Stone was on the deck of the *Jewell*, and Master Codington, one of the passengers ask'd Dirke, as Dirke did thinke, about the noise. And Dirke told him the name of this noise in Dutch. For Master Codington had in the voyage been lerning from Dirke manie words of the Lubeckers and Flushingers speech, which Dirke knew verry well. And so whan Master Codington saide, What do you Dutch call that, Dirke said, 'Nixie Shmalt,' I do not know how to spel it, but it meaneth the Wail of the Water Spirits, or the Water Spirit is chiding. But Master Codington thought it was the name of the iland, and set it down on a map he had Nix his Mate Iland.

"And after that, in order to account for the name, Dirke did saie that your Massachusets peple had made up a fairy Tale about a Captaine Nix and hys mate, and a Kyling and a Hanging and a Sheriff and a necke-speche which was a prophecy, and how the prophecy was fulfilled, and it was all a Tale of a Tub, for there was no Captaine Nix, and he had no Mate, and the Mate did not kyl the Captaine, and he was not Hanged, and did not make any speche or prophecy.

"And manie a time did I heare my Grandsir Edward Burbeck say This was a Name which had Made a Storie, and not a Maid which had named a Storie, and wolde laugh, for he was a right merrie soule.

"This shal go by the Smack which hath brout out Winter's stockfish from youre towne.

"And may God have you in his keeping dear Niclass. From your loveing friend,   RICH: BURBECK.

"To Nicklass Merrit, at Marble Harbor in the province of Massachusets."

Let us close the chapter by adding this powerful poem, written in 1888 for the "Journal of Education."

NIX'S MATE.

"The tide runs strong, and the sea grows dark,
   Hark ye, Pilot! (Cling, clang, cling!)
The night-wind freshens and drives the bark;
      (Cling!)
The sluggish fog-horns fill the air,
And fitful is the beacon's glare,
And near us lies an island bare.
   Hark ye, hark ye!"
      (Cling — clang — cling!)

"Quiet, lad! 'tis the bell buoy tolls
As the heavy sea beneath it rolls.
The lights are bright on the long sea-wall:
I know the reefs where the breakers fall,
And I know where there are no rocks at all."

"But the isle is black, without shoals or sands,
   Hark ye, hark ye! (Cling, clang, cling!)
And black on the rock the beacon stands.
      (Cling!)

And the bell-buoy's voice has a warning tone,
And flares the light on the pile of stone:
What makes the isle so black and lone?
　Hark ye, hark ye!"
　　　　　(Cling — clang — cling!)

"That island, boy, was once fresh and green,
The fairest isle in the harbor seen;
'Tis the ghost of an isle that you yonder see:
Now the bell strikes one, now the bell strikes three,
And the night shade falls, and the wind blows free.

"The trees are gone, the fields, the shore,
And the heron comes to the reef no more;
No sea-gull's wing to the rock dips down,
Nor petrel white, nor sea-mew brown,
Nor boat stops there from port or town."

"Do you know the rocks of the reft sea-wall? —
　Hark ye, Pilot!"　(Cling, clang, cling!)
"I know where there are no rocks at all."
　　　　　(Cling!)
"Then, Pilot, we're safe; so tell to me
The tale of this isle on the haunted sea,
While the bell strikes one, and the bell strikes three;
　Hark ye, hark ye!"
　　　　　(Cling — clang — cling!)

"Listen, boy! the tide runs fast
Where the green isle lay in the years long past.
There once a gibbet the moon shone through,
And its iron frames the high winds blew, —
There the crimes of the sea received their due.

"Old Nix was a captain, hard and bold,
And he reaped the sea, and gathered gold:
He gathered gold, but one windy night
They found him dead 'neath the gunwale light,
And his mate stood near him, dumb and white.

"And his mate they seized, — a young sailor he, —
And charged him with murder upon the sea.
And they brought him here where the island lay,
Where the gibbet rose o'er the windy bay:
'Twas more than an hundred years to-day."

"O Pilot, Pilot! how dark it grows!
　Hark ye, hark ye!　(Cling, clang, cling!)
Across the bay the fog-wind blows.
　　　　　(Cling!)

The beacons turn in the fog-clouds drear,
And my head is dulled with nameless fear:
They did not hang that sailor here?
  Hark ye, hark ye!"
            (Cling — clang — cling!)

"Here lay the ship, and the island there,
And the sun on the summer oaks shone fair;
And they took him there 'mid the chains to die,
And he gazed on the green shores far and nigh,
Then turned his face to the open sky,

"And he said, 'Great Heaven, receive my prayer;
The shores are green, and the isle is fair:
To my guiltless life my witness be:
Let the green isle die 'mid the sobbing sea,
And the sailors see it, and pity me.

"'In her old thatched cottage my mother will spin,
And dream of her boy on the coast of Lynn,
Or watch from her door 'neath the linden-tree;
O Heaven! just Heaven! my witness be,
Let the island beneath sink into the sea!

"'Let it waste, let it waste in the moaning waves,
With its withered oaks and its pirates' graves,
Till it lie on the waters black and bare,
The ghost of an isle 'mid the islands fair,
Where bells shall toll, and beacons glare!'

"He died, and the island shrank each year:
The green trees withered, the grass grew sere;
And the rock itself turned black and bare,
And lurid beacons rose in air,
And the bell-buoy rings forever there.

"The bell-buoy rings in the moaning sea,
And it now strikes one, and it now strikes three!"
                    HEZEKIAH BUTTERWORTH.

Rainsford Island.

THE ANTINOMIAN ELDER.—AN ANCIENT SUMMER RESORT.—THE BOSTON ALMSHOUSE.

SEVEN miles from town, and half a mile from Long Island, the pleasant little island of Rainsford rises from the harbor, near the entrance of the Western Way, with hardly a dozen acres of soil, drawn out for half a mile, and indented with many a pretty cove and miniature bay. Its two bluffs are connected by a low and narrow isthmus, from which the all-devouring sea receives continuous repulses, along the line of the sea-wall. Its first white resident appears to have been Elder Edward Raynsford, to whom the island was probably granted in 1636, at the request of Owen Rowe, of London, who wrote to Governor Winthrop, asking that "Mr Ransford may be accommodated with lands for a farme, to Keepe my cattle, that so my stocke may be preserved." He was the first ruling elder of the Old South Church, a large landholder on Long Island, and one of the substantial men of the Colony. There is a tradition that he came from a very good English family, and that his brother, Sir Richard Rainsford, succeeded Sir Matthew Hale as Lord Chief Justice of the King's Bench. Nevertheless, the colonial authorities disarmed him, in 1637, for heresy. (What mountains of revolvers and brooms would fill the State House, if that dereliction were similarly punished to-day!) Yet, though a heretic, and possibly even an Antinomian, it is said that the good elder bought his little domain of its Indian lords, preferring a just title to one founded on the right of might. Here he lived during many years, with his wife and children, until 1680, when he died; and eight years later his wife was buried in King's Chapel Burying-Ground. After her death the island-property was divided, passing through many hands, until, in 1737, Boston bought it, of the Lorings of Hull, for £570, "to be used and improved for a publick hospital for the reception and accommodation of such sick and infectious persons as shall be sent there by order." A hospital was erected, having four rooms on a floor, and a proper person put in charge. Until 1852 Rainsford's Island was used as a quarantine.

As early as 1677, just after the close of King Philip's War, a vessel was quarantined in Nantasket Roads, with the small-pox; but sundry people from the villages about the harbor boarded her, and the dread infection was soon let loose in Massachusetts, nearly a thousand persons falling victims.

This grim lesson taught the Colony people the need of stricter quarantine regulations; and, after several attempts elsewhere, they established their lazaretto on this sequestered islet. It appears to have been under the joint control of Boston and Massachusetts; and the keepers of the Light-house and the commanders of the Castle had orders to send there all vessels in which contagious diseases were found.

Occasionally junketing-parties visited the island, even in those ancient days, on a variety of pretexts. Ezekiel Price tells us, in his diary, that, on Sept. 2, 1778, he went down the harbor to Hospital Island, with the selectmen and other Boston gentlemen, and "had a view of the French fleet then in the harbour, as well as those stationed in Nantasket Harbour; they made a very formidable appearance, and were disposed so as to protect us from any approach of the British Navy."

Nearly three-quarters of a century ago, the sweet singer of the harbor thus apostrophized "Rainsford's pleasant little isle:"—

> "The sailor here when dire disease
> His body has opprest;
> May lie upon the bed of ease,
> With kind attentions blest.
>
> "Here Welch, the son of healing art,
> Will due prescriptions give;
> And use each mean to soothe the heart,
> And make the suff'rer live.
>
> "Here sprightly youth may exercise,
> Upon the bowling green;
> When no rude storms deform the skies,
> And nature shines serene.
>
> "Long may the legislative care,
> Thy kind protection be;
> And long may Mercy's hand prepare,
> Her dwelling-place in thee."

On Great Head stands the Old Mansion House, built in 1819, which was for many years the chief summer resort in the harbor, and has given comfortable shelter to many well-known Bostonians of the old *régime*. The town authorities allowed the keepers to take boarders, when no infectious diseases were upon the island; and the fever and small-pox hospitals were often crowded, besides the old mansion. It must have been a grewsome summer-resort, and abounding in suggestions not conducive to hilarity; yet our grandfathers appear to have found real and lively pleasure here. The North Bluff (or Great Head) also has the superintendent's house, the old dead-house, and several other buildings, besides the wharf at which the city steamboat touches. These houses are now mainly used for pauper women. The West Head is that part of the island west of the narrow isthmus, and is devoted to pauper men. Here is the long, low building erected for the Fever Hospital, and generally known as the Bowling Alleys.

The imposing Greek temple on high ground beyond was the Small-Pox Hospital, and not (as its appearance indicates) the shrine of the tutelar divinity of the harbor. It is a stone building, and dates from 1832. Near by is a high promontory of slate projecting to the southward into the harbor, and sheltering two pretty coves. The graveyard is on West Head, and

Rainsford Island.

has monuments nearly a century and a half old, many of which bear pathetic records. Here are buried most of the old keepers of the island, and many sailors and officers of foreign ships, who have ended their voyages here. Up to a date well within the present century, it was the custom for Boston families to send their members, when taken with dangerous infectious diseases, to the island, whence they were tolerably certain never to return. Numbers of these unfortunates rest in the local cemetery. Although within sight of the spires of their home-town, they were rigidly isolated on this dreary strand, and allowed to drift down into the darkness of death without the comfort and support of their neighboring friends and relatives. Many years ago a remarkable stone tomb was discovered here, containing a skeleton and an iron sword-hilt. Dr. J. V. C. Smith, who, as Port Physician, spent many years on the island, wrote a fanciful account of this grim treasure-trove, suggesting a strange history.

In 1852 the State took possession of Rainsford, for a pauper colony, and spent about $100,000 in buildings and improvements. The State institution was broken up in 1866, and its inmates went to the inland almshouses.

In 1872 Boston bought the island and all its buildings, for $40,000, and the large hospital was converted into a city almshouse. Up to the year 1882 a number of ex-soldiers, Massachusetts veterans of the Secession War, were kept here, living on the cold bread of municipal charity. At that time they were transferred to the new Soldiers' Home, on Powder-Horn Hill, Chelsea, where they can pass their broken old age in honor and peace, and free from the taint of pauperism.

In the good time coming, when chronic poverty shall have become a matter only of tradition, this beautiful and picturesque little gem of the sea, with its rocky shores and snug coves, and its noble view out on the Atlantic, may become once more an abode of summer pleasure, resorted to by the elegant patrician descendants of the plain shopkeepers who used to weather the dog-days in the Small-Pox Hospital forty years ago.

Peddock's Island and its Tragedy.

GRAPE AND SLATE ISLANDS. — NUT ISLAND AND ITS ARTILLERY. — HANGMAN'S ISLAND.

THE most conspicuous object in the view from the west end of Hull is the quiet and peaceful Peddock's Island, where, between two bold grassy bluffs, several snug houses are seen, clearly outlined against a background of dark-green orchards. Here dwell the Cleverlys, who, father and son, have piloted vessels into Weymouth and Quincy for half a century. From their sitting-room windows they look down Nantasket Roads and seaward, and watch their vessels coming in. From the East Head a magnificent view is gained over the lower harbor, and down on to Fort Warren, only a mile away. This fine hill is separated from Windmill Point and the Hotel Pemberton by the narrow and rushing strait of Hull Gut, a quarter of a mile wide. Thence the island rambles away to the south-west, hill and dale and isthmus, with four miles of coast-line, to within less than a mile of the shores of Quincy. The semi-insulated bluff of Prince's Head long supported the ponderous ironclad targets upon which Norman Wiard's great guns played from Nut Island, their hurtling missiles tearing and piercing the iron plates as if they had been pine planks.

Not one in ten thousand of the happy summer idlers who sail by Peddock's know that it was once the scene of a tragedy of terrible results, which were thus recorded two hundred and fifty years ago: "It fortuned, some few yeares, before the English came to inhabit at new Plimmouth in New England; that upon some distaste given in the Massachusetts bay, by Frenchmen, then trading there with the Natives for beaver, they set upon the men, at such advantage, that they killed manie of them, burned their shipp, then riding at Anchor by an Island there, now called Peddocks Island in memory of Leonard Peddock that landed there (where many wilde Auckies haunted that time which hee thought had bin tame), distributing them unto 5 Sachems which were Lords of the severall territories adjoyninge. They did keep them so longe as they lived, onely to sport themselves at them, and made these five Frenchmen fetch them wood and water, which is the generall worke that they require of a servant. One of these five men out livinge the rest had learned so much of their language, as to rebuke them for their bloudy deeds, saying that God would be angry with them for it; and that hee would in his displeasure destroy them; but the

Salvages (it seems boasting of their strength,) replyed and say'd, that they were so many, that God could not kill them. But contrary wise in short time after, the hand of God fell heavily upon them, with such a mortall stroake, that they died on heapes, as they lay in their houses; and the living that were able to shift for themselves would runne away, & let them dy, and let there Carkases ly above the ground without buriall. For in a place where many inhabited, there hath been but one left alive, to tell what became of the rest, the livinge being (as it seems) not able to bury the dead, they were left for Crowes, Kites, and vermin to pray upon. And the bones and skulls upon the severall places of their habitations, made such a spectacle after my comming into those partes, that as I travailed in that Forrest, nere the Massachussets, it seemed to mee a new-found Golgotha."

In these words does Morton, one of the earliest settlers, narrate the tragedy of Peddock's Island, and the Divine wrath which, as the savages believed, came upon the red tribes. The *auckies* spoken of were probably great auks, a strange penguin-like bird, which Dr. Elliott Coues says was once common on these shores, but cannot now be found south of Labrador. Somewhat later, Morton received a more circumstantial account of the massacre of the French sailors from a chief who was engaged in the terrible work. "The Salvagis seemed to be good freinds with vs while they feared vs, but when they see famin prevail, they begun to insult, as apeareth by the seaquell; for on of thay^r Pennesses or Chef men, Caled Pexsouth, implyed himself to Learne to speek Einglish, obsarving all things for his bloudy ends. He told me he Loued Einglish men very well, but he Loued me best of all. Then he said, 'you say ffrench men doe not loue you, but I will tell you what wee have done to y^m. Ther was a ship broken by a storm. Thay saued most of they^r goods & hid it in the Ground. We maed y^m tell us whear it was. Y^n we maed y^m our sarvants. Thay weept much. When we parted them, we gaue y^m such meat as our dogs eate. On of y^m had a Booke he would ofen Reed in. We Asked him 'what his Booke said.' He answered, 'It saith, ther will a people, like French men, com into this Cuntry and driue you all a way, & now we thincke you ar thay.' We took Away thay^r Clothes. Thay liued but a little while. On of them Liued Longer than the Rest, for he had a good master & gaue him a wiff. He is now ded, but hath a sonn Alive. An other Ship Came into the bay wth much goods to Trucke, y^n I said to the Sacham, I will tell you how you shall have all for nothing. Bring all our Canows and all our Beauer & a great many men, but no bow nor Arrow Clubs, nor Hachits, but knives vnder ye scins y^t About our Lines. Throw vp much Beauer vpon thay^r Deck; sell it very Cheep & when I giue the word, thrust yor knives in the French mens Bellys. Thus we killed y^m all. But Monnsear Ffinch, Master of thay^r ship, being wounded, Leped into ye hold.

We bidd him com vp, but he would not. Then we cutt thay^r Cable &
ye Ship went Ashore & lay upon her sid & slept ther. Ffinch cam vp &
we killed him. Then our Sacham devided thay^r goods and ffiered they^r
Ship, & it maed a very greeat fier. Som of our Company Asked y^m 'how
long it was Agoe sinc thay first see ships?' Thay said thay could not tell,
but thay had heard men say ye first ship y^t thay see, seemed to be a floting
Iland, as thay suposed broken of from the maine Land, wrapt together w^h
the roats of Trees, with some trees upon it. Thay went to it with thay^r
Canows, but seeing men and hearing guns, thay maed hast to be gon."

The Pilot's House.   Peddock's Island.

Many years later traditions of these events lingered around the Bay, and
pieces of French money were found near the Indian villages of Dorchester. But no record can be found of Leonard Peddock, who has left so
great a monument in our harbor.

In 1634 the island was granted to Charlestown, for twenty years, to keep
cattle upon. The rich, sweet grass on the bluffs seems to have been very
kindly food for domestic animals; for in May, 1775, there were 30 cattle
and 500 sheep here, which a raiding party of amphibious American infantry
swept off, and carried to the mainland. The next year 600 militia of Boston
and the Old Colony encamped here, to guard the harbor entrance. In spite
of Sir Edmund Andros's dictum, that an Indian deed to land was of "no

more value than the scratch of a bear's claw," the people of Hull were careful to secure a grant of the island from one of the last Massachusee sachems; and the domain was early taken from Charlestown and given to Nantasket, whose people divided it up, each taking four acres.

In 1778 the great French fleet of the Count D'Estaing, battered by storms and by British guns, took refuge in Boston Harbor. While the vessels were being refitted, large numbers of the soldiers and sailors were set ashore on the islands, where they erected fortifications. Soon afterwards a British fleet of a hundred sail approached the harbor, but were fain to turn to sea again when they saw the island-forts. There is a tradition that the outer head of Peddock's was fortified at this time; and very faint remains of the old intrenchments are still pointed out. As Chevalier states in his history of the French navy, "Des batteries étaient déjà commencées sur quelques-unes des nombreuses îles qui avoisinaient la rade." As he previously gives a minute description of the French forts at Hull and George's Island, this paragraph must refer to other localities near Nantasket Roads, of which Peddock's afforded the best site for defensive works.

There are grewsome traditions of wrecks on these bold shores, one of them relating to a plague-ship which drifted into the northern cove. It was perhaps thought best to have a domain so associated with suffering and death placed under some form of ecclesiastical supervision, and Peddock's became a part of the parsonage-lands of Hull. About twenty years ago it was bought by Miss Sallie Jones of Hingham, who now owns the entire island save a narrow strip of eight acres. There is a landing-stage near Cleverly's house; and in August camping-parties frequent certain parts of the island, their white tents making pretty contrasts with the dark bluffs. Peddock's is a series of lenticular hills, almost insulated from each other, and joined only by low bars. The hotel guests at Hull enjoy the results of the cattle grazing along these curving highlands, and the fruits and vegetables of the little farm. Nor are the higher senses without satisfaction here; for one of Foxcroft Cole's best paintings (much admired at the St. Botolph Club) portrayed the lovely view down the glen back of the houses, and the luxuriant orchard, with its network of wind-twisted boughs.

In the southern port of the harbor, beyond Peddock's, are several interesting little islands, rarely visited by summer explorers, yet each helping to make up the lovely panorama of blended sea and shore. Grape Island, a rather pretty and fertile islet, lies off the mouths of the two Weymouth Rivers, and covers about fifty acres, which are gracefully disposed in two swelling hills. About a furlong distant, to the eastward, rise the thickets and ledges of Slate Island. Grape has been for many years the abode of an eccentric old fisherman whom the harbor people call Captain Smith (a maritime simplification of his true name, which was Amos Pendleton), and who is distinguished equally for his dangerous temper, his Munchausen stories of a past life of crime, and his complicated and ingenious system of profanity. He claims to have been for many years an officer of a slave-ship, and afterwards of a smuggler on the Spanish Main; and, to the few visitors who could win his confidence, he told blood-curdling stories of battles with cruisers, and long flights over Southern seas, with English or Spanish men-of-war in hot pursuit, long-toms roaring, and slaves dying by scores in the hold. The scene would change from the coast of Africa to the bayous of Louisiana, or the lagoons of South America; but everywhere the story was of horror and bloodshed. Captain Smith has a sinister reputation among the yachtsmen and fishermen of the harbor; and many stories are told of his firing upon invaders of his ancient solitary realm, and planting bird-shot in inconvenient localities. But the writer of this chronicle wandered at will over the domains of this sanguinary hermit, from the great

Peddock's Island.

bowlders on the eastern point to the shell-heaps which the savages left here so long ago, and up the grassy hills, nor heard nor saw the legendary shot-gun which holds four yacht-clubs at bay. Here and there bevies of horses were enjoying the rich pasturage; the perfume of the noble forest on the adjacent Hingham shore came off on the land-breeze; and in the hollow, near the cold spring and the deep water on the south of the island, nestled the snug little house, among its vegetable-gardens.

This was one of the favorite haunts of the Indians, who, like their successors in the land, delighted in large and juicy clams, skilfully baked among hot rocks and fragrant sea-weed. Ring after ring of these stones has been found here, set up edgewise, with beds of clean beach-gravel in the enclosed spaces. Here the careful searcher may still find stone tomahawks, with which, in long-past days, the red epicures broke the clam-shells, while they enjoyed their jovial feasts, and made inscrutable and polysyllabic Massachusee jokes. The esculent clams are still found in great numbers on the western bar.

In 1775 four small British vessels came down from Boston, and anchored off this point, to the intense alarm of the Old-Colony towns, over whose peaceful plains the roar of alarm-guns, the rapid clanging of guns, and the bickering of drums were quickly heard. The rumor fled down the country-side, that 300 red-coats were marching on Weymouth; and all the houses in Old Spain were deserted by the people. Nearly 2,000 well-armed minute-men assembled to cover the towns; and when they found that the object of the naval expedition was the hay on Grape Island, a strong force of rural musketeers put off in boats brought round from Hingham, intending to engage the enemy, and save the Yankee forage. But the raiding-party made haste to get upon their vessels, and sailed away to Boston, happy in the acquisition of several tons of fine hay. Meantime the whole country was aroused, the minute-men made hundreds of ineffectual pot-shots at the scarlet harvesters; and the British schooner-of-war cannonaded Eastward Neck with all her might.

Slate Island, comprising about twelve acres, and nearly nine and a half miles from Boston, is difficult of access except at high tide; but when reached the aptness of the name is evident, for its slaty ledges run far out into the water, their black edges fringed by the light spray. The little beaches are covered with splinters and slabs of slate, which are ground and beaten to and fro by the waves, when they surge around these silent shores. The venerable divine who wrote "New-England's Plantation," in 1630, spoke with enthusiasm of the existence of "plentie of Slates at the Ile of Slate in *Masathulets* Bay." Yet a year later Government ordered that no slate should be taken therefrom without permission. In 1650 the island was granted to William Torrey, with a reservation that "any man shalbe free to make use of the slate." It remained in his possession only two years, passing then by grant to Hull.

Around the coast rise the ragged and irregular ledges of slate, well-nigh concealed in places by a luxuriant growth of brown sea-weed and masses of kelp, which seem only floating upon the water's top, though they cling so closely to the rocks below, giving to the island an appearance as if hidden dangers were continually lurking around it. Clambering over the rocks, and across the tiny beaches covered with splinters and fragments of slate, and passing many ancient excavations, one suddenly gets entangled in the high bushes which cover and crown the little island, making of its crest a hopeless jungle. Here, in July, grow the rarest and sweetest red-raspberries, and the perfect golden-rod, —

> "Graceful, tossing plume of glowing gold,
> Waving lonely on the rocky ledge;
> Leaning seaward, lovely to behold,
> Clinging to the high cliff's ragged edge," —

and the sad little purple aster, which dares to stay later than either of the others, until the chilling frosty breezes come down the Bay. On the north and west, towards Grape Island, are low gray cliffs of slate-rock, tier after tier, standing upon edge, or slanting backward or forward like ancient time-worn and weather-beaten tombstones. Here schooners load with the slate; and one may see the quarries, all along, from which they have taken the material for countless cellar-walls and underpinnings. Were its quality better, who knows but that Slate Island, with its rocks and flowers, might vanish as utterly as Nix's Mate has done?

In a rude little hut near the southern shore long dwelt a strange hermit, whose lonely and sequestered life was the subject of many winter-evening stories among the peaceful farms of Hingham. Here was a solitude to which Thoreau's hermitage, surrounded with friendly flowers and fraternal trees, and visited often by respectful Concordians, was as lively as Scollay Square after a *matinée*. In this poor anchorite "the Ile of Slate" may have found its romance, sealed to the world.

Nut Island lies in Quincy Bay, 7½ miles from Boston, a little to the north of Great Hill on Hough's Neck, and was sometimes called Hough's Tombs on the queer old eighteenth-century charts. It rises

Peace and War, Nut Island.

sharply on one side into a tall, slightly concave highland, the top of which is fairly rounded and covered with green grass and summer flowers, and slopes gently down again to the water on the other side. Just at the foot of the cliff are one or two sturdy trees, a few deserted cannon, a wharf and track, and three fishermen's huts. The guns are immense, and some of them have been exploded by the great tests to which they were subjected. Yonder are the sand-banks which seem to have stood unyielding their heavy fire, though not so the iron plates lying thereabouts, bent, broken, and pierced through. Many experiments in ordnance have been tried on this sequestered islet; and one can see faintly in the distance on Prince's Head the bluff at which the shots were aimed, although they sometimes fell wide of their mark, ricocheting over the waters, and dropping into the waters about Hull. One of these huge missiles even cut the spile from the upper wharf, startling the good people of Hull, and disturbing the quiet of their peaceful little cemetery on the hill-slope, where it finally landed. This shot weighed 400 pounds, and with great labor was hauled to the hotel, only to be reclaimed by the United States. In October, 1876, a Wiard gun fired a 531-pound shot through 12 inches of solid wrought-iron plates on the Prince's-Head target, 1,650 yards distant. Not far from half a million dollars were spent in the experiments made here by Norman Wiard, in endeavors to find the gun of the future. Here occurred the famous tests of the fifteen-inch breech-loading rifle, made at South Boston, and found to have a range of six miles, and power to drive a shot through twenty inches of iron plate. The newly adopted hydraulic gun-carriages also received their most efficient tests here.

It is very important to have such a testing-ground for heavy ordnance in this vicinity, since the chief manufactory of American fortress-guns is at South Boston. Here, at the famous Alger Foundry, the process of gun-making has been studied as a science for fifty years, during which time 2,000 pieces of heavy ordnance and 500,000 projectiles have been made for the United-States Government. Of these the number furnished during the late Secession War were 700 bronze guns and howitzers, 700 iron guns, 332 of the great Rodmans (of ten-inch calibre and larger), and a few heavy rifles. Here also were made the fifteen-inch Rodmans, weighing twenty-five tons each, with wonderful powers of endurance in long firing. Among these were the guns with which the *Monitor* fought the *Merrimac*, the splendid armament of the *New Ironsides*, and some of the heaviest pieces at Fortress Monroe.

A short bar connects the island with Hough's Neck on the south, and the shallow strait may be forded at low tide. Some years ago a merry party of summer pleasurers drove down here, and essayed to navigate their horse and carriage to the island. But the tide was too far advanced; and the vehicle capsized in deep water, and left several of its occupants to drown. The view from Nut Island is very pretty towards Hough's Neck, across the fields and treetops, and past the towns and villages beyond to the distant Blue Hills; and the air is fragrant with the odors from the flowers and fruits of the shore. Morton, "the Lord of Misrule," wrote that " There are divers arematicall herbes, and plants, as Sassafras, Muske, Roses, Violets, Balme, Laurell, Hunnisuckles, and the like, that with their vapors perfume the aire; and it has bin a thing much observed that, shipps have come from Virginea where there have bin scarce five men able to hale a rope, untill they have come within 40 Degrees of latitude, and smell the sweet aire of the shore, where they have suddainly recovered." And he should certainly know, for he was familiar with every thing about his home, and especially with this locality. Morton tells this little story of himself and Bubbles, the berated " Master of Ceremonies " at Merry-Mount: " To-

SKETCHES ON NUT ISLAND.

gether Bubbles and hee goes in the Canow to Nut Island for brants, and there his host makes a shotte and breakes the winges of many. Bubbles in hast and single handed, paddels out like a Cow in a cage; his host cals back to rowe two handed like to a pare of oares, and before this could be performed, the fowles had time to swimme to other flockes, and so to escape; the best part of the pray being lost, mayd his host to mutter at him, and so to parte for that time discontended." There are still many fowls at Nut Island, apparently not in the least disturbed by guns greater than Morton's; and could the jolly lord return now with Bubbles, he might perchance think more of the shooting and less of the fowls.

Hangman's Island stands well out in Quincy Bay, with open waters on all sides. It is hardly more than a reef, with deep channels all around, and a convenient strip of beach on the south. Here are several snug little huts of fisher-folk; and among the rocks are patches of corn, potatoes, and other vegetables in their seasons, among which the crickets chirp merrily during the long summer days. Here and there bloom clusters of wild flowers, leaning over the dark ledges, and outliving the gales; and occasionally an adventurous bird, flying from the mainland, rests on the beaten crags. The origin of the name of this inhabited rock is obscure, and hardly invites speculation. Perhaps some of the ancient pirates met their fate here, and the gloomy tragedy is thus commemorated. On a chart published in London in 1775, it is called *Hayman's Island*, and covers a much larger area than at present.

Far in-shore, on the broad flats which stretch out from Mount Wollaston, rises the narrow and singularly curved Half-moon Island; and on the east side of Hough's Neck is Raccoon Island, an irregular tract of ten acres, overlooking the broadenings of Weymouth Fore River. Well out in the centre of the Bay, east of Nut Island, Sheep Island breaks above the blue plain of waters, with its two acres of level ground, whereon, in ancient times, the farmers of the adjacent mainland kept their little flocks, securely fenced by the surges of Massachusetts Bay. Many years ago it bore the name of Sun Island, but it is difficult to imagine why. The snug little domain is now frequently occupied by camping parties, whose tents are visible from the Nantasket and Hingham steamboats, running close by to the eastward.

Less than a mile distant, across the channel, rises the high round hill of Pumpkin, Bumpkin, or Ward's Island, a conspicuous green dome, arabesqued with daisies and thistle-tops, and covering nearly fifty acres. It was bequeathed by Samuel Ward to Harvard College, in 1682, and still belongs to and yields an income to the University.

The Penal Colony of Deer Island.

GODIVA'S HEIR. — THE CHRISTIAN INDIANS. — ANCIENT MERRYMAKINGS. — BOSTON'S PRISONS AND CHARITIES.

 EVER was fairer site found for a convict-colony than Deer Island, at the mouth of Boston Harbor, which has at different times been the abode of thousands of unwilling guests, in its great municipal buildings, — the House of Reformation for juvenile offenders, the House of Industry, and the Almshouse. It is a little continent in itself, with the tall bluffs of North, East, South, and Graveyard Heads, and the high ridge of Signal Hill, with many an incipient cape and miniature bay. There are also two ponds of fresh water amid the environment of salty waves; whereof one is known as Ice Pond, since it yields large stores of ice for the summer use of the islanders; and the other as Cow Pond, because the cattle of this penal colony find in it their daily drink. The island is nearly a mile long, and covers 184 acres, with a broad margin of flats. It is $4\frac{1}{2}$ miles from Long Wharf, and nearly a mile from Nix's Mate and Long-Island Head, across Broad Sound. On the west, Shirley Gut separates it from Point Shirley, in Winthrop, with a rushing strait of salt water, narrowed down at one point to 325 feet across, where occasionally a few of the more daring boys, tired of their island prison, have swam across, or drowned in the attempt. If safely landed on the opposite side, they are almost sure to be re-captured by the officials, when they always say, "We were only goin' home to see the folks, and comin' right back." On the side where the waves of the Bay dash against the bluffs, the National Government has built a costly and massive stone sea-wall. The *débris* from the bluffs, in stormy weather, had already formed two long bars; one running towards Point Shirley, and the other towards the Graves. The dark pyramidal beacon well out in the water towards Long Island marks the site of the southern tip of ancient Deer Island, which has been washed away for hundreds of feet.

> "The waves unbuild the wasting shore:
> Where mountains towered, the billows sweep."

Four years after Boston was settled, a traveller spoke of "Deare Ilande, so-called because of the Deare which often swimme thither from the Maine, when they are chased by the Woolves. Some have killed sixteen Deare in a day upon this Ilande." About the same time Morton of Merry-Mount wrote thus, in similar vein: "On all these [deare] the Wolfes doe pray continually. The best meanes they have to escape the wolfes is by swimming to Ilands, or necks of land, whereby they escape; for the wolfe will not presume to follow them, untill they see them over a river; then being landed, (they wayting on the shore) undertake the water, and so follow with fresh suite." A more modern romancer gives a vivid account of Sir Harry Vane, Endicott, and Winthrop, and their Pequot slaves, hunting the deer here, with arquebuse and arbalest. Then there were high forests and grassy glades, swamps and thickets, all over the island. Although Motley speaks of moose on the South Shore, these were the common Virginian deer, such as now abound in the Plymouth woods. In 1634 this fine game-preserve was granted to Boston, together with Long and Hog Islands, for £2 a year; and a year later Spectacle Island was included, and the annual tribute reduced to 4*s*. Massachusetts has never reclaimed this valuable piece of property from Boston, in whose possession it has since remained. In 1636 the Bostonians were given permission to cut wood here; and so the gallant groves, which had so long breasted the north-easters, went down before the Puritan axes. Five years later the island became a pound, in which to keep stray domestic animals; and a building was erected to shelter them. In 1644-47 it was leased to Penn and Oliver, for £7 a year, which went to the school-fund; and later Bendall hired it for £14 a year. In 1655 the cutting of wood was prohibited; and seven years later the lease reverted to Sir Thomas Temple, a reputed descendant of Earl Leofric of Mercia and Lady Godiva of Coventry, and cousin of the famous Sir William Temple. After his several years in New England, he returned home, and befriended the colonies at court. Once when King Charles was upbraiding Massachusetts for having coined money, a sovereign prerogative, Sir Thomas showed him a pine-tree shilling. "But what is this tree upon the coin?" exclaimed the irate monarch. To whom the knight rejoined, "That is the oak in which Your Majesty found shelter;" and Charles, greatly pleased, cried out, "They are a parcel of honest dogs!" Sir Thomas's great-grand-nephew, born on one of the harbor islands, became famous as Sir John Temple, Surveyor-General of Customs in England. A town in New Hampshire was named for him. Certainly it is a strange and noteworthy dispensation which makes of one of our islands the birthplace of a descendant of Lady Godiva. His father, Robert Temple, came to New England in 1718, and built a very handsome mansion on Noddle's Island. He married the daughter of Captain John Nelson of Long Island; and the granddaughter of this noble couple, the daughter of Sir John Temple, was the mother of the Hon. Robert C. Winthrop.

One of the native proprietors of Deer Island was Winnepurkitt, the last sagamore of Lynn, who married the daughter of Passaconaway, the renowned chieftain of the New-Hampshire tribes. It will be remembered that Winnepurkitt was the hero of Whittier's poem of "The Bridal of Pennacook," who dwelt where, —

> "faint with distance came the stifled roar,
> The melancholy lapse of waves on that low shore."

He became sachem in 1633, and in 1676 was transported to Barbadoes, — a deadly change from his cool and breezy northern shores. In 1685 the Indian chiefs Wampatuck (grandson of Chickataubut) and David (son of Sagamore George) were well paid to give a quit-claim of the island, which, however, Sir Edmund Andros endeavored to wrest from its tenant.

No sadder scene has New England ever witnessed than Deer Island

The House of Industry, Deer Island

in 1675-76, when, during the panic caused by King Philip's War, Massachusetts tore the Christian Indians from their inland villages, and confined them upon this bleak and dreary strand. The penalty of death was enacted against any who should leave this gloomy prison, and if any one should help them to escape he should be punished "as a man-stealer." Yet the Province appointed officials to go down regularly, and keep them well fed and supplied. Eliot, their saintly apostle, said that the Indian Christians went to their captivity "patiently, humbly, and piously, without murmuring or complaining against ye English," sailing on the downward tide at midnight, from the present site of Watertown. Through the dreary winter, their chief sustenance was fish and clams; their only shelter the scanty thickets and the lee sides of the bluffs. Out of this 500 martyrs to English distrust very many died, and were sadly buried by the moaning and misty sea. Later in the winter, as town after town was destroyed by the hostile tribes, and homeless fugitives poured even into Boston, the hard-pressed Provincials sent down to Deer Island, asking for volunteers. Many of the captives came forward, and were armed and sent to the frontiers (there were 50 in Capt. Hinchman's company alone); where they fought their red brethren with equal valor and skill, so that they slew 400 of them, and rescued many white captives. As Gen. Gookin then said, they "turned ye balance to ye English side, so that ye enemy went down ye wind amain." In May, 1676, the surviving women and children and old men were returned to their villages in honor. Thereafter the island was used as a prison for hostile Indians captured in war. Some of these Christian Indians, and many of the captured heathen, were sent into slavery in the West Indies, from whence they never returned. Others were sold at Tangier, and elsewhere on the African coast; and Eliot, the saintly apostle, followed them, even in their distant Saracen prisons, with his letters and counsels.

Eighty years later a nobler sight was seen, when a splendid naval procession emerged from Broad Sound, and, rounding the east point of Deer Island, bore away for the north-east, to the victorious siege of Annapolis Royal. It included the frigates *Success*, *Mermaid*, and *Siren*, and 33 transports, in which were upwards of 5,000 British and Provincial soldiers. Another score of years passed by, and the old comrades became antagonists, when His Majesty's army was blockaded in Boston. In June, 1775, Major Greaton captured a British man-of-war's barge and crew here, and carried from the island 800 sheep and many horses,—very useful supplies for the Continental army at Cambridge, and sorely missed by the hungry red-coats up the Bay. In 1813 fortifications were erected here by the Boston militia, to prevent a naval attack by Broad Sound or Shirley Gut. The island was then well known as a summer resort, and had a notable hotel and ballroom, with swings, bowling-alleys, and other familiar adjuncts of modern excursion life. This was a favorite resort of the picnic-parties of that period; and here frequently came the annual excursion of the West Church of Boston. In 1823 the last of these trips was made, "accompanied by a very large and respectable number of citizens. . . . The day was fine, entertainment very good, and agreeable to all." The interest of the locality was probably not lessened by its ghastly tradition, which was rehearsed with bated breath by the people of the lower islands. Dominie Brown thus hints at it:—

> "For oft I've heard the story told,
> How ghost, without a head;
> Here guards some thousand pounds in gold,
> By some strange fancy led."

In the spring of 1882 a band of Zuñi Indians from the mysterious pueblos of New Mexico visited Deer Island, to perform their strange religious ceremonies on the shores of "The Ocean of Sunrise," and to fill their ancestral vases with the sacred water of the sea. They were attended by 300 citizens, including many prominent divines and scholars. Advancing far out on the rocks, they chanted strange songs of prayer, and offered sacrifices to the waves, praying, "Make the roads of life for ourselves and for our children to be prolonged." These ceremonials were continued upon the beach after the tide had driven them shoreward; and Mr. Cushing, who had long been a resident of Zuñi, was there initiated into the high religious order of the Kaukau, an order which is many centuries old.

The construction of municipal institutions began in 1847, when Boston

Convicts at Work.

built here several large buildings for sheltering Irish emigrants, of whom more than 10,000 landed between January and July. The terrible scourge of ship-fever made formidable ravages among these new-comers, hundreds of whom died upon the island, and were buried and forgotten. About three years later the large city building was erected, at a cost of $150,000. In 1858 the House of Reformation was established; and the buildings of the farm-school and the asylum for pauper girls date from 1869.

The main building is a large brick edifice, with three wings projecting from a high central block crowned with a cupola, and is the most conspicuous object in the outer harbor. In its western front is the home of the superintendent and his family; and the great nave and transepts of this cathedral of Lucifer are occupied by the cells and dormitories, kitchens and dining-rooms, workshops and schoolrooms, of the army of the criminal classes. Here, also, is the spacious chapel, where religion finds a harder and more hopeless (but more necessary) task than under the splendid towers of Trinity Church, or in the solemn aisles of the Cathedral of the Holy Cross. It is, however, a pleasing and pathetic sight when the long lines of uniformed boys file into the galleries, and sing their hearty songs to the music of the band which has been recruited from their own ranks. The schools connected with the reformatory institutions are widely famed for their efficiency and perfect equipment, and yearly give 300 or more boys and girls

A Lively Sea.

(from 7 to 19 years of age) thorough instruction. Most of these are reformation children and truants.

From the main building a broad avenue nearly two miles long runs to the wharf and around the island, past the various buildings, each one of which, though sad and unpleasant in its suggestions, is full of interest. In the greenhouse, perhaps the only building free from a prison atmosphere, are beautiful flowers of all kinds and varieties, and a little family of pretty tame squirrels. In front of the nursery, one of the smaller buildings, is a pretty garden, where in early spring peep out long lines of graceful little snowdrops, and brilliant, many-hued crocuses. Here are the poor little children, left homeless almost as soon as born: but tenderly cared for, spending a part of each day in the airy kindergarten, loving their dolls, or driving their tin horses until wearied, when the bright sunshine and air of the island is freely granted them in the play-grounds. Their ages vary from less than three to five or six; but all, from the smallest up, wear the dull uniform of charity. On the hill-slopes are the vegetable-gardens, abundant and successful; and here are raised enormous mangel-wurzel beets, some of which weigh twenty-five or thirty pounds each, and lie heaped up on the floor of the barn to assure the incredulous visitor. In the barns or on the hill are the gentle-eyed cattle; and, if one cares to see an endless number of pigs, an entire building is devoted to them on the southern point.

The drive around the island is everywhere beautiful, with the deep blue of the sea stretching out beyond, the distant isles dotted over the bay, and the white sails of vessels appearing upon the horizon, returning home from distant ports. The light-house stands out whitely, on its centre of rocky islands; and the flag over Fort Warren seems merely a speck of bright color. The eye returns again to the nearer surroundings, and perhaps rests

Scene at Deer Island.

on the queer brown seals sunning themselves on the rocks, and looking so much a part of them, that, but for their sudden disappearance into the water, one would not dream they were anything else. Yet they come in such numbers to one of the rocky little coves of the island near the sea-wall, that the bay has taken their name to itself. Nearing the wharf again, the view at the sunset hours is very charming, when the sky is reddening over the golden-domed hill, the crown of Boston, and the gulls are flying away seaward, while the sails of vessels at anchor, or sailing home, brighten with color until their very hulls seem all ablaze. As the sun falls lower, the blue hills grow grayer and grayer while the twilight steals over them, until they are lost in haze, and the murmur of the sea alone remains to charm the night.

The dwellers on Deer Island number from 1,200 to 1,500; and they are maintained at an annual cost of $150,000. The average expenditure for each person, deducting the amount earned in the work-shops of the institutions, is $1.96 a week. These are not the desperadoes of the Commonwealth, but rather its chronic unfortunates, the dregs of the great European immigration, — men and women who return here month after month, and year after year, having reached the mournful condition where all sense of shame and responsibility is lost. Perhaps the pure air and rigid decorum, the good food and safe shelter of the city institutions, afford a standing temptation to lure them from the gloomy squalor of the North End. Occasionally a delinquent American, grown uproarious in his cups, finds himself locked in with these thronging miserables, and spends penitential months in honest and monotonous labor. These crowded prison-halls are an example of the survival of the unfittest, — a sign of the growth of a fierce and formidable pauperism under conditions where it has no place and no apology. And yet — for each convict's elevation and purification Paul labored, and Washington fought, and (immeasurably above all else) Christ died.

The Deer-Island Ferry-Horn, Point Shirley.

Fort Warren, the Key of the Harbor.

GEORGE'S ISLAND. — THE GREAT FORTRESS. — SOUTHERN CHIEFTAINS. — GARRISON LIFE.

THE granite- and iron-covered George's Island is a little over six miles from Boston (seven by the channel), and covers 35 acres, defended by a long sea-wall, and rising to a bluff 50 feet high on the eastward. It is about a third of a mile south of Lovell's and Gallop's Islands, and a mile from Hull. The main ship-channel flows close under it on the north, and on the south are Nantasket Roads. The present name was given nearly two centuries ago, perhaps in honor of Captain John George, a prominent merchant and town functionary of Boston about the year 1710. The chief distinction of the locality at the present time is the fortress which covers the greater part of it, and is one of the most formidable defences of the eastern seaboard.

The proprietary history of George's Island may be stated in a few words. It was claimed by and granted to James Pemberton in the seventeenth century; he having made "proofe vppon oath, according to law, that he had possession and improvement of the s^d iland by the consent & approbation of the antient inhabitants or planters residents in or about the Matachusetts Bay above fower & twenty yeares agoe." From his family it passed into the possession of Samuel Greenleaf, whose daughter Hannah sold it to Elisha Leavitt, in 1765, for £340. The latter bequeathed the island to his grandson, Caleb Rice of Hingham, who sold it to the United States in 1825.

George's was so far from the Boston of the Puritans that it is not conspicuous in the town and colony records, and received but few and infrequent notices. It seems to have been an appanage of the fleet rather than of the colony, and all its old associations were with the shipping. On a fair August day in 1690, Judge Sewall and a large party of provincial officers went down "to see the Lieut. Generall Muster his Souldiers on Georges Island," and also inspected the fleet lying in the roads. Soon afterwards the ships and regiments sailed away to Canada, on Phips's unsuccessful expedition. 21 years later, when Sir Hovenden Walker's huge squadron and army lay in the Roads, their sick men were landed on the adjacent islands, and placed in impromptu hospitals. The first fortification on this site was erected in 1778, and consisted of a large earthwork, commanding the eastern approaches to Nantasket Roads. Its object was to protect the fleet of the Count d'Estaing, then lying at anchor in the harbor, from an attack by British cruisers, many of which then haunted the outer sea. Among the French ships were one of 90 guns, another of 80, and six of 74 each; huge floating castles, which had just been roughly handled by Earl Howe's fleet off Newport, fighting in a tempest. Many of their guns were landed here to arm the battery with. The great British fleet lay off the harbor, with Earl Howe and Sir Henry Clinton on board, and had some design of dashing in and engaging the crippled sea-lions of France among the islands; but the show of formidable shore-batteries deterred them, and thus an event which would have been invaluable for this Handbook was lost.

All the marines of the fleet, and large detachments of sailors, were landed on George's and at Hull, and set to work to fortify the approaches to the channels where the French vessels lay at anchor. On George's they erected six mortars and two batteries, one of eleven 14-pounders, and the other of eight 18- and 24-pounders, which could cross their fire with the thirty-gun fort on Nantasket. The largest of the frigates near by was the *César*, which had 60 men killed and 100 wounded in the recent naval battle, and now floated in the light-house channel, badly cut up.

In 1778 there were pilots living on George's, for Commodore Tucker's log speaks of them. Twenty years afterwards the island was the home of Thomas Crane, who had a stock-farm here, and also frequently entertained parties of summer excursionists. Here was born his famous son, Thomas Crane, who dwelt on this narrow realm for seven years, and often revisited it after he had become one of the greatest capitalists of New-York City. In May, 1882, the virtues and successes of this typical Yankee were made the theme of a noble oration by the younger Charles Francis Adams.

About the year 1833 the National Government began the construction of a first-class fortress here, to command the approaches to the harbor, and cover the city at a safe fighting distance. In August, 1847, the new military works were inspected by Robert J. Walker, the Secretary of the Treasury, although they were not finished until about three years afterwards. Gen. Thayer, who designed this, and the other modern forts hereabouts, was a native of Braintree, and for many years Superintendent of West-Point Military Academy. The United States kept him in Europe for five years, studying the Continental fortresses and military systems; and from 1833 to 1857 he was the constructing engineer of the defences of Boston. When the Secession War broke out, the Government felt great concern because the drawings and working-plans of Fort Warren could not be found; but, after Thayer's death, they turned up between the leaves of one of the huge old volumes of his military library. He is buried at West Point; and the tower of the handsome academy which he bequeathed to Braintree is conspicuous from many points in the harbor of Boston.

In 1861 there were no guns mounted on the fort; but Governor Andrew hurried the Second Battalion of State troops to the island, and applied to Col. Rodman for cannon. Gen. Peirce commanded here in May, and Gen. J. Andrews succeeded him. Great labor was performed by the volunteers, to make the deserted fort formidable; for the State authorities had lively fears of a Southern Armada steaming up Nantasket Roads, to demolish the city of Charles Sumner and Wendell Phillips. The *Cambridge*, *Pembroke*, and other vessels sent out at that time with Massachusetts troops, were well equipped with ordnance, and commissioned as armed transports; and the State school-ship received a battery, to act as a coast-guard. Even the Ancient and Honorable Artillery Company volunteered their services "for coast defence;" and the British residents of Boston formed a corps for

Fort Warren.

the same purpose. The regulars, scattered by companies over a territory greater than the Roman Empire, had more imminent service to perform; and the civilians of the Puritan capital sprang to arms, like their ancestors, the minute-men, and worried themselves into a saving knowledge of the use of great guns.

In May, June, and July, 1861, the Webster Regiment (12th Mass.) lay in camp here. Five of its companies were from Boston, one from Gloucester, and four from the Old Colony. Its colonel, the son of Daniel Webster, was killed in the battle of Groveton; and eighteen of its officers died from wounds received in the field. The thorough training given within these grim fortress walls made the Twelfth one of the most trusty regiments in the hard-buffeted Army of the Potomac. But the discipline of the garrison, and the imposing dimensions of the Rodman guns, did not fully comfort the good people up the Bay. Great alarm was felt at the defenceless condition of the port; and the General Court voted $1,500,000 to fortify the Massachusetts coast. State agents in London purchased many heavy Blakely guns for Fort Warren, which were afterwards sold to Chili, and helped to beat off the Spanish iron-clads from Valparaiso. Just after the raid of the rebel iron-clad *Merrimac* down Hampton Roads, the National authorities ordered Governor Andrew to seal up Boston Harbor, by sinking hulks at its entrance, so that hostile war-vessels might not be able to enter. This panicky despatch passed unheeded; but a complicated and ingenious system of obstructions was arranged, so that the harbor could be blockaded from within at very short notice. It did not tranquillize the perturbed Bostonians to hear, later in the war, that Jeff Davis had said, at Atlanta, that the *Alabama* and four other cruisers were about to run into Boston Harbor, and drop a few shells into the State House. He added that, "The forts may try to play ball a little, but the ships are such fast sailers they will not hurt them much."

Meantime, Col. Justin Dimick, the gallant old West-Point officer in command at Fort Warren, had converted his militiamen into a tolerably efficient garrison. As colonel of the First Artillery and a veteran of the Florida and Mexican wars, he should have been the first martinet in the army; but he preferred to look upon the pranks of his boys with a kindly tolerance, provided their military duties were well done. It happened, therefore, that from this happy garrison proceeded one of the most powerful influences which made themselves felt in the national armies during that long and weary war. The famous song of the national armies, "John Brown's body lies mouldering in the grave," was composed, and first sung, at Fort Warren, by the glee club of the Second Battalion Light Infantry, in the spring of 1861. It was adapted to an old Methodist camp-meeting tune, somewhat altered in form; and the Brigade Band at the fort was the first that played it. The singers entered the Twelfth Regiment, which marched through Boston, New York, and Baltimore, to this grand chorus from a thousand throats: and the music ran through the Army of the Potomac, nor ceased until grim and powder-blackened choirs had chanted it in Texas and Alabama, and down the great Mississippi, and on all the flowery coasts of the Gulf, and through the Carolinas, and along the streets of conquered Richmond. From Fort Warren came the Marseillaise of our emancipating revolution. As Admiral Preble says, "Few people, aside from those who kept step to its strains when leaving home for the battle-field, and sang it around the smoky camp-fire during the long dull nights and days of army life, know the extent of its popularity, and the deep hold it took upon the soldier's heart. It spread from regiment to regiment like wildfire. No song gained so firm a hold upon the troops; and it is safe to say that it was sung by every regiment — cavalry, infantry, and artillery — of the Army of the Potomac."

A few months after the war broke out, the dreaded rebels began to pour into the fort by hundreds, — not in storming-parties, but as prisoners of war, tributes to the prowess of the Northern infantry. Many Confederate officers and civilians of high rank suffered imprisonment here during those terrible years of fraternal strife. Prominent among these were Kane, the chief of police of Baltimore; Mayor Brown; and a number of Virginians from Fairfax and Loudon Counties. Other civilians who were under suspicion of disloyalty were immured within these grim walls, side by side with the gray-uniformed officers who had been swept in from hotly contested battle-

The U. S. Frigate "Constitution."

fields. Here were many political prisoners, gathered from the towns of the North, and charged with disloyalty to the United States. Among these appeared Judge Flanders and his brothers, of Malone, N.Y.; Robert Elliott, of Freedom, Me.; Ex-Captain H. L. Shields, of Bennington, Vt.; Hon. P. C. Wright, of St. Louis; Wm. H. Winder, of Philadelphia; Dr. MacGill, of Baltimore; and several members of the Maryland Legislature. In November, 1861, the steamship *State of Maine* brought here from Fort Lafayette 110 political and 645 military prisoners, who were provided with snug quarters in the casemates. In the accounts which many of these gentlemen have written of their life in Northern Bastilles, they credit Col. Dimick and his Massachusetts garrison with uniformly kind and considerate treatment, in marked contrast with the *régime* at Fort Lafayette. Here also were the famous rebel emissaries, Mason and Slidell, who had been captured by the U. S. S. *San Jacinto*, while on their way to Europe in an English mail-steamer. The threatening attitude of the British Government compelled the United States to release them; and on the morning of Jan. 1, 1862, the garrison was paraded under arms, with their backs to the gate, while the prisoners and their secretaries were conducted to the wharf, in a howling winter storm. They were carried across Massachusetts Bay in the tug *Starlight*, to Provincetown, where the British war-vessel *Rinaldo* took them on board. During the dreary weeks which they spent on this icy strand, the portly and jovial Mason and his lean and dyspeptic companion solaced themselves by unnumbered rounds of poker, and swore and spat, and spat and swore, continually, to the great and increasing amazement of their orthodox guardsmen. A horrible little triangular dungeon in the casemates was long occupied by Keene, a sailor who had endeavored to blow up the U.S. frigate *Congress*, with all on board. Many other prisoners were incarcerated in the demi-lune, just outside the main gate of the fort.

There were 800 Confederates here in the winter of 1861-62, most of whom had been captured by Burnside, in his campaign of Roanoke Island. It was found necessary to maintain a vigilant watch down the Bay, and the outer picket-line had orders to keep off all boats. The garrison from November, 1861, to May, 1862, was a battalion of volunteers from Hingham, Concord, Boston, and Gloucester, afterwards converted into the Thirty-second Massachusetts Regiment, and full of heroic deeds at the Second Bull Run, Antietam, Gettysburg, Petersburg, etc. Gen. Buckner, the head of the Kentuckian Knights of the Golden Circle, was sent here in February, 1862, after surrendering Fort Donelson and 16,000 men to Gen. Grant; and remained in captivity until the end of the summer. Gen. Tilghman, who surrendered Fort Henry, in Kentucky, was also imprisoned here for six months. Buckner, an old West-Point professor and Mexican veteran, was a precise type of the "ramrod soldier;" but Tilghman was a merry, happy-go-lucky fellow, once an officer in the old Dragoon Regiment, and distinguished for services at Palo Alto and Matamoras. Less than a year after his release, he was killed in one of the deadly Mississippi battles. Through the long and dreary winter, when the island was covered with glare ice, there were a considerable number of North-Carolinians here in duress; and an unhappier crowd was never seen in Boston Harbor. In February they went South to be exchanged; and their places were occupied by "long, gaunt men, given to wearing sombrero hats, and chewing tobacco,"— the Tennesseeans captured at Fort Donelson. The batteries here fired a grand salute when the news of Grant's victories came up; but it took them so long to get ready that (as the second in command said) "the

Alabama might have steamed into Boston Harbor before we could have brought any guns to bear on her." The entire supply of fixed ammunition at this time in the fort was thirty rounds; and when the Governor came down they could fire no salute, for lack of powder. In May, 1862, the garrison consisted of 374 men, including the Cadet corps from Boston and Salem; and held under guard 146 prisoners of war. Among these was Gen. John Pegram, captured by McClellan in West Virginia, and after his release mortally wounded in one of the battles near Petersburg. Still another Virginian visitor was Admiral Barron, of the Confederate navy, who passed under the yoke at Fort Hatteras. Twelve other officers of the Southern navy shared his captivity, under the dear old flag which, in spite of their temporary wrong-headedness, they must have always loved, — the flag of their own Washington and Jackson and Scott and Taylor and Decatur and Maury.

In May, 1862, the fort received a lot of prisoners from the battles below New Orleans, including six officers of the rebel iron-clad *Louisiana*. Gens. Gautt and Hanson were also among the casemate-lodgers; and many

The Bug Light at Low Tide.

officers of the Texas, Louisiana, and Tennessee volunteers. The shivering Confederates found themselves in a place where the East Wind was king, and Cotton had no regal powers. The garrison, by education comfortable townsmen, who had never felt the sleet rattle around Mackinaw, or the furnace-blasts of the gales blowing from the Gulf around Pensacola and the Tortugas, endured here new and distressing climatic conditions. The sentry-posts were often made untenable by the dashing of the waves, and the guards had to be replaced by patrols. No wonder that the unfortunate sentinels saw mysterious shapes, so that an order was posted at the guard house, "denouncing severe punishment in any case where ghosts were allowed to pass a beat without challenge and arrest."

Slowly, as this vague solution of town train-bands crystallized into disciplined infantry, the men found new themes to interest them, and arouse a genuine military enthusiasm. In Col. F. J. Parker's "Thirty-second Regiment" there are many interesting details of garrison-life here, and stories of bluff old Col. Dimick. He says, "To one who thoroughly explores the island, there will recur vivid reminiscences of the mysterious castles of romance and of history. He will find here a sally-port, a postern, a drawbridge, and a portcullis. Here, too, are passages underground and in the walls; turret staircases, huge vaulted apartments, and safe and dark dungeons. ... It only needs a dark and windy night to make almost real the description of the Castle of Udolpho, with its clanging sounds of chains, its sweeping gusts of air, its strange moanings and howlings, and the startling noise of some sudden clang of a shutting door reverberating through the arches."

The militiamen were often called away for serious service, and acted with soldierly steadiness and resolution. When Banks was driven down the Shenandoah Valley, and Stonewall Jackson menaced Washington, the garrison of Fort Warren was hurried to the front, and the famous Boston battalion, the Corps of Cadets, took its place. During the draft-riots in Boston a company of artillerists from Fort Warren was in the thick of the fight at the North End. At the close of 1863 the fort contained 78 cannon: including 30 32-pounders, 13 8-inch and 4 15-inch columbiads in barbette, and 16 8-inch columbiads and 14 100-pound Parrott rifles in casemates. The garrison was composed of 700 volunteer artillerymen. Four months later the armament consisted of 101 guns. Later in the war the prisoners included many desperate blockade-runners, officers of Longstreet's corps, and guerrillas from Morgan's command. Major Cabot's battalion garrisoned the works, and guarded these captives, 172 in number, besides giving much attention to practice with the great guns. An order to send this command South was disregarded; as it was feared that the bright, brave fellows in captivity here, among whom were some expert artillerists, might possess themselves of the fort, and empty its well-filled magazines against Beacon Hill.

In August, 1863, a daring attempt at escape was made. Among the prisoners then confined in the casemates were the officers and crews of the rebel privateers *Tacony* and *Atlanta*. Of these, four officers and two others succeeded in squeezing themselves through the loophole which opened from their prison, and dropping into the moat at night; and then, skilfully evading the sentinels, they gained the shore. Thomas Sherman and Prydé, quarter-gunner of the *Tacony*, started to swim across to Lovell's Island;

but the night was intensely dark, and the tide ran out like a mill-race, and neither of the men was ever heard of again. Lieuts. Thurston and Alexander, of the *Atlanta*, crossed to Lovell's on a rude raft, intending to capture a boat, and return for their comrades. Reaching the shore more dead than alive, they waited there until their strength came back, and then rowed out in a dory, and got on to an anchored sailboat. This frail craft bore them out of Boston Harbor at gray dawn, and they were well down on the Maine coast before a United-States revenue-cutter overhauled them. Two others, Capt. Reed of the *Tacony*, and Major Saunders of the rebel army, waited by the shore for the lieutenants to sail in for them, until the day broke,

The United-States Revenue-Cutter.

and they were recaptured. The fort was at that time still commanded by Col. Dimick, the same gallant officer who preserved Fortress Monroe from seizure at the outbreak of the war.

Among the guests of the "Yankee Bastille" during the last two years of the war were Major-Gen. Edward Johnson, captured with his whole division at Spottsylvania; Gen. Wm. L. Cabell of Virginia; Gen. George W. Gordon; Gen. John S. Marmaduke; Gen. Henry R. Jackson of Georgia, formerly American minister at Vienna; Gen. T. B. Smith; Gen. I. R. Trimble, who lost his foot at Gettysburg; and Gen. Adam R. Johnson. Another restless prisoner was Harry Gilmour, the dashing Baltimorean, whose cavalry so often scurried around the flanks of the national armies.

The most serious attack upon the fortress was made by minions of the law from Boston, bringing a writ of *habeas corpus* to release a political prisoner. Being refused passage on the Government steamboat, they hired a sailboat, and approached the island, to find a detachment of the garrison on the wharf, under arms, and compelling the legal invaders to keep off and return to town empty-handed. About the middle of April, 1865, there came to the island a large group of officers captured by Phil Sheridan, and including Lieut.-Gen. Ewell and Gens. Eppa Hunton, Kershaw, Barton, Corse, Simms, and De Bose. In the same boat came the rebel Commodore Tucker, and several other officers. During the following June, 288 prisoners of war were released, after taking the oath of allegiance to the reunited Republic.

In 1865 the fortress received no less a prisoner than Alexander H. Stephens, the Vice-President of the Confederate States, who remained under guard here for five months. His fate was not severe; for this captivity took place in the summer and early autumn, and was solaced by many kind attentions from the gentlemen of Boston. The fallen chieftain philosophically devoted himself to the study of the Bible and of Cicero, probably as good companions as he could have found in his native Georgia; and emerged from this season of politico-military penance to become a true and valuable citizen of the United States. He was the last of the famous prisoners of state here. At the beginning of 1864 Major Stephen Cabot of the Massachusetts Heavy Artillery was in command, and had a garrison of 763 men and 131 prisoners of war. In September, the garrison and prisoners remaining about the same in numbers, Major A. A. Gibson of the 3d U. S. Artillery took command. Early in 1865 the command of the post passed to Major H. A. Allen, 2d U. S. Artillery. Later in the year the commanders were Major John U. M. Appleton and Capt. C. F. Livermore of the Massachusetts Heavy Artillery. Then Major Gibson, U. S. A., commanded for four years. Among the regular officers who have since governed the fort have been Truman Seymour, formerly a division-commander in Florida, Carolina, and Virginia; Major George P. Andrews of the 5th Artillery (1873-75); Major Mendenhall of the 1st Artillery (1877-79); Lieut.-Col. C. L. Best of the 4th Artillery; Major La Rhette L. Livingston, Capt. J. P. Story, and Capt. Joseph B. Campbell.

Fort Warren is connected with the city by the U. S. steamer *Resolute*, Capt. Loring, which makes three trips each way daily, between Central Wharf and the fort-pier, touching at the upper fortifications if there is occasion. During the winter she has lively work in battling her way through the drifting harbor-ice, or facing the fierce north-easters which sweep down the Bay. The garrison of the fort is composed of Batteries H and K, of the 4th Artillery. In 1882 it also included the famous Battery F, which was organized in March, 1776, and in 1882 received a superb guidon of red and white silk, velvet, and gold fringe, from the grandson of its first captain, Alexander Hamilton. As Gen. Hancock said, in presenting the flag, "An unbroken chain of honorable and valuable services, beginning before the Declaration of Independence, and extending through all the wars of the United States down to the present time, runs through this battery's spotless history."

The walls of the fort are of hammered granite, and present a very imposing appearance, frowning over the deep ditch, and cut through here and there by loop-holes for musketry and flank defence. The main work is surrounded by a moat fifty feet wide, beyond which are minor outworks, — a curtain on the north, a ravelin on the south, and a formidable water-battery on the north-west, fairly glowering over the ship-channel. The fort mounts 300 guns, 70 of which can concentrate their fire on any point in the channel. Of course there are vessels afloat that could live through such an attack, but they would certainly require a long convalescence and careful nursing afterwards. After passing through such a fiery vortex, they would perhaps hardly yearn to encounter the enfilading cannonade of the inner forts, and the reproaches of the rubicund Ancient and Honorable Artillery Corps on Long Wharf.

Rocks on the Outer Islands.

The enclosed space is six acres, of which the parade-ground covers about five acres. The great pentagonal fortress, with its bastions at each angle (commanding the ditches), is composed of casemated walls, in which, and protected by enormous thicknesses of masonry and earth, burrow the barracks, hospital, magazine, storehouses, ice-house, cook and mess rooms, cisterns, and a battery of heavy guns facing the sea. These are lighted from howitzer embrasures, musketry loop-holes, and windows opening on the parade. The walls, with their casemates, attain a thickness of sixty feet. The officers' quarters are two-story stone buildings on the north-west side of the parade; and the doors nearest the portal were those leading to the prisons of the rebel officers and prisoners of state. Above the casemates are the ramparts, sheltered by massive parapets and traverses, and sustaining long lines of 10- and 15-inch guns. As rapidly as possible the stone faces of the fort are being masked behind outer ramparts of earth, into which the largest missiles may sink harmlessly. The granite walls themselves could hardly stand a dozen modern broadsides. The channel at this point has well been called "an ocean Thermopylæ," and merits a worthy defence. The South-Boston Iron Company have made preparations for manufacturing for this fort one or two 54-ton breech-loading rifle cannon, 30 feet long, and of enormous power. It is uncertain, however, when the armament will be increased. The huge guns now mounted are not valued for their long range or penetrating power, but have a well-won reputation for delivering an almost irresistible *smashing* fire, which, at the short range of the ship-channel, would be exceedingly destructive, even to iron-clads. They are mounted in pairs, with impenetrable traverses protecting each couple, and have the best atmospheric appliances for preventing dangerous recoil. Here and there are rifled Parrott guns of the heaviest calibre, whose power of piercing is counted upon to complement the crushing blows of the Rodman missiles. In the water-batteries, great numbers of 10-inch guns are placed as closely together as the carronades in an old-fashioned ship's broadside; too close to be adequately worked, but making a very imposing line of iron for the contemplation of passing yachtsmen and in-bound steamships.

The garrison is concentrated United States, — an island of pure nationalism. The half-score of officers, whose families and pets and flowers make bright home-lights amid the gloomy granite walls, are before all else Americans, — not Virginians, nor New-Yorkers, nor Texans. Each of them is a man without a State, without a city, but with all centred in the Republic. Among them are veterans of Mexico and the South, and former officers of garrisons in Alaska and Arizona, and along the Atlantic seaboard for a thousand miles. They are here this year; next year they may be at Fort Jefferson, or among the Texan lagoons, or back on the Columbia River. The child that is born at Alcatraz cuts his teeth at Fortress Monroe, learns his letters at Fort Marion, wears his first boots below New Orleans, and mounts his first pony in the South Park of Colorado. There is small space for local attachments to grow. Meanwhile the officers, transplanted from one sea-girt, rock-walled fortress to another a thousand leagues away, lose their sectional pre-dispositions, and become United-States men, and, secondarily, Fourth-Artillery men, or Tenth-Infantry men, or what not. One can imagine them, in their snug quarters under the ramparts, discussing the defence of Fort McHenry, or the siege of Mexico, or repeating traditions of the Legion of the West and the wars among the Everglades. Their children, the curly-headed cherubs now romping across the parade-ground, or peeping through the sally-port, when they grow old and gray, and command American posts on Hudson's Bay or the Bay of Campeachy, under a flag of a hundred stars, may tell their legends of the War of the Great

Rebellion, with Grant and Sherman and Sheridan as their demi-gods, and the Fourth Artillery as their vengeful Spartans.

Regardless of the opinions which military and naval persons may entertain about this bristling fastness, the peaceful *literati* who densely populate the adjacent towns have looked upon this scene with varying minds. In Dominie Brown's ancient poems of the harbor, this apostrophe scintillates: —

> "Of George's Isle; oh, muse, now speak,
>   Whose lofty southern shore
> Secures a ship from whirlwinds bleak,
>   Until the storm is o'er.
> . . . .
> "When the poor sailor, wet and cold,
>   And with fatigue opprest;
> This happy island does behold,
>   He happy feels and blest."

In Hovey's "Causerie," there is a funny account of "a solitary soldier who stands guard down at the end of the sandbar that makes the tip end of the island that Fort Warren stands upon. Sailing by, the other day, Causeur was commenting on the uselessness of keeping a man standing there broiling in the hot sun, with nothing whatever to do but lug his musket up and down the beach. 'Nothing to do!' exclaimed his companion. 'Don't you suppose he's got to protect government property? Just let a clam stick his head up anywhere, and he'd shoot it off quicker'n scat. Government property's got to be protected, I tell you.'"

In a different mood of Concordian objurgation, when passing Fort Warren, Thoreau anathematized it as "a bungling contrivance. Wolfe sailed by the strongest fort in North America, in the dark, and took it. . . . All the great seaports are in a boxing attitude; and you must sail prudently between two tiers of stony knuckles before you come to feel the warmth of their breasts."

After poetic pathos, and broad fun, and crusty philosophy, we may be refreshed by Howells's kindly picture of the two Boston forts: "of the air of soft repose that hangs about each; of that exquisite military neatness which distinguishes them; of the green, thick turf covering the escarpments; of the great guns loafing on the crests of the ramparts, and looking out over the water sleepily; of the sentries pacing slowly up and down, with their gleaming muskets."

Once more, how daintily Charles Dudley Warner touches the popular sentiment with regard to the locality, saying: "What a beautiful harbor it is, everybody says, with its irregularly indented shores, and its islands! The day is simply delicious when we get away from the unozoned air of the land. The sky is cloudless, and the water sparkles like the top of a glass of champagne. We intend, by and by, to sit down and look at it for half a day, basking in the sunshine, and pleasing ourselves with the shifting and dancing of the waves. Now we are busy running about from side to side, to see the islands, — Governor's, Castle, Long, Deer, and the others. When, at length, we find Fort Warren, it is not nearly so grim and gloomy as we had expected, and is rather a pleasure-place than a prison in appearance. We are conscious, however, of a patriotic emotion, as we pass its green turf and peeping guns."

Fort Warren is perhaps the most interesting object in the lower harbor. — not so much, indeed, for what it has been, or is, as for what it represents, and may be. There is no other garrison of the United-States Army in the Commonwealth; and no other point so insures the security of the Yankee metropolis. At present, it is regarded mainly as a notable object in the sail down the harbor; and has a keen interest for thousands of people who pass the summer in its vicinity, and nightly hear its evening guns, and see the splendid garrison-flag sink downward, flaming in the last rays of the setting sun. Here and there among these are gray old citizens, prosperous merchants or professional men of Boston, who start up involuntarily as the blare of the fort-bugles floats across Nantasket Roads, remembering long-past echoes of the same wild melodies on the red plains of Virginia or among the jungles of Louisiana.

The Surf-Beaten Brewster Islands.

THE LIGHT-HOUSE. — THE MIDDLE AND OUTER BREWSTERS. — THE GRAVES. — THE OUTER ISLANDS.

UT at the mouth of Boston Harbor, between the main ship-channel and Broad Sound, is a group of seven picturesque rocky islands, called the Brewsters, and nearly two miles in length from north to south. Near them are many submerged rocks and ledges, some of which are full of peril to mariners, while others are famous as fishing-grounds.

Here, indeed, one may realize, the year round, what Charles Kingsley meant, when he said: "New England is, in winter at least, the saddest country, — all brown grass, ice-polished rocks sticking up through the copses, cedar scrub, low swampy shores, — an iron land which only iron people could have settled in. The people must have been heroes to make what they have of it."

Scientific persons have stated that this group of sea-swept rocks is the *débris* and foundations of an ancient island, larger than any now in the harbor, which once occupied this area, and has been destroyed by the storms of immemorial ages. They received their name about the year 1621, in honor of the famous Elder Brewster, at whose house in Scrooby the primitive Pilgrim church used to meet, before its flight to Holland and then to America. He was for years the only preacher and teacher at Plymouth, and enjoyed the highest respect among his austere brethren. The islands were granted to Hull in 1641; and eleven years later to Leverett (afterwards Governor of Massachusetts), in compensation for money which his patriotic father put "into the common stocke in the beginning of this plantation." Somewhat later the General Court restored them to Hull, giving Major Leverett a better and less inaccessible domain; and in 1686 mariner Coomes of Hull sold the entire archipelago to John Loring, for £4. It would seem that Mr. Loring got the worst of such a bargain.

Charles Dudley Warner says that "these outer islands look cold and wind-swept even in summer, and have a hardness of outline which is very far from the aspect of summer isles in summer seas. . . . Upon the low [adjacent] shore-line, which lies blinking in the mid-day sun, the waves of history have beaten for two centuries and a half, and romance has had time to grow there." Here, on the stern outer guards of the metropolis, amid the wild wash of the waves, one may read with understanding Stedman's magnificent "The Lord's Day Gale," and comprehend its thrilling refrain: —

> "New England! New England!
> Thou lovest well thine ocean main!
> It spreadeth its locks among thy rocks,
> And long against thy heart hath lain;
> Thy ships upon its bosom ride,
> And feel the heaving of its tide;
> To thee its secret speech is plain."

The Great Brewster, the innermost island, is mainly composed of a lofty and conspicuous bluff, half of which has been eaten away by the sea. It covers about twenty-five acres, and has a stone wharf, a bit of ancient ruin, and the summer-villa of the Hon. Benjamin Dean. A contented family lives on the island throughout the entire year. Further encroachments of the waves have been checked by a noble sea-wall, built by the United States, at great cost. The projection of Little Hill has been nearly worn away by the sea, and now contains only an acre and a half. Rich grass and clover cover the bluff, and columbines and other dainty flowers thrive. The view from the crest is very impressive, and gives a bird's-eye prospect of these rocky islets. A curving gravelly ridge, 1½ miles long, and covered at high tide, runs thence to the Bug Light; and a short bar, which may be traversed at low water, leads to the Light-House Island. The Great Brewster was bought by the city of Boston in 1848, for $4,000; and the part which lies about the sea-wall pertains to the United States. Mr. Dean has leased the island from the city, and spends parts of his summers here.

The Bug Light stands on the end of the long bar which runs out from the Great Brewster, rising from the water at low tide like a great wall, and sometimes traversed by pedestrians along its entire distance. It is a snug little house, on heavy iron supports, like stilts, and sustains a fixed red light, visible for seven miles. It was built in 1856, to warn vessels against the dangerous Harding's Ledge, which lies off Point Allerton. One of the best studies which Halsall has painted represents this picturesque beacon, in the midst of the roaring sea. At one time, when shepherds followed their calling on these islands, a large flock of sheep were driven out on the bar by excited dogs, and kept there, huddled together in terror, until the rising tide drowned them all. The Light-House Island, once known as the Little Brewster, or Beacon Island, is a trifle over eight miles from Boston, and about 1¼ miles north of Point Allerton, across the main ship channel. As early as the year 1679 there was some kind of a beacon on the Great Brewster; for Dankers and Sluyter, the Dutch Labadist envoys, said that they observed one on the highest of the islands, twelve miles from Boston, which could be seen from a great distance. In 1713 the Bostonians

BOSTON LIGHT.

began to hold town-meetings about establishing a beacon at the mouth of the harbor, since its want "hath been a great discouragement to navigation, by the loss of the lives and estates of several of His Majesties Subjects." The General Court ordered its construction, and provided that all vessels coming in from abroad, or clearing therefor, should pay a penny a ton towards the cost. This was in the first year of King George I.'s reign. Hull granted the island for this purpose, "being censable that it will be a genarall benifit to Trade;" and the light-house was built, at a cost of £2,386. The first keeper of the light was George Worthylake, who was drowned while sailing up to town, with his wife and daughter, in 1718. All three were buried on Copp's Hill; and Benjamin Franklin, then a North-End lad, wrote a doleful poem describing their fate, and entitled "The Light-House Tragedy."

About the middle of the last century an ingenious system of guarding the port was devised, whereby the men stationed at the light-house should signal to Castle Island the approach of suspicious or hostile vessels by hoisting and lowering the Union Jack. If the number of these unwelcome craft reached four, the Castle alarmed the town, and then the flaming torches on Beacon Hill called in the country yeomanry. In this manner Boston was given six hours in which to parade her train-bands and man her batteries.

There was hot fighting hereabouts in the summer of 1775. Major Vose, of Heath's Continental regiment, landed here from whale-boats, under the fire of the British frigates and barges, and took seven prisoners, besides burning the barn on the Great Brewster, and partly destroying the light-house. Another and more serious attack was made a few days later, by Major Tupper and 300 Continentals, who stormed the little redoubt, killing and wounding 12 men, and capturing 2 cannon, 33 marines, and a party of carpenters. But the tide went out, and left their boats high and dry; and several good American soldiers were lost in fighting the man-of-war barges which pounced down upon them. At last they got afloat, and rushed across the channel to Hull, covered by the fire of the Yankee guns there, which sank one of the hostile barges. In general orders, Washington commended Tupper's men for "their gallant and soldier-like behavior;" and Col. Barré rose in the British Parliament, to complain that "they burn even the light-house, under the nose of the fleet, and carry off the men sent to repair it." The light-house built in 1716 was repaired in 1757, after a fire, and stood until 1776, when it was blown up by the retreating British marines, having been held by them for three months after the evacuation of Boston. The present structure was erected in 1783, and is 98 feet above the sea-level.

The island is not so grim as it appears from the channel, whence it appears foreshortened. There are three acres of ground, with a neat vegetable-garden; and it is a brisk little walk from the light-house to the house where the keepers and their families live, or to the wharf where boats make landing. The light-keeper, a veteran of the Mexican wars, keeps his snug principality with military order and precision, and has a profound and loving admiration for the great night-signal which seems the *raison d'être* of the island. The lantern is a very costly piece of French workmanship, containing 336 pieces of glass, and protected from the weather by great windows of thick and clear plate-glass. Nothing can be allowed to dim this outer window; and the snow, driving against it on winter nights, must be frequently cleared away, so that the brilliant beams may shine out unimpeded. The light is a revolving one, and is visible for sixteen miles in clear weather. Near the light-house is a great steam fog-horn, whose dismal bellowings warn the mariners for leagues offshore, in thick weather. The

On the Outer Brewster.

ancient minute-gun, which this more powerful appliance has superseded, rusts by the shore. Occasionally the wharf is visited by a swarm of boarding-house runners, in long-boats, who dash out thence upon foreign vessels entering the Roads, to lure the sailors to their dens in the North End. These are the stuff that pirates are made of, — bronzed and scarred fellows, with sinister faces, and language which the Puritans would have hung them for.

Hence the shapely pilot-boats are seen, cruising out and in, and towards the capes, and in their fair symmetry meriting the eulogy given by Capt. Basil Hall, of the Royal Navy: "Our ingenious friends, the Americans, have contrived a set of pilot-boats which are the delight of every sailor. . . . They are truly 'water-witches;' for, while they look so delicate and fragile that one feels at first as if the most moderate breeze must brush them from the face of the ocean, and scatter to the winds all their gay drapery, they can and do defy, as a matter of habit and choice, the most furious gales with which the rugged seaboard of America is visited in February and March."

The Middle Brewster is a high and rocky islet, with about ten acres of arable soil hidden behind its cliffs; and the groups of fishermen's red-roofed houses, and the tall white summer-house of Mr. Augustus Russ, perched on the highest point, make a pleasant picture amid the surrounding desolation. Forty years ago there were no houses on the rock; but subsequently a small colony of fishermen settled here, by their favorite fishing-grounds, and not without occasional chances at wrecking. Here, also, the patrician yachtsmen and other guests enjoy ease with dignity during the dog-days, and are entertained with free hospitality in the Russ villa. The snug little steamer *Galatea* is used by the proprietor in making trips to and from his island-home. Halsall, the marine-painter, has spent many months here; and often visits the locality in the most inclement winter season, as well as during the lovely summer days, finding true artistic values in all views of the sea at this close angle. Notman, the photographer, has spent two seasons on this secluded islet, attracted by the peculiar grandeur of the scenery, which has been likened to parts of the rocky coast of Cornwall. Only a single fisherman now lives here, and the houses of his former companions have been endowed with enough of piazzas and dormer-windows to make them available as summer-cottages. On the southerly side is the only good landing, made by removing the surface-rocks, and leaving a bit of beach, sheltered by an outlying reef. The narrow and rather difficult passage between the Middle and Outer Brewsters is known as the Flying Place, and foams like a caldron when a heavy sea is on. In 1828 the brig *Jachin*, bound in from St. Martha, with a full cargo, got tangled among these rocks in midwinter, and was wrecked on the Middle Brewster, with loss of life.

About ten years ago the Middle Brewster was owned by three fishermen in undivided thirds, and their rights were bought up by Mr. Russ. A small corner still belongs to one of these toilers by the sea; and the remainder pertains to the above-mentioned gentleman, who reserves this marine park, enwalled by the Atlantic, for his summer home. Here the long sunny days glide away very peacefully, while the great fleets pass in and out through the adjacent channel, each with its own story of distant seas.

"Yon deep bark goes
 Where Traffic blows
From lands of sun to lands of snows:
 This happier one,
 Its course is run
From lands of snow to lands of sun.

O happy ship,
 To rise and dip,
With the blue crystal at your lip!
 O happy crew,
 My heart with you
Sails, and sails, and sings anew!"

The view from the flagstaff, on the highest point of the island, includes a vast horizon of sea, with the rugged adjacent islands, the inland hills of Saugus and the Middlesex Fells, and the crowded highway of nations close at hand. The geological structure of these islands is very interesting to scientific persons; since it has no affinity with that of the contiguous mainland, but represents, with its dark granites and porphyries, a totally different epoch of the building of the world.

The Outer Brewster is a pile of frowning rocks, enclosing several acres of fertile soil, in which is a fine spring of fresh water. Dr. Shurtleff says that "this island is one of the most romantic places near Boston, far surpassing Nahant in its wild rocks, chasms, caves, and overhanging cliffs." Several attempts have been made to use the rocks of the Outer Brewster for building purposes; and a massive little edifice on City Square, Charlestown, is walled with this sea-soaked material. There is a pond on the island, attaining, in rainy weather, very respectable dimensions. The right-hand side of the western cove has a singular rock-formation, called the Pulpit, from which the Rev. East Wind delivers very powerful addresses. In the northern cove are the remains of the unfinished canal, cut through the rock by

Whistling Buoy. Off the Graves.

the late Gen. Austin, with some wild idea of forming an artificial harbor. It once had a gate at its entrance, and made a tight and secure little dock. Mr. T. Dean's description is the best ever written of it: "In truth, it is a noble island. Its jutting rocks and cavernous recesses were now invisible; but its grand position and imposing front, as it stood darkly revealed against the cloudy sky, seemed to give it a heroic charm. The ocean-waves approaching Boston here meet the foremost champion of the port. Majestic and alone it stands forth on the 'perilous edge of battle when it rages,' and sternly encounters the maddened billows which seek another prey. Even now the seas came stealing along its rugged side, making a line of white, again and again bursting into spray as they met some vexatious rock. We neared the canal. This is a deep fissure extending across the eastern part of the island. The northerly end forms a long, deep, aisle-like gap in the Brewster, with sufficient depth of water, when the tide is up, to float quite a craft well within the limits of the island. On the seaward side of the entrance, rugged, isolated rocks break somewhat the force of the seas; but, in a troublous time, they seem only to fret and aggravate the jealous waves. It was not without difficulty that we found the entrance; but at last we entered safely, and rowed slowly up the watery path of the canal. The sound of the waves diminished as we advanced; and when at last our skiff gently touched the shore within the walls of rock that had opened to receive us, the grating of her bow upon the shingle was the only sound we heard. Stepping ashore, we gazed about us. Here, at the end of inland navigation, the canal expanded into a little cove, favored with water only at the higher stages of the tide, and having a ribbon of shingly beach. The stillness was oppressive. We were on the leeward side of the island, where the wind came shorn of its strength, down low between the lofty walls of rock. No trees were nigh, to rustle in the breeze, nor grasses tall to bend and sigh. Even the sound of the waves at the entrance of the canal seemed to the ear like the far-off murmur heard in ocean-shells. The softly-heaving bosom of the water, the breathing of the Titanic sea, apparent even here, alone relieved the death-like stillness."

When Gen. Austin owned the island, about the year 1840, and took from it the stone used in macadamizing the Warren Bridge, there were two or three inhabitants here, with six head of cattle and fifty sheep. The house was afterwards burnt by rowdies from Boston. About the year 1861 a fisherman named Jeffers came to this solitary islet, with his wife and children, and built a rude dwelling near the rocky lines of House Beach. On a terrible November night, as he was trying to get to his home, in a dory, with two men from the Middle Brewster, the frail craft was wrecked near the mouth of the canal, and Jeffers and one of his companions sank in the roaring sea. The stricken widow soon afterwards left the island, and their house was burned down. This is the most inaccessible island in the Massachusetts archipelago, and many lives have been lost in trying to land upon it. There is no shelter nor anchorage; and occasionally, after a long storm, the fishermen find on its rocks fragments of decks and masts, the only memorials of all-destroying wrecks. This lonely and legend-haunted rock has been called the home of the East Wind, that worst of scourges in winter and spring, and most delightful of blessings in summer. Often during the scalding days of July and August the Outer-Brewster zephyrs go trooping up the harbor, bearing life and refreshment through all the town, and dispelling its muggy vapors and exhalations.

The Shag (or Egg) Rocks are a group of formidable ledges, rising from the waves south of the Brewsters, and very dangerous to mariners, many of whom have lost their lives here. "At midnight, on the 3d of November, 1861, the ship *Maritana*, laden with a rich cargo, and bearing many human lives, struck on the Shag Rocks.... The forward part of the vessel jammed in

Villa of Augustus Russ, Esq., on the Middle Brewster.

among the rocks, and held fast: the stern was in deep water. There was a driving snowstorm when she struck, and it was very cold. The wretched passengers, who at one time were safe on the inhospitable rocks, were persuaded that the vessel would hold together, and, impelled by the piercing cold, returned to the ship, and were lost." At seven in the morning the vessel broke in two; and 25 of her crew and passengers, including several women and children, were drowned. Their bodies were thrown up on Light-House Island days afterwards. Thirteen persons clung to the rocks until the next day, when they were gallantly rescued by Samuel James of Hull, in a small dory, and placed on board a pilot-boat. Many other disasters have happened on these rocky fangs, but none so terrible as this. On a stormy March night of 1861 the schooner *Enterprise* drove in on to the Egg Rocks, and was very quickly broken in pieces. Some years earlier a rich French merchantman struck here in a gale, and was utterly destroyed with her crew.

On the night of January 31, 1882, the *Fanny Pike* of Calais struck here during a terrific north-east snow-storm. A very heavy sea was running; but the crew succeeded in getting on the rocks, where they lay for ten hours, after which they were heroically rescued by Bates and Bailey, the light-house keepers, and Charles Pochaska of the Middle Brewster. These gallant rescuers received diplomas and rewards from the Massachusetts Humane Society.

The Graves are a group of black and frowning ledges, north-east of the Brewsters, in the sea, and entirely swept by the surf during heavy weather. They are marked by a huge whistling buoy, whose mechanism is such, that the waves which rock it to and fro drive the air through a narrow space at the top, making a sound that can be heard for miles. It is indescribably weird and mournful, varying in compass from a vast sigh, almost too vague to locate, but pervading all the adjacent sea, to a long and blood-chilling moan, or a wild and long-drawn shriek. It is as if all the dead men whose lives have been drowned out of them on these gloomy ledges, still haunted the scene, with articulate wailings. Yet, on a still day, light yachts run out around the rocks, and touch the great buoy.

The Graves were named in honor of Thomas Graves, who came over in command of the *Talbot*, the vice-admiral of Winthrop's fleet. Afterwards, in 1643-44, he commanded the *Trial*, the first large vessel built in Boston, in her long voyages to Bilboa and Malaga. The *Trial* was built by Nehemiah Bourne, who, after some years' residence at Boston, returned to England, and became rear-admiral in the Parliament's navy. Shurtleff says that the Graves were named for the British Admiral Graves, who made himself so disagreeable to our American ports during the Revolution, and is said to have touched these rocks. This cannot be accurate, however; for they bear their present name on the chart made in 1689, nearly a century earlier. The fishermen on the adjacent islands believe that the resemblance of the rocks to tombstones, rising in somewhat regular forms from the sea, and whitened by layers of limestone, has given reason for the name.

Outside of Point Allerton, about two miles, is the dreaded Harding's Ledge, which was anciently known as Conny Hasset Rock, and remains one of the most formidable dangers of the Bay. It becomes partly bare at low water, and is marked by an immense bell-buoy. The new bell is forty feet above the water, and its deep pealing is heard at a great distance. Among the most serious losses which this black Harding's Ledge has inflicted on our commerce was that of a great ship which was wrecked here, with serious loss of life, some years ago. In 1876 a large iron steamship also struck on this grim rock. Only a year or two ago the Govern-

A Calf-Island Woman spearing Flounders.

or Cony, laden with pig-iron and kerosene, missed stays, and struck the Ledge so plumply that she went down almost instantly, leaving only her upper masts in sight.

The mournful peal of the bell breaks through the gray solitudes with that strange pathetic harmony which Lucy Larcom has thus described: —

" The vessels are sunk in the mist;
    And hist!
Through the veil of the air
    Throbs a sound,
Like a wail of despair,
That dies into stillness profound.

All muffled in gray is the sea;
    Not a tree
Sees its neighbor beside
    Or before;
And across the blank tide,
Hark! that sob of an echo once more."

Calf Island is just north of the Great Brewster, and was anciently known as the North Brewster. It covers ten acres, and has several small houses and a lonely grave. Nature has not been lavish here; but her kindlier touch appears in a pretty grove of wild cherry-trees, and artists find here a great variety of choice subjects for studies. Among the rugged ledges of basalt which front the surf, there are several pretty bits of beach where landing may be made. In years not long past, sometimes, of a pleasant summer Sunday, scores of boats, dories, and yachts would make a rush from the city to this sequestered spot, and their crews would congregate in a dense circular crowd on the greensward. From the general scattering apparent if the harbor-police boat approached, it was evident that these summer-tourists were not on the best terms with the law; and the general belief is, that the art of pugilism had here a favored shrine. A half-dozen

Lobsterman's House, Calf Island.

lobstermen and their families now live on the island, under the paternal and eccentric sway of Captain Turner.

About a hundred feet northward, and accessible hence at low tide, rises the barren rock of Little Calf Island, fringed with weedy ledges. To the north is the narrow strait of Hypocrite Passage, through which small boats frequently run.

Green Island is the most northerly of the group, and has a small area of grassy earth in a great bowl of rock, and a long and gravelly South Point. When Samuel Choate, mariner, had reached his fiftieth year, in 1845, he settled on this islet, hardly larger than a vessel's deck, and built a rude hut, where he lived for twenty years, subsisting mainly on fish and muscles. During the famous storm of 1851, this maritime hermit was taken off by a pilot-boat, for his fast-anchored deck was submerged by the furious tide; and in 1865, old and feeble, he was removed to a charitable home.

CLIFFS ON THE OUTER BREWSTER, AT LOW TIDE.

This group of gaunt and jagged rocks, each with its bit of history, but mainly endowed with tragic interest, are the remotest outer guards of the western St. Botolph's Town, and around them flows the swelling tide of her great commerce. Myriads of weary mariners have welcomed them with joy, sailing inward from far-distant seas. Standing upon their strong bul-

On the Middle Brewster.

warks, you may hear the bands playing in summer plaisance at Hull, the distant bugles of Fort Warren, and the ghostly murmurings of the Graves; and

"Hark to the sailor, singing as he rocks,
A mote upon the mighty ocean swell."

The Bug Light.

Bits of Harbor History.

HISTORIC VIGNETTES.—OLD-TIME EXCURSIONS.—ART AND LITERATURE.—
BOSTON'S COMMERCE.

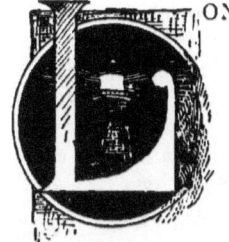
LONG ago Peter Peregrine (the celebrated Dr. E. C. Wines) wrote thus : " The sea-view of Boston, which I had the opportunity of contemplating as we passed down the bay, is superb. I can recall but two similar views—those of Genoa and of Naples—worthy of being compared with it. And while, in some points of the comparison, the superior beauty of the latter must be confessed by all, there are others in which the Boston view indubitably surpasses them. The almost innumerable green and fertile islands, sown broadcast over the surface of the bay, constitute a feature in the prospect, to which neither of the views referred to furnishes any parallel. . . . The number of islands reminded me of the Cyclades, though it must be confessed, that, in their appearance, nothing could well be more dissimilar than those of the Ægean Sea and Massachusetts Bay." In a similar but more temperate vein, N. P. Willis remarks that Boston Harbor has been likened to the Bay of Naples; and charitably adds that " it may be mentioned in the same day." We have also the testimony of a cultivated gentleman from Southern Italy, that paragon of lands of beauty; for Raffaelle Capobianco, the priest of the Neapolitan frigate *Urania*, described " the wonderful and picturesque bay" of Boston, as his fine old Bourbon man-of-war ascended its island-mazes, amid salutes from all the batteries. He especially admired Bunker-Hill Monument, which, he said, was " commenced by the celebrated engineer, O'Donnell Webster, under the presidency of the famous Lafayette."

When the Abbé Robin, a chaplain in Rochambeau's army, sailed into the harbor, he wrote: " A favorable breeze sprang up, and brought us safely into the roadstead of Boston. In this roadstead, studded with pleasant islands, we saw, over the trees on the west, the houses rising amphitheatre-like, and forming along the hillsides a semicircle of nearly half a league : this was the town of Boston."

More than two centuries before these wise priests sailed up through Nantasket Roads, and in the very dawn of its history, the saints took possession of Massachusetts Bay and its inner harbor; and on the most ancient maps this broad expanse of water bore their names, emblazoned across the uncertain space between Cape Cod and the mainland. On Fernando Columbus's map, dated 1527, Massachusetts Bay is called the Bay of St. Antonio. Apolonius's Antwerp map of the New World, dated 1566, calls it the Bay of St. Christoval (and Cape Cod is Cape de Trafalgar). On Hood's map, of 1592, it is the Bay of San Christoforo. Twenty years later the Dutch explorers named Boston Harbor, Fox Haven, in honor of one of their ships, the *Little Fox;* and about the same time Champlain called it the River du Guast, and Captain John Smith named it the Charles River. In 1608 Champlain's little French ship anchored off Noddle's Island; and he thus described the country: "We observed many smokes along the shore, and many Savages running up to see us. Sieur de Monts sent two or three men in a canoe to them, to whom he gave some knives and paternosters to present to them; with which they were greatly pleased, and danced several times in acknowledgment. We could not ascertain the name of their chief, as we did not know their language. All along the shore there is a great deal of land cleared up and planted with Indian corn. The country is very pleasant and agreeable, and there is no lack of fine trees. . . . As we continued our course, large numbers came to us in canoes from the islands and mainland." This visit of Champlain is neatly described by a local antiquary: "When they left the harbor of Boston, the islands and mainland were swarming with the native population. The Indians were, naturally enough, intensely interested in this visit of the little French barque. It may have been the first that had ever made its appearance in the Bay. Its size was many times greater than any water-craft of their own. Spreading its white wings, and gliding silently away without oarsmen, it filled them with surprise and admiration. The whole population was astir. The cornfields and fishing-stations were deserted. Every canoe was manned, and a flotilla of their tiny craft came to attend, honor, and speed the parting guests: experiencing, doubtless, a sense of relief that they were going, and filled with a painful curiosity to know the meaning of this mysterious visit."

Capt. John Smith says of his Charles River: "They find that faire channell to divide itselfe into so many faire branches as to make forty or fifty pleasant islands within that excellent Bay. . . . We found the people in those parts verie kinde; but in their furie no lesse valiant. For, upon a quarrell wee had with one of them, hee onely with three others crossed the harbor of Quonahassit [Cohasset] to certaine rocks whereby wee must passe, and there let flie their arrowes for our shot, till we were out of danger."

During the next decade, several parties of adventurers sailed into the harbor, seeking locations for new colonies on this virgin soil. Standish reconnoitred the coast in 1621; Weston's men came to Weymouth in 1622; exiles from Plymouth founded Hull in 1622; and Morton's scapegrace colony of Merry-Mount began in 1625.

Many a vessel had sailed into the harbor, from the time of Thorwald to that of Champlain and Standish; but the arrival which was great with destiny for these shores occurred in the beautiful late summer of 1630, when Governor Winthrop's fleet sailed in, coming around from Salem. The picturesque high-sterned vessels, almost Elizabethan in their antique models and rich quaint decorations, with abundance of flags fluttering from their low masts, and scores of fierce little four-pound cannon protruding from their port-holes, made a brave show as they sailed up the harbor, while the rich flush of a July day rested on the embowered islands and the graceful hills of Shawmut. Foremost rode the admiral-ship, *Lady Arbella*, of 350

The Old Tewksbury House, Point Shirley.

tons, with 28 guns, and in all points well equipped; next came the vice-admiral, the *Talbot*, with the remaining vessels closing in behind.

Mr. Beecher once said that "God seems to have picked out the hardest territory on the globe for the Puritans to inhabit. He placed them on the sterile soil of New England, and told them to show what they could do; and they have shown it to the world." At first they took a grave view of this dispensation; and Cotton Mather himself reported that Boston, "the Metropolis of the whole English Empire . . . was at first proverbially called *Lost-Town*, for the mean and sad circumstances of it." Ship after ship ascended the Bay, each with its precious cargo of immigrants, self-exiled for conscience' sake, and finding joy in freedom, even on a rugged and empty continent. The sentiment is clearly set forth in "*Margaret Smith's Journal:*" "As we passed the small wooded islands, which make the bay very pleasant, and entered close upon the town, and saw the houses and orchards, and meadows, and the hills beyond covered with a great growth of wood, my brother, lifting up both of his hands, cried out, 'How goodly are thy tents, O Jacob, and thy habitations, O Israel!' and for my part I did weep for joy and thankfulness of heart, that God had brought us safely to so fair a haven."

If, on the one hand, Dummer's words describing the Massachusetts land as "bare creation" were doubtless true, the compensation was set forth, and the victory assured, by Stoughton's expression, "God sifted a whole nation that he might send choice grain over into this wilderness." Even saintly Herbert wrote that, —

"Religion stands on tiptoe in our land,
Ready to pass to the 'Merican strand."

One of the most homely and pathetic scenes of this exodus is that portrayed in "The Wonder-Working Providence of Sion's Saviour in New England," where the women of Boston are shown in the act of digging clams on the harbor-flats, "where they daily gathered their Families food with much heavenly discourse of the provision *Christ* had formerly made for many thousands of His followers in the wildernesse."

In 1633 Wood wrote the following good description of Boston Harbor, in his "New-England Prospect:" "This harbour is made by a great company of islands, whose high cliffs should cut the boisterous seas; yet may easily deceive any unskilful pilot; presenting many fair openings and broad sounds, which afford too shallow water for ships, though navigable for boats, and pinnaces. It is a safe and pleasant harbour within, having but one common and safe entrance, and that not very broad; there scarce being room for three ships to come in board and board at a time; but being once in, there is room for the anchorage of 500 ships. The seamen having spent their old store of wood and water, may here have fresh supplies from the adjacent islands, with good timber to repair their weather-beaten ships."

The Indians still visited the harbor to see the wonders of the new civilization, and the author of "Naomi" represents their canoes as continually flitting up and down among the islands. Josselyn, the delightful gossip, thus describes (in 1638) one of their sea-boats: "We had the sight of an Indian pinnace sailing by us, made of birch-bark, sewed together with the roots of spruce and white cedar (drawn out into threads), with a deck, and trimmed with sails top and top-gallant very sumptuously."

When the fleet lay in the Roads, in 1636, the Rev. Hugh Peters entertained the sailors with most edifying sermons. Peters was the successor of Roger Williams in the First Church at Salem, and in after-years became more famous as a colonel in Cromwell's Parliamentary army. He grievously insulted King Charles I., who lay at the time a prisoner under sentence of death, and after the Restoration was executed in the Tower of London.

In 1643 Capt. Carman's ship came into the Roads, amid great rejoicings. She had been attacked by a Turkish corsair, of 26 guns and 200 men, off the Canary Islands, and escaped only after a very desperate battle. A hundred of the Saracen pirates boarded her at one time; but half of them were driven into the sea, and the rest fled back to their own decks.

In 1652-55 several ships entered the port, bearing sad exiles, sent hither by Cromwell's order, to be sold as slaves. They were Irishmen and Scots, captured by the victorious Parliamentary armies (many of them at the battle of Dunbar), and torn from their homes to encounter the grievous hardships of servitude.

The terrible witchcraft troubles, which desolated the Massachusetts towns, did not spare the harbor of Boston. After Thomas Jones's wife had been executed as a witch, he resolved to fly from such a cruel country, and went on board the ship *Welcome*, then at anchor in the stream. "The weather was calm, yet the ship fell to rolling, and so deep it was feared she would founder. Great weight was placed on one side to trim her, and she would heel over on the other side.

Governor Winthrop.

The County Court was then in session, and, hearing that the husband of the executed witch was on board, sent officers to arrest him. No sooner was the warrant shown, than the rolling of the ship began to stop; and after the man was in prison it moved no more." Other supernatural terrors stalked abroad in the harbor. Weird corpse lights were seen, dancing along the heights of Governor's Island; ghastly human forms walked on the waves beyond the Castle; and mysterious voices were heard mingling with the night-winds.

"I write the *wonders* of the *Christian Religion*, flying from the depravations of Europe, to the American Strand,"— says worthy Cotton Mather, in Homeric vein, at the beginning of his "Magnalia Christi Americana;" and in the chapter headed "Pietas in Patriam," he describes the gathering of the great colonial fleet in Nantasket Roads, in 1690, when 32 vessels and 2,000 men were assembled there, and Sir William Phipps sailed away at their head in the ship *Six Friends*, 44 guns, to take Quebec, the western citadel of the abomination of Rome. But, after much hard fighting, Phipps returned to Boston with the remnants of his discomfited fleet, and publicly said, "The things which befell me on this expedition are too deep to be dived into."

Numberless unfortunates were driven into this port during the early days, and found the grim Puritans most sympathetic and helpful. In simple language, the old records tell many a plaintive story: "There are lately arrived fifteen French families, with a religious Protestant minister, who are in all — men, women, and children — more than fourscore souls, and are

The Police-Boat, Boston Harbor.

such as fled from France for religion's sake; and by their long passage at sea their doctor and twelve men are dead, and by other inconveniences the living are reduced to great sickness and poverty, and therefore objects of a true Christian charity. Also, fifty persons — men, women, and children — which were by the cruelty of the Spaniards driven off from Elutheria (an island of the Bohemiahs), naked and in distress." Sometimes the compassion of the townsmen took a singular turn, as when a cargo of negroes, mostly women and children, torn from the coasts of Madagascar, were brought into port more dead than alive. These, as it is recorded, "were sold as slaves to magistrates, ministers, and people of distinction." Probably their descendants, sable or part bleached, are now not without honor in Anderson Street.

In 1711 Nantasket Roads saw a more splendid sight than it ever had before, when the vast armada of Admiral Sir Hovenden Walker anchored there for several weeks. The fleet was composed of 15 men-of-war and 6 store-ships, with 40 transports and 7,000 soldiers, many of them Marlborough's veterans; and the troops were landed, and encamped on the harbor islands. In July the expedition sailed away, filled with high hopes of the conquest of Canada; but when it reached the mouth of the St. Lawrence a terrible storm broke over it, and several transports and 1,000 soldiers

The Fire-Department Boat, Boston Harbor.

were lost. The pious Franco-Canadian Catholics saw in this disaster the hand of God, as the Puritans also referred the destruction of the Duc d'Anville's fleet to the same agency; and Queen Elizabeth's Episcopalians likewise recognized a similar impartial Providence in the loss of the Spanish Armada.

Bennett, in 1740, thus describes the harbor and its islands: "At the entrance of the bay there are several rocks of great magnitude, the tops of which appeared considerably above the surface of the water at the time of our passing by them. There are also about a dozen little islands all in view as we approach the town, some of which are as fine farms as any in the whole country. This town has a good natural security, in my opinion; for there is great plenty of rocks and shoals, which are not easy to be avoided by strangers to the coasts; and there is but one safe channel to approach the harbor, and that so narrow that three ships can hardly sail through abreast; but within the harbor there is room enough for five hundred sail to lie at anchor."

In 1745 a body of 2,000 French prisoners from Louisburg were brought into Boston, where they were held in captivity for some time, and then sent to France. Three years later another singular company came into port from Louisburg and Quebec. These were the people of New England, many hundreds in number, who had been torn from their homes, and led into captivity in the northern forests and fortresses of Canada. They were now coming home with great joy. In 1775 several ships entered the Roads laden with Acadians, the gentle and pious peasantry whom the Provincial generals had driven from their homes, into a weary and perpetual banishment. Here might have been Evangeline herself, sadly gazing upon the sharp black rocks of Massachusetts Bay. In 1758 came the grandest fleet which Boston Harbor had ever seen, when Sir Jeffrey Amherst, a veteran of Fontenoy, and conqueror of Louisburg, brought in his great expedition. He landed 4,500 choice British soldiers, who marched hence to Albany and Montreal.

In 1768 two Irish regiments and twelve men-of-war from Halifax entered the Roads, where they were put in order of battle, and sailed up the harbor, with cannon run out and loaded, to overawe rebellious Boston. The Continental lines which surrounded Boston in the landward towns were continued on blue water by the minute-men of the sea, the gallant privateers of Marblehead and other ports. When a royal frigate approached, these marine militia crowded on canvas, and fled into the adjacent coves; but when a transport or troop-ship appeared, they bore down on her, with the pine-tree flag waving saucily from the fore, and their little batteries of 6-pounders barking. Many a rich prize was taken thus, and others were even cut out of the harbor, and borne off to Yankee ports. A royal brig, heavily laden with provisions and artillery, and with 3,000 muskets and 2,000 broadswords in her cargo, fortunately ran the gauntlet of the Massachusetts fleet, and anchored in Nantasket Roads; but a particularly audacious Plymouth privateer cut her out, and escaped to sea with the prize, although pursued hotly by several British men-of-war. The *Lee* of Marblehead captured four inbound British vessels in a single week of December, 1775; one of which, the *Nancy*, laden with artillery, ammunition, and intrenching-tools, became almost the salvation of Washington's ill-equipped army. In April, 1776, the *Hancock* captured in the Bay a British brig from Cork, laden with provisions, and another from the Azores, deeply freighted with wine and fruit. Later, she took the Scottish brigantine *Peggy*, 8 guns; and during the year forty vessels surrendered to the gallant little *Hancock*. Some of these were armed, and carried valuable cargoes. On Sunday, March 17, 1776, the great British fleet dropped down the harbor from Boston and Charlestown, and anchored in Nantasket Roads, where it remained for ten days. On board were 11,000 soldiers and sailors, 1,019 self-exiled Bostonians (including 102 civil officers and 18 clergymen), and 105 loyalists from the country towns. It was a beaten and dejected army, and a worried fleet; but the saddest feature was this great company of Boston *emigrés*, who preferred their king to their native land, and departed into perpetual exile. How

View from the Jerusalem Road.

their tears must have flowed as the familiar islands dropped astern, one by one, and the Puritan spires faded away in the west, and the noble crests of the Blue Hills sank beneath the horizon!

When the fleet sailed away, Commodore Banks with the *Milford*, 50, and several other war-vessels, remained to blockade the port. Mrs. Adams wrote that "the *Milford* frigate rides triumphant in our bay, taking vessels every day, and no Colony or Continental vessel has yet attempted to hinder her. She mounts but twenty-eight guns, and is one of the fastest sailers in the British navy. They complain we have not weighty metal enough, and I suppose truly." The day came for this last remnant of hostile occupation to be removed, when Gen. Lincoln's Continentals and coast-guards suddenly opened a simultaneous fire on the fleet from half a dozen headlands and islands, and knocked many a great splinter out of the natty frigates. The crashing broadsides of British iron did not silence the Massachusetts guns; and the whole squadron, from high-decked flag-ship down to little tender, were soon fain to spread their towering canvas, and fly away to sea.

On the day after the first anniversary of the battle of Bunker Hill, the Massachusetts brig *Defence*, 18 guns, captured the transport *John and George*, 6 guns, and 120 men, off the mouth of the harbor. In the same week the American privateers captured the transport *Arabella*, in the same locality, with 200 British soldiers on board. This conquest was the result of a hard naval battle, during which Major Menzies and 18 men were killed. Only the day after Campbell's Highlanders were captured off Long-Island Head, another transport ran into the harbor, with 112 fine Scottish soldiers on board. When she was alongside the light-house a privateer-schooner pounced upon her, and led the unhappy plaidies into Boston.

In 1779 the celebrated Penobscot expedition rendezvoused here, and lay in the Roads for several days. The French fleet and army had declined to attack the British stronghold at Castine; and so Massachusetts collected here her whole naval strength, — 19 armed vessels, with 324 guns, and 20 transports, with 1,300 soldiers. None of these snug little Yankee frigates ever saw the harbor again; for a British squadron pounced upon them as they lay off Castine, and destroyed the entire outfit.

When the French fleet lay in the harbor, in 1778, blockaded by Lord Howe's powerful squadron, Gov. John Hancock gave the officers a grand breakfast at his stately house on Beacon Hill; and they returned the compliment by a banquet on their flag-ship, at which Madam Hancock was a strangely honored guest. "As the wife of His Excellency was seated at the table, on which was spread an elegant collation, on board the vessel of the French commander, he requested her to ring a small bell which he handed her. She did so. This was the preconcerted signal for a general salute from all the guns of the fleet. She was startled alike out of her official dignity and personal propriety by the deafening peal of artillery that ensued." For three months the vast line-of-battle ships lay at anchor here; and Massachusetts called out nine regiments of militia to aid in defending them against the British armada outside.

Once a clipper-schooner, laden down with powder for the use of our armies, attempted to run the blockade. She had been ingeniously disguised as a rough and dirty coaster, with torn sails and littered deck, and all her men out of sight; and her shrewd captain carried on the following dialogue with the commander of the cruiser that overhauled him: —

"Heave to, you —— Yankee!" cried the English officer from the quarter-deck. "Why the devil didn't you do so when I fired a shot across your bows?"

"Didn't know what you were arter," called out a slovenly-looking individual at the helm; "didn't think you was goin' to fire right into our little schooner, that wa'n't a-goin' to do you no harm."

"What schooner is that?" called the amused officer.

"*Pretty Sally;* named for my wife, to hum."

"Where do you hail from?"

"*Taunton, good Lord!*"

"What's your own name?"

Sea-View, from Atlantic Hill, Nantasket.

"Captin Silas Slocom; and I ain't ashamed of that name, nohow nor nowheres."

"What sort of a cargo have you got aboard?"

"Long-faced gentry — there's a critter grunting now; barn-yard fowls — didn't you hear that one crow jest now? long sarse and short sarse; and near abouts a bar'l o' potatoes I got down East."

"Well, strike: why don't you strike?"

"Strike, hey? I ain't got nobody to strike, 'less I strike brother Jonathan, and I guess he'd strike back; I just struck little Fidelle, and knocked him overboard, plaguy clumsy-like it was, and our Sally'll be all-fired sorry, I kin tell ye; and if ye don't want no more of me, I'll be gettin' along, for it's e'ena'most night now."

"This is a poor, harmless kind of fellow," said the British officers in council, "carrying home provisions to keep his family from starving. He really isn't worth taking, and it would do us no good and him a great deal of harm if we brought him aboard and sunk his old rattle-trap." The naval commander sung out, "Heave ahead there, old fellow! and don't let us catch you again, or it'll be the worse for you." Off went the clipper up the harbor, and soon moored alongside the wharf at Boston, with her precious cargo.

It was in the summer of 1780 that a formidable naval battle occurred off Boston Light, when the British 50-gun ship *Sagittaire* pounced on a French convoy bound inward from Newport to Boston. The frigate which guarded the little fleet carried but 32 guns; yet it boldly attacked the hostile ship, while the merchantmen, laden with spars and naval stores, bore away up the harbor. Three French men-of-war lay off Castle Island, but they made no attempt to aid their overmatched sister-ship, and the battle went on for over an hour, while the sacred height of Beacon Hill was covered with Bostonians, watching the combat with spy-glasses. At last the roar of artillery ceased, and the French flag descended from the mast-head of the *Magicienne;* and, during the subsequent hours of that beautiful morning, the rigging of the two vessels was repaired, and the dead sailors were thrown into the Light-house Roads. Some hours later the French fleet made sail, and chased the British frigate and her prize to Halifax, whence they returned empty-handed, ten days later.

In 1781 the French army which had fought so gallantly for us in the Southern campaigns marched into Boston, in grand state: the Bourbonnais Regiment, uniformed in white and gold; the Soissonnais Grenadiers, in white, red, and pink, with waving plumes, commanded by Count Segur, afterwards a peer of France, whose Memoirs are so well-known; the Saintonge Regiment, in white and blue, led by Count de Custine and the Prince de Broglie, both of whom were guillotined during the French Revolution; the four battalions of the Royal Deux-Ponts Regiment, in white, red, and gold, led by Count de Deux-Ponts, afterwards made famous at the battle of Hohenlinden; Lauzun's famous Legion, whose chivalric leader was afterwards guillotined; the Royal Artillery, in blue and red, most of whose soldiers remained with Washington to besiege New York; the Engineer Corps, in blue and gray; and other brilliant companies, with bands of music, white lily-flags, and all the paraphernalia of old-time warriors. Among the leaders were Vioménil, who was slain afterwards, while defending the Tuileries; the Chevalier de Lameth, who became a soldier of the Empire; the Marquis de Champcenetz; the Count de Dumas; Berthier, afterwards a marshal under Napoleon; and many other famous nobles and warriors. It has been reported also that Bernadotte, afterwards king of Sweden, was a soldier in this army. The young Marquis of Talleyrand-Perigord marched as a volunteer among the Grenadiers. This martial host embarked on the French fleet in the Roads. There lay the *Triomphant, Couronne,* and *Duc de Bourgogne,* all 80-gun ships; the *Hercule, Souverain, Neptune, Bourgogne, Northumberland, Bravo,* and *Citoyen,* all 74-gun ships-of-the-line; and the frigates *Amazone* and *Néréide.* On Christmas Eve, 1781, this splendid little army left the harbor, when the French fleet, ten vessels in all, mounting 754 guns, put to sea, headed by the *Triomphant.*

In the summer of 1782 the British frigate *Albemarle* cruised in the Bay,

A Coaling-Station on the Nantasket-Beach Railroad.

and made sad havoc with the coasting-vessels; although its commander, Nelson (who afterwards became the most illustrious of English admirals), was as lenient as his instructions would allow, and often released the unfortunate little sloops and schooners that were brought under his guns. Pleasant stories are still extant, in the Old Colony, of Lord Nelson's courtesy and kindliness.

In 1787, 1788, and 1789, the harbor of Boston was the winter-quarters of the French fleets in the Western Atlantic, since there they were safe from the fearful hurricanes of the West Indies. In the latter year, the same in which Washington visited Boston and was snubbed by Gov. Hancock, the

French vessels in the harbor were the line-of-battle ships *Leopard* and *Patriot*, with several frigates; and the British man-of-war *Penelope* lay in the roads at the same time.

During the Revolutionary War, the harbor was a nest of saucy privateers, of which this port alone had 365 sail, by which many hundreds of British vessels were captured. Among these were such strangely named craft as the *Sturdy Beggar*, *Charming Sally*, *American Tartar*, *Reprisal*, *Viper*, *Lizard*, and *True Blue*. The State of Massachusetts also had ten well-armed war-ships, which cruised very effectively on the outer seas. In the War of 1812 Boston sent out many privateers, roaming the Atlantic in search of British merchantmen or small cruisers. If the main channel was blockaded, these gallant little war-ships would scurry out Broad Sound, or creep through Shirley Gut, and run for the Capes, with all sail set. Oftentimes they lurked in the lee of the islands until propitious gales had driven the blockaders out of sight, and then away they went:

> "A randy dandy, dandy, oh!
> And a whet of ale and brandy, oh!
> A rumbelow, and seaward, ho!
> And cheer, my merrymen, all, oh!"

The port was blockaded during nearly all the time of the War of 1812-15, but the American frigates ran in and out without much difficulty. Among those who thus escaped the British fleet were the *United States*, *President*, *Congress*, *Hornet*, *Frolic*, *John Adams*, *Argus*, *Nautilus*, *Rattlesnake*, and *Siren*. The *Constitution* passed in and out seven times. It was from the Roads that the *Constitution*, 44, sailed, in August, 1812, on the cruise which resulted in her capture of the British frigate *Guerrière*, 49, after a most spirited naval battle, commemorated in the song beginning:—

> "I often have been told
> That the British seamen bold
> Could beat the tars of France neat and handy, O!
> But they never found their match,
> Till the Yankees did them catch,
> For the Yankee tars for fighting are the dandy, O!

> "Oh, the *Guerrière* so bold,
> On the foaming ocean rolled,
> Commanded by proud Dacres the grandee, O!
> With as choice a British crew
> As a rammer ever drew,
> They could beat the Frenchmen two to one so handy, O!'

The British had laughed enough at a navy which they said was composed of "half a dozen of fir frigates with bits of striped bunting tied to their mast-heads;" and so soon Capt. Hull was able to announce the capture of the *Guerrière*, dating his despatch, "Off Boston Light."

During a considerable part of the War of 1812, guard-boats were stationed here every night, with rockets, which they were to send up in the event of the approach of hostile ships. In case of such an alarm, the reserve forces encamped at South Boston were to be hurried into the forts, with field artillery; and the frigates in the inner harbor were to bear down on the

View across Hull Bay, from Peddock's Island.

channel. Fortunately the rockets were not needed, and the liveliest night in Boston Harbor is still to come.

The Navy Club of Harvard College commemorated a tradition that one day during the War of 1812 the senior class was enjoying a sail in the lower harbor, when their little craft was pounced upon and captured by the boats of one of the British blockaders. After a brief captivity, the pining lads were set free, and returned to Cambridge with their love of adventure thrown far in abeyance. For thirty years or more thereafter, the Navy Club sailed down the harbor on every recurring Artillery-Election day, but His Britannic Majesty's mariners troubled them no more. The Lord High Admiral of Harvard was always the young gentleman who had the most friends in his class and the most enemies in the Faculty, and who had been suspended at least once.

Here the *Independence*, 74, the flag-ship of the Mediterranean squadron, with the *Erie, Chippewa,* and *Lynx,* set sail, under command of stout old Bainbridge, in 1815, on the expedition against Algiers and the Barbary powers. One of the strangest tragedies of the harbor was the destruction of the *Canton Packet* in 1817. This fine ship was about to sail to the East Indies, with a valuable cargo and $400,000 in specie; and on the day before

Scene near Nantasket.

departure her negro steward demanded permission to go ashore, to enjoy the revels of Artillery-Election day. This privilege was denied him, and he secured a novel revenge. When the crew were ashore, he fired a pistol into the casks of gunpowder which composed a part of the cargo, and blew up the ship, losing his own misanthropic life in the general ruin. The explosion alarmed the whole town, and garbled traditions of the blackamoor's achievement were narrated for half a century afterwards.

In 1844 the harbor was frozen over to Castle Island, and thence nearly to Broad Sound, with huge fields of ice choked up in the lower channels. Tents and booths were set up on the level icy plain; fast horses made their best time on this novel race-course; and thousands of skaters glided hither and thither, in every direction. Many vessels were blockaded, and among them the Cunard steamship *Britannia;* and to effect their release the merchants of Boston paid the ice-cutters of Fresh Pond $15,000 to cut a canal of great length, 150 feet wide, down which the *Britannia* moved to the distant sea, escorted by cheering crowds. The work took 500 men three days.

When the Massachusetts volunteers were embarking here for the southern sea-board, during the Secession War, many a ship passed down the harbor, laden with the pride of the State, — its brave and patriotic young men, bound for the insurrectionary cities. In dreary November of 1862, the 50th and 51st Massachusetts Regiments sailed from Boston, the one for New Orleans, the other for Newbern. In May and June, 1863, the 54th and 55th Regiments, both of them composed of negroes, sailed from the harbor for

Distant View of Atlantic Hill.

the Carolina coast, where the first-named won immortal fame by its charge on Fort Wagner. There was much suffering here during the long October storm of 1863, when the 3d, 5th, and 8th nine-months Regiments, and the 43d, 44th, 45th, and 46th Regiments of Massachusetts volunteers lay in transports in the Roads, waiting for a chance to get to sea. At last they sailed away, and down to Newbern, where the Carolinas welcomed them with blander skies, which have now for well-nigh twenty years arched over the graves of many of their number.

Turning from these more serious concerns to study the chief uses for the harbor, as far as the average Bostonian goes, we find that the custom of sailing down these blue reaches for pleasure has come down to us from the very heart of the Puritan days. As far back as July, 1687, Judge Sewall came down the harbor with a party "to Alderton's Point, and with our Boat beyond, quite out of the Massachusetts Bay, and there catch'd fresh Cod." Throughout the Provincial period, other parties of grave gentlemen are occasionally seen indulging in the same exciting but apostolic pursuit; and perhaps, although the worship of Nature had not then come into vogue, they sometimes looked with a kindly eye on the grandeur of the sea and sky. In a letter written nearly a century ago, this passage appears: "The gentlemen, sometimes by themselves, and sometimes in company with ladies, spend the day partly on the water and partly on some of the islands in this very delightful harbor." In the Massachusetts Historical Society's volume for 1810, it is said that the islands were at that time much resorted to by pleasure-parties from the towns on the main, who went down in small sailboats, and had quiet family and society picnics by the water-side.

The first steamboat in the harbor was the *Massachusetts*, a Philadelphia-built vessel, which made several trips to Salem, and one to Hingham in 1816. On July 4 the *Daily Advertiser* noted that she took a party of excursionists "to sail about the islands in this harbor." But the people fought shy of this new method of travel, and the enterprise resulted in a heavy loss. The next winter she was wrecked on the North-Carolina coast. In 1818 the *Eagle* ran as an excursion-boat in Boston Harbor. Many were the vessels, large and small, that succeeded them; until now, when every variety of pleasure-craft that goes by steam is found here, from the huge excursion-boats, carrying thousands of passengers daily on their decks, to the wasp-like little steam-launches which skim up and down among the islands. The Secession War caused a partial suspension of the excursion business; for the best of the steamboats were sent away into the Southern seas as despatch-boats, and for other warlike uses. But now the fleet is larger than ever, and all its resources are taxed to the uttermost. There are steamboats running several times a day to Hull, the Pemberton, Downer Landing, and Nantasket Beach. The *Anita* makes several voyages daily to Nahant. The *Longfellow* crosses Massachusetts Bay to Provincetown. Other boats there are making daily trips to Plymouth, on the South Shore, and to Gloucester, at the end of the North Shore. The Carnival of Boston is two months long, and is enacted on the waters to the eastward; and many are the thousands of citizens who richly enjoy the keen and bracing air of the sea, and derive from it enduring benefit.

Among the excursionists have been many very notable persons, who have recorded their impressions in varying phrases. Harriet Martineau, in her "Western Travel," took this practical view of the seaward suburbs: "The scenery of Massachusetts Bay is a treasure which Boston possesses over and above what is enjoyed by her sister cities of the East. New York has a host of beauties about her, it is true, — the North River, Hoboken, and Staten Island; but there is something in the singularity of Nahant, and the wild beauty of Cape Ann, more captivating than the crowded, fully appropriated beauties around New York. In summer and autumn, when the Southerners, who cannot afford to board, are panting and sickening in the glare, among sands and swamps, the poorest of the citizens of Massachusetts may refresh himself amidst the sea-breezes on the bright promontories or cool caverns of his native shore." Another famous Englishwoman, Lady Mary Wortley Montague, gave us this pretty little vignette: "In returning through the harbor of Boston from Nahant, we were full of admiration of its scenery: the many lovely islands with which it is beautifully studded, and the superb view of Boston itself, so nobly surmounted by its crown-like State House, enchanted us."

Here, too, among these green Hesperides, over-arched with a sky fairer even than "the tempest-proof pavilions of the deep Italian air," many of the foremost American artists have found their inspiration. Allston's calm and saintly eyes have rested upon them with satisfaction; Copley and Stuart often surveyed the blue harbor from the Boston hills; Hunt, Norton, and

View toward Boston, from Old Fort, Point Shirley.

Foxcroft Cole have found many of their best scenes between Long Wharf and Point Allerton; and the younger marine-painters, Halsall, Lansil, Webber, and others, discover abundant material here for many beautiful pictures. The venerable George L. Brown, whom the Romans called "The American Claude," lived until recently in South Boston, where his studio overlooked the Bay; and he painted the scene outspread before him with a brush dipped in Venetian sunsets. Some of his harbor-pictures needed only the insertion of two or three gondolas and the inevitable Salute domes to pass for scenes on the Lagoon. He was right in doing so; for the vivid coloring is equal in both the eastward-facing ports, Venice and Boston, although with us somewhat harder and clearer. Here Dante could have found that rare vagation which he called *il tremolar della marina*, as well as in the seas off Pisa or Ravenna. Certainly one of the most impressive of modern historical paintings is Halsall's "Arrival of Governor Winthrop's Colony in Boston Harbor," depicting in glowing colors the scene which the poet describes in the ballad of "The Lady Arbella:" —

> "The low islands part, as an opening door,
> And they glide in and anchor in sight of the shore;
> Where the wild flower's fragrance, the strawberry's scent,
> With the music of song-bird and billow is blent."

Nor have the poets of New England remained uninfluenced by the charms of the "lovely innermost nook of Massachusetts Bay." This element appears most strongly in the works of Longfellow, many of whose poems were written near the rocks of Nahant, where he watched the white caps, the flying birds, the distant sails, —

> "Till my soul is full of longing
> For the secret of the sea,
> And the heart of the great ocean
> Sends a thrilling pulse through me."

Whittier gives his deepest study and sweetest songs to the Merrimac and the coasts of Newbury and Hampton, but has found grace to paint this pretty picture of Boston Harbor: —

> "Broad in the sunshine stretched away,
> With its capes and islands, the turquoise bay;
> And over water and dusk of pines
> Blue hills lifted their faint outlines."

No nobler naval song has ever been written than Holmes's "Ay, tear her tattered ensign down!" and many another ballad, like "The Wasp and the Hornet" and "The Steamboat," and many a breezy allusion in his other poems, attest the inspiration of the adjacent narrow seas. Who does not remember the last verse of his "Boston Tea Party"? —

> "The waters of the rebel bay
> Have kept their tea-leaf savor.
> Our old North-Enders in their spray
> Still taste a Hyson flavor."

Lowell is the viking of the poets. He finds inextinguishable joy in donning a tarpaulin suit, and sailing down through the island-passages, and far out into the Bay, in one of the swift pilot-boats which cruise between the capes of Massachusetts. The voice of the northern sea is heard even in "Sir Launfal;" it breaks, now and then, into the rural "Biglow Papers;" it throbs grandly through the "Commemoration Ode;" and in the Appledore poems and "The Voyage to Vinland" the wild rush of whitening waves is heard. As far back as 1842, while at Nantasket, Lowell wrote his "Siren-song."

Dana, one of the foremost poets of a half-century ago, whose "Buccaneer" is one of our classics, had his beautiful rural home on the North Shore, within view of Boston Light. In previous pages we have seen Thoreau wandering down Nantasket Beach, and Stoddard lingering on the Hingham wharves, and the author of "America" enjoying summer rest at Hull.

Hawthorne was for years officially connected with the harbor and its commerce, and spent many a day on its blue expanses, and among its sea-browned mariners. Dr. Loring tells a quaint story of the great author's life here: "An attempt on the part of a rough and overbearing sea-captain to interfere with his business as an inspector of the customs in charge of his ship was met with such a terrific uprising of spiritual and physical wrath that the dismayed captain fled up the wharf, and took refuge at the feet of him who sat at the receipt of customs, inquiring, with a sailor's emotions and a sailor's tongue, 'What, in God's name, have you sent on board my ship as an inspector?'"

The Lobsterman.

Daniel Webster made many journeys down the harbor, on the way to his beloved home on the Marshfield coast, and acknowledged the deep and controlling power which the adjacent seas exercised over his spirit. In one of his letters, written from a great distance, he breaks through his prolonged sentences about contemporary diplomacy and statecraft, with the passionate cry, "Oh, the sea, the sea! — and Marshfield!"

John Lothrop Motley was familiar with every cove and islet inside of Point Allerton, especially to the southward of the ship-channel; and his early novel of "Merry-Mount" is incomparably the best description of the strange people on the islands and headlands in the ante-colonial days. Mr. Howells has given many a cheery day to the overflowing life of Nantasket, which he has described with inimitable pleasantry and appreciation, especially in that marvellous study of *bourgeois* life, "The Rise of Silas Lapham," so many of whose scenes are laid on this strand, where the patrician Tom Corey visits Irene Lapham.

But, whatever may have been its incidental interest in other ways, the chief value of Boston Harbor to America is found in its intimate connection with commerce and the navy. The naval constructor who searched the Yankee harbors for a site on which to build a navy-yard must have borne in mind Admiral Montague's declaration that "God Almighty made Noddle's Island on purpose for a dockyard;" for he reported that "Boston, from the natural strength of its situation, the great number of ship-carpenters in its vicinity, and of its seamen, must always remain a building-place, and a place of rendezvous for our navy of the first importance; while the rise of tide, eleven feet, would greatly lessen the expense of emptying a dock. . . . The outer harbor of President and Nantasket Roads affords a large and safe haven for large fleets from the weather; and the inner harbor, safe from winds, freshets, and enemy, could be securely fortified at an easy expense." The first vessel built at the new navy-yard was the sloop-of-war *Frolic* (in 1813), whose broadsides made mournful music for many a British craft. In 1815 the three-decker *Independence*, 74, was launched, amid great rejoicings. After so many years, she has retired into peaceful repose as receiving-ship of the Mare-Island Navy Yard in California. The *Constitution* and *Argus* were built at adjacent private yards. The *Argus* fought many gallant battles on the Tripolitan coast and in the War of 1812, and was at last captured in the English Channel, by H. B. M. brig *Pelican*, in 1813. In 1826 the *Warren* was launched here, and soon afterwards sailed to the Far East, where she did memorable service against the Greek pirates in the Ægean Sea.

The Bell-Buoy.

The next year the handsome sloop-of-war *Falmouth* was built here. Among other war-vessels launched at Charlestown were the *Cyane*, *Porpoise*, *Plymouth*, *Marion*, *Alligator*, *Boxer*, *Bainbridge*, *Erie*, *Princeton*, and the line-of-battle ship *Vermont*. At this yard were built (in 1842 and 1854, respectively) the famous war-ships *Cumberland* and *Merrimac*. After years of service in foreign seas, the two vessels met in deadly conflict, off Fortress Monroe; and the *Cumberland* sank, amid the horror of the whole naval world. In 1858, from the upper ship-house, the historic war steamship *Hartford*, Admiral Farragut's favorite flag-ship, was launched.

During the Secession War many famous vessels were built at the Navy Yard, including the iron-clads *Monadnock*, *Nahant*, *Nausett*, *Nantucket*, *Canonicus*, *Casco*, *Chimo*, *Shawnee*, *Squando*, and *Suncook*. Of the thirty other frigates built here during the same period, and, as it were, born into Boston Harbor, the most notable were the *Wachusett*, which captured the rebel-gunboat *Florida;* the *Huron*, whose fatal wreck is still remembered;

CHARLESTOWN NAVY YARD

the *Tallapoosa*, *Winooski*, *Ashuelot*, and *Housatonic*. Thirty steamers and numerous sailing-vessels besides were refitted here for naval purposes. Most of these were prizes, captured by the blockading squadrons off the Southern ports. Among them was the formidable rebel ram *Atlanta*.

The receiving-ship, lying off the yard, is the famous old frigate *Wabash*, which won many a hard knock during the Secession War. Beyond here are the vast dry-dock, rolling-mill, brass-works, rope-walk, barracks, gun-park, and battery of thirty cannon. Here rest the remains of the huge double-turreted iron-clad *Miantonomoh;* and in one of the ship-houses the ancient three-decker *Virginia* stood on the stocks for more than half a century. In the stream, towards Chelsea, long floated the decaying old war-ships *Ohio*, *Iowa*, and *Connecticut*.

The maritime enterprise of Boston began early. It was but a year after the founding of the colony, that Gov. Winthrop launched the barque *Blessing of the Bay;* and in 1635 the ship *Seafort*, 400 tons, was built. At first, the price of passage from London to Boston was £5: and goods were freighted at £4 a ton. Winthrop's colonists came over under this schedule. The average time of passage was sixty days. The first trading-vessels went to the Indian country for corn, and presently Dutch ships began to come in heavily laden. A profitable commerce sprang up with the Dutch and Swedish towns on the Delaware and Hudson: with Fayal and Madeira, and the Isle of Sable. Ships came in continually from England: there were 298 of them that arrived in the first ten years, bringing 21,200 passengers, from whom descended the chief New-England families of to-day. Lord Bellomont reported, in 1698, that the town owned 194 sailing-craft, adding, " I believe I may venture to say that there are more good vessels belonging to the town of Boston than to all Scotland and Ireland." In 1738 there were 41 topsail vessels built here.

For many decades Massachusetts was the Holland of America, the headquarters of the carrying-trade by sea; and Boston had fully 500 sail of vessels, excluding fishing and coasting craft. The commerce with Britain, the Dutch colonies, Surinam and Martinique, was large and lucrative. As early as 1720 the royal customs officers reported an average of 24,000 tons of shipping as clearing from Boston yearly. After the Revolution an active trade sprung up between this port and the Isles of France, China, and India; and many a neat little ship of 300 tons started hence on the long voyage, with supercargoes from the then rising families of Derby, Shaw, Perkins, and Silsbee. The *Columbia* sailed in 1787, and discovered the famous Oregon river which still bears her name; exchanged her cargo of Yankee wares for otter-furs brought in by the Indians: called at the Sandwich Islands; visited Canton, where her furs were exchanged for tea; and in 1790 sailed up Boston Harbor, firing Federal salutes. She was attended in this great voyage by the 90-ton sloop *Washington*, the first vessel of her class to circumnavigate the earth. The brig *Hope* then sailed for the Northwest Coast and China, and in her voyage discovered the Marquesas Islands. In 1790 the arrivals from abroad at this port numbered 455 vessels, exclusive of 1,200 sail of coasters; and in a single day as many as 70 vessels left the harbor, bound for all parts of the globe. Most of these Indiamen were well armed, and had officers of naval grades, and large crews, competent to protect their cargoes, which were usually valued at several hundred thousand dollars. In the words of the time, these gallant little frigates were "prepared to fight their way for rich cargoes." In the East they were annoyed by Chinese and Malay pirates; in the Mediterranean, by Barbary corsairs; and on the high seas everywhere by British and French frigates and letters-of-marque. Their voyages were through such vast distances that they had need to be prepared for all manner of receptions. Many were the Boston ships that rounded Cape Horn; traded their Yankee cargoes for otter-furs and other products of the North-west Coast; sold them in China for teas and silks; crossed to Valparaiso, and left parts of these precious goods in exchange for copper; carried the metal to England; and finally felt the waters of Nantasket Roads ripple along their keels, with each supercargo rejoicing in a profit of a quarter of a million dollars made for the owners out of the venturesome voyage.

At the Harbor's Mouth.

At last the Napoleonic decrees and the War of 1812 came, inflicting severe blows on this flourishing commerce. Not only were there licensed buccaneers on the ocean, but even the home-port was closed by hostile war-fleets. Occasionally a swift Boston Indiaman would dash through the blockaders, and enter the harbor safely, deep-laden with silks and teas from Canton. In this manner the *Rambler*, *Jacob Jones*, and *Kamaahmaah* escaped the *Grampus* and *Glendower*, British frigates which were watching for them in the Bay. They went up through the islands, firing salutes from their batteries, and waking the echoes of the Blue Hills with guns that had roared in the China seas, or off the Polynesian coral-reefs.

The Cunard Line of ocean steamships was founded in 1840, and for eight years Boston was their only American port. Here came in, bi-weekly, the *Unicorn, Britannia, Acadia, Caledonia,* and other Cunarders, — awkward paddle-wheel boats, largely filled up with coal-bunkers. Twice (in 1844 and 1857) the harbor was frozen up; and each time the citizens had long canals cut through the ice, down to Nantasket Roads.

In 1844 Train's Liverpool packets began their voyages, which were made regularly once a month for many years. These were handsome Medford and East-Boston ships, and formed a large fleet. The same firm which founded this line now runs the Warren Line of steamships. Another class of vessels made the long voyages to Riga, Cronstadt, and other Russian ports; carrying sugar and cotton, and bringing back hemp and iron. This trade began as early as 1783, and continued for three-quarters of a century.

In 1855 the commerce of Boston had reached its height, and 541,644 tons of shipping were owned here. The rise of New York as a centre of commerce, the unwise local legislation of Massachusetts, and the depredations of rebel privateers, seriously injured the sea-trade of Boston. In 1879–80 even the Cunarders were withdrawn from this port. In 1869 not a single steamer sailed from Boston to Europe direct. Of late years the current of commerce has changed, and now the sailings of steamships for Europe average more than one a day. In 1880 there were 196 steamships from Boston to Liverpool alone, upwards of 40 each to Glasgow and London, and 37 to Hull and West Hartlepool. Various new branches of commerce have arisen under these new conditions. In 1875 the first shipment of cattle was made to England, and this trade now amounts to $10,000,000 a year. Low rates in freighting cotton hence have caused its export value to rise from $135,000 in 1870 to over $7,000,000 in 1881. The total value of Boston's exports in 1850 was $7,000,000; in 1881 it had risen to $72,000,000. The great merchants and railway strategists of the port claim that it has better terminal facilities than any other American city; and are firm in the faith that it will never occupy a relative position lower than its present one, that of second port of the United States. Between 1869 and 1881 inclusive the foreign vessels entering the port brought in upwards of a quarter of a million of immigrants. Now such enormous steamships as the *Parisian* and the *Hooper* frequently enter the harbor, — vessels so huge that all the members of Gov. Winthrop's colony could be carried upon one of them, and yet its decks would be lonely. Professor Mitchell reported that Boston has the best harbor in the world, perfectly land-locked, and shielded from heavy winds, and possessing many advantages, besides being a day's sail nearer Europe than New York is. There is, therefore, great reason to hope that Nantasket Roads may become an avenue of nations, the portal of a grander Venice of the West, the kindly rival of the New-York Narrows.

Many years ago, in an attempt to break a galling blockade by British men-of-war, the great naval battle took place between the *Chesapeake* and *Shannon*, on June 1, 1813, which resulted in one of the best ships of the American navy being conquered and carried away within sight of Boston Light.

While the *Shannon*, 38, Capt. Broke, had been cruising off Boston Harbor, her crew received careful drilling and practice in target-firing, and reached a high and efficient state of discipline. The U. S. frigate *Chesapeake*, 38, Capt. Lawrence, lay in port, and Broke sent in a manly challenge for her to come out and fight; but, before this missive reached its destination, the American ship was already standing out to sea. The *Shannon* had 330 men and 52 guns (firing a broadside of 550 pounds); the *Chesapeake* had 379 men and 50 guns (542 pounds in a broadside). The crew of the American vessel were, however, unpractised, half-drilled, and dissatisfied on account of not receiving prize-money due. At one o'clock the *Chesapeake* rounded Boston Light, and stood off after her antagonist. About four hours later she hauled up, nearly off Marblehead, and soon opened fire on the approaching American. The action immediately became very hot, and broadside after broadside roared from either ship, at close quarters. In the first six minutes the *Chesapeake* suffered terribly in men and material; the decks were almost hidden by flying splinters, hammocks, and other *débris;* Lieut. Ludlow had fallen; and Capt. Lawrence, mortally wounded by Lieut. Law of the British marines, had been carried below, exclaiming, "Don't give up the ship!" Twelve minutes after the first gun was fired, Capt. Broke boarded the *Chesapeake*, followed by 20 men; and after some hot fighting with scattered parties of American sailors and marines (the Portuguese and other foreigners who composed a part of the crew having fled between decks), the stars and stripes were hauled down.

The battle lasted just fifteen minutes, during which the *Chesapeake* was struck by 362 cannon-shot, and lost 61 men killed and 85 wounded; and the *Shannon* received 158 cannon-shot, and lost 83 men in killed and wounded. Capt. Broke, who had been severely wounded, was made a baronet; and the chief American officers, Lawrence and Ludlow, were buried at Halifax with military honors. The hills and headlands from Hull to Marblehead had been covered by thousands upon thousands of spectators of this mighty naval duel; and when the British flag was seen rising through the cannon-smoke to the mast-head of the *Chesapeake*, a profound grief took possession of the assembled multitudes, who had never doubted that the gallant Lawrence would bring the Britisher captive into Boston Bay. Not long after the close of the war, of which this was so sad an episode, new departments of commerce came into existence; and it was but a few years before steam-vessels appeared in the Bay.

After glancing briefly at a few historic, naval, and commercial facts, let us take a purely contemplative view, in the little poem on Boston Harbor, written by Robert Southey, once Poet-laureate of England. The lines record, in placid Lake-country measures, the descriptions of the scene given to Southey by his Boston friend George Ticknor.

> "Scattered within the peaceful bay
>   Many a fair isle and islet lay,
> And rocks and banks which threatened there
>   No peril to the mariner.
> The shores which bent around were gay
> With maizels, and with pastures green,
> And rails and hedge-row trees between
>   And fields for harvest white,
> And dwellings sprinkled up and down;
> And round about the clustered town,
>
> Which rose in sunshine bright,
> Was many a sheltered garden spot,
> And many a sunny orchard plot,
>   And bowers which might invite
> The studious man to take his seat
> Within their quiet, cool retreat,
>   When noon was at its height.
> No heart that was at ease, I ween,
> Could gaze on that surrounding scene
>   Without a calm delight."

Ralph Waldo Emerson shall have the last and highest word in this chapter of mosaics and fragments: —

> "The rocky nook with its hill-tops three
>   Looked eastward from the farms,
> And twice each day the flowing sea
>   Took Boston in its arms;
> The men of yore were stout and poor,
> And sailed for bread to every shore.
>
> "The waves that rocked them on the deep
>   To them their secret told:
> Said the winds that sung the lads to sleep,
>   'Like us be free and bold!'
> The honest waves refuse to slaves
> The empire of the ocean caves."

The Outer Reefs.

Plymouth, the Land of the Pilgrims.

THE PILGRIM MONUMENT — THE ANCIENT TOWN — THE CLIFFORD.

DOWN to the quaint, picturesque and memorable old town of Plymouth, the most ancient settlement in New England, it is but an hour and a half from Boston by the Old Colony Railroad, passing through Hingham and Cohasset, Scituate and Marshfield, and other venerable and moss-grown villages. It would be difficult to name any other place in America with such a profoundly interesting historical event as that which has made the name of Plymouth Rock forever famous in the annals of devotion and freedom. Upwards of thirty thousand persons come hither every summer, making reverent pilgrimages to the cradle of American civilization. For these, and for all who love the antique and historic, Plymouth has well-nigh unrivalled attractions. Here is the renowned Rock, down by the waterside and the wharves of the small local shipping, and overarched by a stately granite canopy, in whose top are the bones of several of the Pilgrims. Up in the village rises the massive fire-proof structure of Pilgrim Hall, consecrated to relics and memorials of the first colonists, — Lucy's great picture of the Embarkation from Delft; Halsall's new painting of the Mayflower in Plymouth harbor; the Winslow portraits; Governor Carver's chair, the sword of Miles Standish; and many other mementoes of the olden time. Near this shrine is the country court-house, with rare records and documents of the seventeenth century

Leyden Street, Plymouth.

The harbor before the town is sheltered by a league-long strip of sandy beach, north of which are the well-known points of the Gurnet and Saquish, with their light-house, ruined fort, and farm-houses. Further in, towards the Duxbury shore and the landing-place of the French Atlantic telegraph, the green slopes of Clark's Island rise over the clear waters, where the Pilgrims passed a day or two in secure rest before attempting the unknown perils of the mainland beyond. The scenery about the bay and harbor is as pleasing as the historical reminiscences are interesting, and there are plenty of snug sail-boats and smacks, with experienced skippers, to take people out on these quiet waters.

On a noble hill near the Samoset House rises the Pilgrim National Monument, a vast pile of carved granite, crowned by a very impressive statue of Faith, forty feet high, and the largest stone figure in the world. This magnificent work of art cost thirty thousand dollars, and was presented by the Hon. Oliver Ames, a native of Plymouth. On the huge buttresses of the monument, adorned with reliefs of scenes in the history of the colony, are colossal statues of Morality and Education; and similar figures of Law and Freedom are to be added in time. America has no other monument so vast, so imposing, so worthy.

North Street, Plymouth.

The great statue of Faith, visible by the mariner far off at sea, like the ancient figure of Pallas Athene on the Acropolis, is pronounced by James Jackson Jarves, the art-critic, to be thoroughly American in meaning and execution, "fittingly representing its purpose in unmistakable grandeur, severity, and simplicity." Mrs. M. E. Blake says: "There is such an inner sense of uplifting in the poise of the whole figure, with her star-crowned brow bared under the eternal majesty of heaven; there is so much of beauty and promise and accomplishment in the beautiful panorama that lies under her gaze, that you reach at last the moral exaltation which Plymouth Rock inspired and sustained in the annals of the country." The vast figure rises over the low hills which shelter Plymouth, like a protecting goddess, full of immeasurable power and invincible strength.

KING'S HANDBOOK OF BOSTON HARBOR. 291

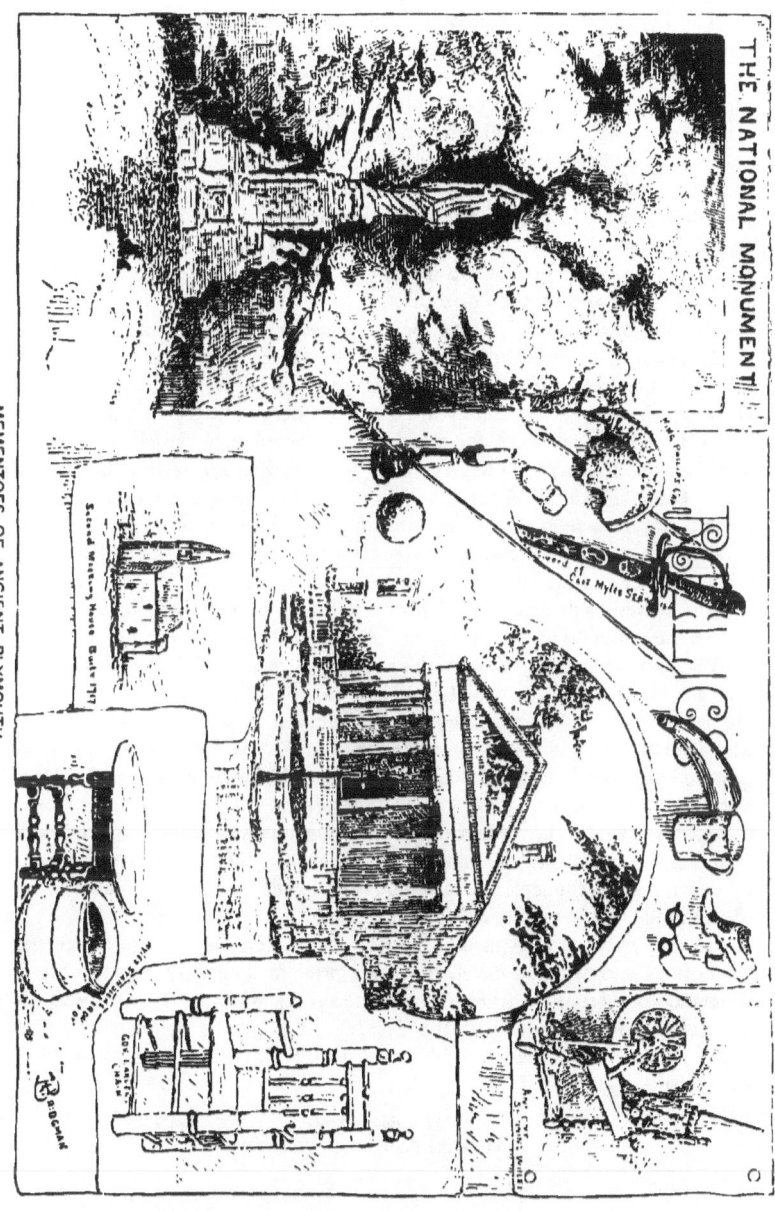

THE NATIONAL MONUMENT.

MEMENTOES OF ANCIENT PLYMOUTH.

The Burying Hill rises above the Unitarian Church, and is one of the most interesting localities in New England. On every side are the tombs and monuments of the founders of the State and their descendants, the Bradfords, Cushmans, and other old families; some of them rather notable memorials, erected by later generations, and others low-lying tombstones, ancient and mossy, and covered with quaint symbols and inscriptions. Above these sacred graves the pleased eye wanders over an exquisite panorama of sea and shore, lonely islands, far-reaching promontories, and distant blue hills, reaching from Captain's Hill on the left, and Manomet Highlands on the right, out across the blue sea to where the sandy strand of Cape Cod bounds the view, low down on the horizon.

On this bleak summit stood (on a site now marked by four stone posts) the fortified log-church and watch-tower, the former bearing six three-pound cannon on its flat roof, and the latter occupied by vigilant sentinels. De Rasiere, who visited the colony in 1627, thus described their church-going: "The lower part they use for their church, where they preach on Sundays and the usual holidays. They assemble by beat of drum, each with his musket or firelock, in front of the captain's door; they have their cloaks on and place themselves in order there abreast, and are led by a sergeant without beat of drum. Behind comes the governor in a long robe, beside, on the right hand, comes the preacher with his cloak on, and on the left hand the captain with his side-arms and cloak on and with a small cane in his hand; and so they march in good order, and each gets his arms down near him."

The rambler among Plymouth's ancient streets will find the dark old Carver-Mitchell, Stevens, and Leach houses, all built before the year 1680; the monument on Training Green, commemorating the Plymouth soldiers who died in the late civil war; Watson's Hill, where Massasoit and fifty grim red warriors concluded a lasting peace with the colonists; and Pilgrim Springs, where the fair Priscillas of the forlorn village came for water in those dreary winter days when the sturdy Pilgrims were beset on every side with dangers, pestilence, famine and the savages. Many other localities in the environs are connected with interesting events in that ancient time, or with legends of the remote and romantic past.

Leyden street was named in memory of the city in the Low Countries where the Pilgrims dwelt for eleven years prior to their desperate venture to America, and here their descendants point out the sites of Edward Winslow's and John Howland's houses, the first church, and the colony's commonhouse. Above the Rock is the bluff of Cole's Hill, the first burial-ground of the Pilgrims, —

> "The hill of hallowed brow,
> Where the Pilgrim sleepeth now."

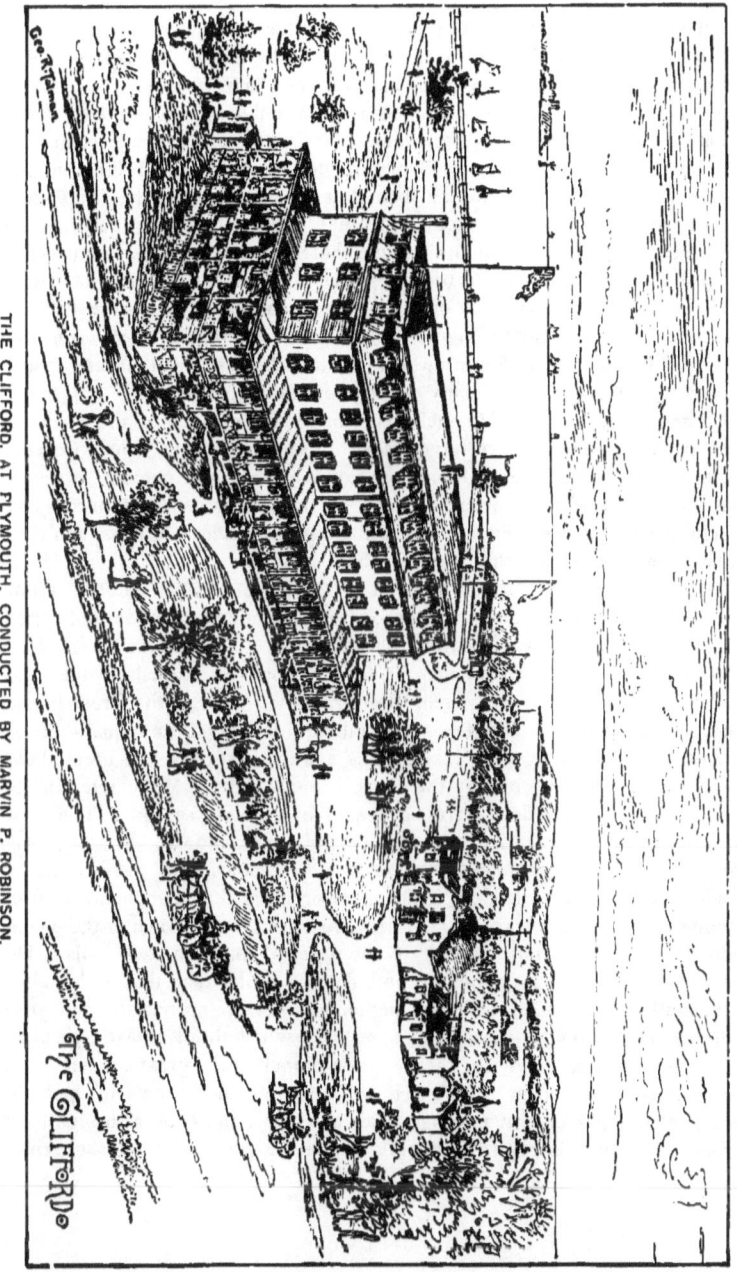

THE CLIFFORD, AT PLYMOUTH, CONDUCTED BY MARVIN P. ROBINSON.

The leisurely visitor in this land of old-time heroism can drive over to Kingston, where Elder Cushman dwelt in godly peace; to Captain's Hill, crowned with the great monumental tower which commemorates Miles Standish, near the remains of his house; to Marshfield, where the tomb and memories of Daniel Webster are found; to South Pond, whence comes the notably good water supply of Plymouth; to the forest-girt Billington Sea, discovered by Francis Billington soon after the landing from the *Mayflower;* to the beautiful and picturesque Manomet Highlands, facing out on Cape Cod Bay; to Duxbury, with its summer-hotels and cottages, and memories of Alden, Standish, and Partridge. Close to Plymouth, in the hamlet of Kingston, was the birthplace of the American navy, for here were built, by the order of the Colonial Congress, the armed brigantines *Independence* and *Mars*, in which Captain Sampson of Plymouth, the first naval officer commissioned by Congress, made many captures on the high seas.

Since her union with Massachusetts, in 1692, the capital of the Plymouth Colony has remained one of the quietest of provincial towns, remote from the main lines of travel, seated beside a shallow harbor, and content to rest in the tranquillity of well-earned repose. Of late years it has attained a considerable fame as a summer-resort, and handsome modern cottages and villas have been erected on the adjacent shores, and the palatial Clifford House looms across the lower harbor. Land is very cheap here, and board is low, and the attractions of the neighborhood are certainly numerous and varied. There is every variety of boating, on salt-water or fresh, with perfect facilities for bathing, and all manner of fishing, from the sea-fish of the outer harbor to the pickerel and perch, trout and black bass of the forest brooks and ponds. Hunters find foxes and rabbits, partridges and quails in the woods, black ducks near the inland lakes, and the best duck and brant shooting in New England out at the Gurnet and down by Manomet. In the adjacent forest forty deer have been shot in a single season. The floral beauties of the Plymouth woods, the home of the mayflower, have long been famous, and beautiful places for excursions, rambles, and picnics abound among its crystalline lakelets, which number more than two hundred, from Billington Sea, two miles out, and nearly five miles around, down to the merest bits of lonely forest-tarns, sacred to the water-lily and the fleur-de-lis. The temperature of all this region is twenty degrees cooler than that of the towns just south of Cape Cod, with cool nights, absence of mosquitoes, and great infrequency of thunder-storms and fogs. These delightful climatic peculiarities are accounted for by the theory that a branch of the great oceanic arctic current from the north is deflected by Cape Cod, and thrown in upon the coasts of the Old Colony, making the air clear, dry, and cool, with high tonic properties. In this regard Plymouth becomes a great summer sanitarium, whose air is full of invigoration and life-renewing properties. The adjacent forest has for many years been known as "The Adirondacks of Massachusetts," and covers hundreds of square miles, extending far down on the Cape, and still in a delightfully primitive condition.

The Pilgrims, long storm-tossed on the wintry sea, on the voyage from Holland to Cape Cod, exiles from Christian Europe, and face-to-face with a continent swarming with warlike pagans, nevertheless, calmly took their time to select a landing-place and town-site, and spent six weeks on the coast, searching for their future home, and meanwhile elaborating the great constitution on which their government should rest. In this snug and tranquil little harbor, bounded by noble highlands, and sheltered from the open sea, they anchored their stanch *Mayflower*, well beaten by winds of autumn and winter, and by waves of unknown seas.

Canopy over Plymouth Rock.

The great summer resort of this region is The Clifford, a vast and splendid hotel at the head of Plymouth Beach, less than three miles from the town. This stately summer palace was erected by the late John L. Tucker of the Tremont House, and is now conducted by Marvin P. Robinson, late of the Hotel Brunswick. It is provided with all the modern necessities, without which life loses so much of its charm, even on the borders of Paradise. The rooms are spacious and home-like; and the bracing air of Massachusetts Bay flows freely along the corridors and piazzas and through the luxurious lounging-rooms and parlors. The house is lighted by gas, heated by steam, and provided with running water. In the vicinity are the best facilities for boating and riding, fishing and hunting, bathing and rambling, and otherwise disposing of the golden hours of summer. But the main thing is the surrounding scenery, which is of very rare and notable beauty and variety, including choice forest and hill landscapes on one side, and on the other lovely combinations of sea and shore, the long curving beach, the high and cliffy bluffs, the distant islands and capes. This is the great charm of the locality, and will cause it in due time to attain a high rank among the New England watering-places. Hillard said that it presented the nearest likeness to the Bay of Naples of any place he had ever seen; and many another veteran traveller has found deep satisfaction in this exquisite region, where marine and woodland beauties are so happily combined in the venerable mother-town of New England.

Since its construction, five or six years ago, the Clifford has grown slowly but surely in the estimation of summer-travellers, and the season of 1883 opened with the brightest prospects, many well-known persons having engaged rooms there. It was somewhere in this section (but not at the Clifford) that Mr. Howells found the *locale* for his romance of " Dr. Breen's Practice; " and the town of " Leyden," which is often alluded to, is no other than Plymouth. But in this great hotel, life is rather sunnier than at Howells's imaginary resort, and every summer-day has its round of varied pleasures. The easy access from Boston renders it quite possible for gentlemen from that city to run down for the night; while the great historic and romantic charm of the locality attract many cultivated persons from remote parts of the country.

A Sea-Trip to the Eastward.

THE EASTERN COAST TO ROCKLAND, BANGOR, AND MOUNT DESERT. — BOSTON AND BANGOR STEAMSHIP COMPANY.

AS early as the year 1823 there was a regular line of steamers between Boston and Bath, and thence to Boothbay, Camden, Belfast, Sedgwick, and Eastport; and ten years later the Boston and Bangor Steamship Company began its operations, its first boat having been the *Bangor*, which was sent to the Mediterranean in 1842, to carry Mohammedan pilgrims, and afterwards became a Turkish frigate. Soon afterward Captain Memnemon Sanford established a new line between Bangor and Boston; which continued under his name until 1882, with no serious interruption except during the Secession War, when most of its boats were chartered for military purposes. In 1882 the corporate name of the "Sanford Steamship Company" was changed to the "Boston and Bangor Steamship Company," of which William H. Hill is President and General Manager. Mr. Hill is one of the senior members of the great banking house of Richardson, Hill & Co., of Boston.

The *Penobscot*, launched at East Boston in 1882, is the handsomest and stanchest steamship east of Boston, and has luxurious accommodations for 560 first-class passengers, and ample protection against perils of fire or storm. There are spacious saloons, covered with Wilton carpet, and furnished in black-walnut; six score of airy state-rooms, besides several bridal suites; breezy promenade-decks, stairways of polished oak, lines of brilliant chandeliers, and a great variety of ingenious and powerful machinery, for different purposes and emergencies. The wheels are provided with Holland Patent Paddles, which obviate the noise and tremor usually noticed on side-wheel steamers. Boston Harbor is justly proud of this noblest of its children. The *Katahdin* is a fine steamship of 1,234 tons, built at New York in 1863, at a cost of $250,000, and with engines of 400 horse-power. It has 70 state-rooms and 210 cabin-berths. The *Cambridge* is a 1500-ton vessel, built at New York in 1867, with accommodations for 450 passengers, commodious saloons and state-rooms, and an abundance of life-boats.

This is also a favorite route to Moosehead Lake and other points in the Maine wilderness which are reached by the afternoon trains from Bangor, and to the mining districts east of Penobscot Bay. A steamship of this line leaves Boston every week-day, returning from Bangor the following day at 11 A.M. The captains, pilots, and other officers of the fleet are all old and experienced mariners, familiar with every mile of the coast, and vigilant to a fault. The fares are very low: the rate from Boston to Rockland and return being but $4.50; to Bangor and return, $6.50; to Moosehead Lake (Mount Kineo House) and return, $12.00; to Bar Harbor and return, $8.00. The wharf is reached by the East-Boston horse-cars.

The New Steamship "Penobscot," Boston and Bangor S. S. Co.

The steamships of this line leave Foster's Wharf, near the foot of High Street, Boston, at 5 P.M., and move down the harbor with stateliness and speed, looking down on the many vessels, steamers, coasters, and yachts which flit in and out among the islands on every side. The course is the same which is described on pp. 21-27, down to Deer Island, where it turns to the north-east, and runs out through Broad Sound, into Massachusetts Bay, with the ragged and rocky Brewster islands and ledges on the right, and the beaches of Winthrop and Lynn on the left. The hills and islands, villages and summer-hotels, of the North Shore are in sight,— Nahant and Swampscott, Manchester and Magnolia; and the tall stone light-houses on Thacher's Island, off the end of Cape Ann, are passed, close at hand, before the summer sunset comes. The course is laid thence across the Gulf of Maine to Monhegan, whose light cheers the darkness of early morning. At dawn the vessel passes White Head, and enters Penobscot Bay, with craggy islands on the right, including the famous Dix Island, with whose granite many Government buildings have been constructed. Soon after rounding the picturesque promontory of Owl's Head, the vessel reaches Rockland, where it connects with the Mount-Desert boat. Thence it goes northward up the bay, toward the noble blue mountains, and touches at Camden, a sort of maritime North Conway, under the lofty peaks of Megunticook. The next landing (in summer) is at Northport, a famous camp-meeting ground, whose newspaper bears the appropriate name of "The Sea Breeze." Beyond this place of tabernacles, the steamer emerges from the thronging islands of Penobscot Bay, and runs across a lake-like inner harbor, of large proportions, to the handsome little maritime city of Belfast, whose houses rise in imposing lines along the hill at the mouth of the Passagassawaukeag River. This locality was settled in 1770, by Scotch-Irish Presbyterians,

Foster's Wharf, Boston.

who were driven away by the British troops nine years later. It is eighteen miles from Camden. After leaving Belfast, occasional glimpses of historic old Castine are obtained on the right, across the bay, with its memories and traditions of the Plymouth Pilgrims, Cardinal Richelieu's gay French soldiers, the wars of D'Aulney and La Tour, the feudal rule of the Baron de St. Castin, the long occupation by garrisons of red-coated British infantry, and the annihilation of a great American fleet by a half-dozen plucky English frigates. At five miles above Belfast, the boat rounds in under the lee of Brigadier Island, and stops at the maritime village of Searsport, on the vast domain once owned by David Sears of Boston. Once more the steamer works out into the bay, with the long Castine peninsula on the eastward. The next stopping-place is Fort Point, with a great summer-hotel looking down across the distant islands and over the blue waters of the upper bay.

Here are the ruins of Fort Pownal, which was built in 1758 by Governor Pownal of Massachusetts, at the cost of the British Parliament, to defend the entrance to the Penobscot River. Seventeen years later, when Yankeedom became rebellious, the British frigate *Canseau* sailed up here; and her blue-jackets destroyed the works and levelled the parapets of the best fort in Maine.

After leaving Fort Point, the course lies up the famous Penobscot River, whose sources lie hundreds of miles away in the deer-haunted wilderness, among bright lakes where no navigation but that of canoes has yet been attempted. Swinging round through the rapid currents of the Bucksport Narrows, the great vessel advances to the wharf at Bucksport, a beautiful old village of farmers, fishermen. and shipbuilders, famous also among the followers of Wesley for its great East-Maine Conference Seminary. On

Steamship "Katahdin," Boston and Bangor S. S. Co.

the opposite shore rise the frowning walls and heavy batteries of Fort Knox, a modern work erected by the Government to seal up the Penobscot River against hostile ships, and protect the vast shipping and lumbering interests of Bangor.

About five miles above is the landing of Winterport, at the head of winter navigation. The river grows more narrow and sinuous, with picturesque highlands near its banks, and the scattered farmhouses of the hardy country-people of Maine. Many vessels are passed in the stream, bound in and out; and the indications of a prosperous commerce increase on every side. A short stop is made at Hampden, which the British fleet captured in 1814, after a most wearisome attempt to catch the flying militia regiments, drawn up here to give battle. The United-States corvette *John Adams* was destroyed during this farcical engagement. A few miles beyond, the steamer reaches (at about noon) her terminal port, the great lumber metropolis of Bangor, twenty leagues from the sea, and crowning a line of graceful hills with the homes of upwards of twenty thousand people. Here the enterprising tourist may take train for the chief points in central and western Maine and the Maritime Provinces.

The swift and stanch steamer *Mount Desert* (belonging to the Boston and Bangor S. S. Co.) leaves Rockland early in the morning, after the arrival of the boat from Boston, and stretches across Penobscot Bay to the central group of islands, which it traverses through the charming scenery of Fox-Island Thoroughfare, touching at several quaint maritime villages, and giving

Steamship "Lewiston," Boston and Bangor S. S. Co.

noble views of the Camden Mountains, the remote seaward cliffs of Isle au Haut, and the bold peaks of Mount Desert. After crossing Placentia Bay it visits Bass Harbor and South-West Harbor, rounds the bold eastern headland of Mount Desert, and runs up Frenchman's Bay, by a long line of spray-whitened cliffs and many a costly villa, to Bar Harbor, the eastern Newport, which is reached in time for dinner (the distance being 65 miles). From thence the course extends to the head of the bay, to Sullivan. This trip across Penobscot Bay is one of the most interesting in America, rich in every variety of marine and coast scenery, light-houses and beacons, straits and bays, and grand mountains, with the electric sea-air sweeping over all. The *Mount Desert* is almost new, and has a wide renown for her speed and her seaworthy qualities. The greater part of her voyage leads through a labyrinth of islands and rocks, along narrow passages swept by the salt tides, and across sheltered bays and fiords, giving the greatest imaginable variety of scenic effects, and a journey full of keen interest. The strange little maritime villages at which she stops — like Green's Landing and Swan's Island — have great attractions for all who delight in out-of-the-way localities, and civilization growing under difficulties of topography and climate; and form a wonderful contrast to the modern palaces and huge hotels, fashionable companies, and ceaseless festivities of Bar Harbor.

The eastward voyage on these great steamships affords a very refreshing change from the summer temperature of Boston and the inland and southern cities, and removes one, in two or three hours, from the torrid zone to the cool air of the ocean, enriched by the intense vitality which comes pulsing in from the distant plains of the outer Atlantic. To leave behind the heated

Steamship "Mount Desert."

pavements and walls, the mephitic drainage, and the myriad noises of the town, and pass out into these vast quiet spaces of the sea, with pure and bracing air on every side, fascinating views, and no care but the coming dinner-hour, affords a change of scene and of life, which, however brief, is rich in physical and mental benefit; and he must be a very unreasonable American who returns from such a voyage without feeling himself a better man.

Noteworthy Boston Firms.

MACULLAR, PARKER, & COMPANY.

The most noted house in its line in this country.

Macullar, Parker, & Company's Entrance.

MACULLAR, PARKER, & COMPANY'S name must always be included in a list of eminent Boston firms, for their great clothing and piece-goods establishment at No. 400 Washington Street is one of the most noteworthy examples of progressive and creditable industry to be found in any city in America. It is only a little less than forty years ago that the business was started in a very small way; and yet to-day the firm give employment constantly the year round to upwards of 600 hands, men and women, in one of the neatest manufacturing establishments in the world, — one, too, in which all reasonable provision is made for the comfort and health of all the employés. The magnificent and commodious building fronts on two streets, — on Washington at Nos. 398 and 400, and on Hawley at No. 81. No adequate idea of its size can be had from a view on the street. Only by passing from one end to the other on all the many floors can the visitor form a correct impression of its magnitude and attractiveness. The floor surface alone amounts to 80,000 square feet, including the space occupied for the engines, boilers, pumps, ventilating apparatus, and carpenter's and machinist's shops. The building is used solely for the manufacturing and retailing of clothing for men, youths, and boys, and the importing and jobbing of piece-goods. The clothing made is sold at retail only by this firm, and in cut, style, trimmings, finish, and goods

MACULLAR, PARKER, & COMPANY.
Nos. 398 and 400 Washington Street.

ranks equal to that made by the leading merchant-tailors. No person is likely ever to enter into this establishment without being able to find a proper fit in thoroughly trustworthy clothing; and every one who patronizes this firm knows that the "one-price" system is positively invariable under all circumstances. It is the constant aim of MACULLAR, PARKER, & COMPANY to furnish the best and most satisfactory garments that can be furnished for the amount charged for them. It is an inviolable rule of the house to satisfy a person, or else not to take his patronage. No false or misleading statement in any particular is ever allowed to be made. People who visit or patronize this firm are never importuned to make purchases, nor is any one ever inveigled into buying things that are not wanted; the constant aim being to find out what the people want, and to supply them accordingly. The

Hawley Street Front of Macullar, Parker, & Company.

custom department of MACULLAR, PARKER, & COMPANY constitutes the largest merchant-tailoring establishment, and the department for the importing and jobbing of woollens and other piece-goods also forms the foremost house in its line, in New England.

SPRINGER BROTHERS' CLOAK ESTABLISHMENTS.
Their Sumptuous New Branch House.

MESSRS. SPRINGER BROTHERS, who are recognized as the foremost fashionable cloak makers of America, have recently opened an entirely new establishment at the corner of Washington and Bedford Streets. It is called a branch house; but this so-called "branch" is a whole establishment in itself, and while it is small in comparison with the other great places of the Springer Brothers, it is nevertheless a very large place when compared with other small houses. This establishment is not a branch in the sense of an agency, but it has been opened by the Springer Brothers to show some of the choice goods for which they have become so famous throughout this country. The building itself has been remodelled throughout, both inside and outside, and is one of the handsomest places of business to be found anywhere in this country or in Europe, and it is destined to become one of the noted sights of Boston. The furnishings, the decorations, the arrangement, and the conveniences are all designed and executed in the best taste, and give evidence that everything has been carried out regardless of expenditure.

Springer, Brothers' Cloak Bazaar, Washington cor. Bedford.

The main establishment of the Springer Brothers is the conspicuous block five stories high, built of sandstone, fronting on three thoroughfares, Essex and Chauncy Streets, and Harrison Avenue, — the site of the former home of Wendell Phillips. The factory buildings are on Green Street, near Bowdoin Square. The firm in busy seasons give employment to over 1,200 operatives. Besides the establishments in Boston, they have branch houses in New York, Chicago, San Francisco, and Dallas, and in Paris. They manufacture every variety of outer garments for ladies, misses, and children, and their goods are unsurpassed by those of any manufacturers in the world; and the trade everywhere look to Springer Brothers of Boston for the introduction of the most stylish and most acceptable garments in their line.

JOHN C. PAIGE'S FIRE INSURANCE AGENCY.
The Leading Agency in New England.

JOHN C. PAIGE is the leading fire-insurance agent in New England, doing the largest business, and representing the greatest amount of capital. Moreover, his offices, occupying the entire building at No. 20 Kilby Street, are unsurpassed for their elegance, convenience, and arrangement. Seventeen years ago Mr. Paige was recognized by the profession throughout this country as a skilful adjuster of fire-losses, and as an experienced general agent. Duties incident to the Great Fire of 1872 brought him to Boston, where he subsequently decided to establish a local insurance-agency in connection with his general agency business; and to-day, by reason of his great ability, varied experience, extreme popularity, and indomitable energy, he has placed himself in the foremost rank of the underwriters in the United States. The companies he represents are the "Imperial Fire of London, Eng.," "City of London Fire of London, Eng.," "Orient of Hartford, Conn.," "Fire Association

John C. Paige's Insurance Building, 20 Kilby Street.

of Philadelphia," "Mechanics Fire of Philadelphia," and the "Niagara Fire of New York." The gross assets of these companies amount to almost fifty million dollars, and the losses they have paid amount to an enormous sum. This agency's business extends throughout the United States; for Mr. Paige is the American resident manager for the City of London Fire, and the Imperial Fire, two great London companies. In the Boston office are about one hundred male and female employees. John C. Paige personally is one of those genial, whole-souled men with whom it is always a pleasure to do business. "Nothing mean about him," never was more fitly applied to any man; and this characteristic is evidenced by his every action in public and private life.

BOSTON ADVERTISING COMPANY.
A Successful Enterprise.

THE BOSTON ADVERTISING COMPANY has already become pretty generally known to Boston people, whether residents or transients, for at all the important entrances to the city this company have secured extensive bulletins, gables, and other means to be used for the making of attractive painted advertisements, so that it is almost impossible to get into or out of Boston without seeing some of these extensive and attractive "paintings."

Laying aside the question of fine art, there can be no doubt that, as a rule, they have put up very many showy advertisements, which do them credit as advertising experts.

The business was established July 1, 1886, only a couple of years ago, by Mr. R. C. McCartney, a man who is well known to the people of Boston, from his various connections with the daily newspapers. When he started this business he saw there was a great field for a competent specialist in newspaper and out-door sign advertising.

The enterprise was well started, and has been pushed with such vigor that the company now control, by lease, nearly all the prominent places in Boston and vicinity for out-of-door advertising. Not only fences, and specially constructed bulletins, but also the gables, roofs, and many sides of houses are used for this purpose, and they have also secured certain extensive rights on steamers and ferries. They are always quick to arrange for the enclosures made around buildings that are in process of erection.

The company place advertisements in leading daily and weekly newspapers, and also in a selected list of magazines and other periodicals.

In addition to placing advertisements in a *gilt-edged* list of newspapers throughout the country, and carrying on the out-of-door sign advertising in New England, they manufacture advertising signs, for which they have a large factory at No. 500 Harrison Avenue, where they make these signs in large or small quantities.

The business of making signs for advertisers has assumed considerable magnitude, and oftentimes they are made in quantities as large as a hundred thousand at a time. These signs are made on metal, wood, and glass.

The business has recently (July 30, 1888) passed into the hands of the BOSTON ADVERTISING COMPANY, a Massachusetts corporation, with a paid-up capital of $25,000. The founder of the business, Mr. R. C. McCartney, is the treasurer and manager, with main offices of the company at No. 8 Bromfield Street.

People who have travelled in Old England will no doubt appreciate the great probabilities of this enterprising concern in New England.

The Literary World.

VOLUME XIX. 1888. $2.00 A YEAR.

A FORTNIGHTLY JOURNAL OF LITERARY CRITICISM,
DISCUSSION, AND NEWS;
DEVOTED TO LITERATURE EXCLUSIVELY.

THE LITERARY WORLD has pushed its way steadily forward to a commanding position. The few competitors which have started after it, from time to time, have dropped out one by one, and it remains to-day the *only*, as it has been so long the *leading*, journal of *literature exclusively*, published in this country.

The special features of the LITERARY WORLD are:—

1. Early and full intelligence about new books and literary enterprises all over the world.

2. Descriptive and critical reviews of all important works published in this country, and a steady view of the more notable issues of the foreign press, British and Continental.

3. Extracts from new publications, and from articles in the periodical press relating to literary topics.

4. A department of *Shakespeariana*, edited by WILLIAM J. ROLFE, who is in personal correspondence with all the eminent Shakespearians in this country and abroad.

5. A department of *Notes* and *Queries*, which is of great value to all who have any thing to do with books.

6. The leading critical reviews in the LITERARY WORLD are the work of scholars, who are widely recognized as authorities in their several departments. The publishers could give the name of several score of such, whose co-operation they have.

7. The LITERARY WORLD is the organ of no school, sect, or party. It is absolutely independent of all trade influence, and owes no man any thing but justice, equity, and truth. It aims to be fearless, friendly, kind, impartial, and trustworthy; to be deemed intelligent rather than "smart," and fair rather than "showy." It seeks the confidence of its readers rather than the applause of the public, and to do honest useful work.

The steady growth of the paper under its present management and policy, both in circulation and influence, shows that its principles and performance are recognized; and it is rapidly coming to be considered an indispensable implement of culture in every well-ordered home.

The LITERARY WORLD only lacks an introduction to make itself a friend.

E. H. HAMES & CO., PUBLISHERS,
1 SOMERSET ST., BOSTON, MASS.

PHOTOGRAPHY.

A. Marshall,

53 Boylston Street,

Studio
Only · Three · Flights · from · Street.

Boston.

CRAYONS, BROMIDE ENLARGEMENTS, ETC.

: : PARTICULAR ATTENTION : :
GIVEN TO
CHILDREN'S PORTRAITS.

ZION'S HERALD.

THE OLDEST METHODIST NEWSPAPER IN THE WORLD.

Rev. CHARLES PARKHURST, D.D., Editor,
ASSISTED BY THE ABLEST OF WRITERS

IT HAS MORE THAN TWO HUNDRED CONTRIBUTORS. ALL DEPARTMENTS ARE WELL ORGANIZED, AND FURNISH INTERESTING READING FOR ALL CLASSES

SECOND TO NO PAPER OF ITS CLASS.

THE SUNDAY SCHOOL NOTES written by Rev. W. O. Holway, Chaplain U. S. Navy, are the **ablest** and most elaborate of any notes published by a denominational paper.

FOR BUSINESS MEN, one of the BEST OF ADVERTISING MEDIUMS. Has probably **60,000 Readers** in New England.

SPECIMEN COPIES FREE. Address

ALONZO S. WEED,
PUBLISHER,
36 BROMFIELD ST., BOSTON, MASS.

Geo. B. Sargent & Son,

REVOLVING SELF-INKING

Rubber Stamps,

Stamps for Dating, Receipting, Banking, and all General Business Purposes.

═══SEAL PRESSES═══

RIBBON STAMPS OF ALL KINDS,

MANUFACTURED AND SOLD BY

Geo. B. Sargent & Son, 15 WATER STREET, BOSTON.

FROST & DEARBORN,

Nos. 8 AND 10 Pearl Street,

BOSTON,

Respectfully invite the patronage of residents and visitors to their

DINING ✻ ROOMS.

WHOLLY REMODELLED AND ENTIRELY REFURNISHED IN 1887.

[*From "King's Handbook of Boston."*]

FROST & DEARBORN'S RESTAURANT is one of the largest, finest, and most popular dining-saloons in the wholesale district. It is situated at 8 and 10 Pearl Street, a short distance from Milk Street, and directly opposite the Pearl-street entrance to the building of the Mutual Life Insurance Company. It was opened in 1873 by Samuel E. Kendall and John N. Dearborn, and was then known as Kendall's Restaurant. Mr. Kendall will be remembered as having kept for a series of years some of the best restaurants that Boston has ever had. One of these was under the Old State House, and in its day was a rival of Parker's. Another was at 8 Congress Square, where he continued for 17 years. This was always patronized by the most prominent business men; and, until destroyed by the Great Fire of 1872, it was considered one of the most successful restaurants in Boston. The present establishment has, from the time when it was opened, met with that success which Mr. Kendall's reputation and experience guaranteed it. In his efforts to conduct first-class restaurants, Mr. Kendall was always greatly aided by John N. Dearborn and Morrill Frost. Mr. Dearborn, for instance, was connected with him for 25 years; and Mr. Frost was in his employ for many years, beginning in 1845 under the Old State House. In 1875 Mr. Kendall died; and Mr. Frost, after being for 21 years the proprietor of the restaurant and news-stand in the Boston and Albany Railroad Depot, became associated with Mr. Dearborn. From the above it is seen that Messrs. Frost & Dearborn have long experience, a good prestige, an admirably furnished and conveniently situated restaurant; and it only needs to be added that their *cuisine* is unexcelled in Boston.

FROST & DEARBORN,

8 and 10 Pearl Street . . . . . Boston.

Type Blocks for Illustrations

Lewis Engraving Co.
65 Essex St.

Manufacturers of   BOSTON.

Illustrations for Books,
Newspapers, Catalogues, Advertisements,
Etc., Etc.

DEAN'S
INTEREST · AND · EQUATION
EXPONENTS.

The most perfect tables ever published for Averaging Accounts and for Computing Interest.

OVER 6000 SOLD.

In use throughout the world.

For particulars address

MOSES KING CORPORATION,
BOSTON, MASS.

www.ingramcontent.com/pod-product-compliance
Lightning Source LLC
Chambersburg PA
CBHW031329230426
43670CB00006B/291